PREVIOUS CONVICTIONS AT SENTENCING

This latest volume in the *Penal Theory and Penal Ethics* series addresses one of the oldest and most contested questions in the field of criminal sentencing: should an offender's previous convictions affect the sentence? This question provokes a series of others: Is it possible to justify a discount for first offenders within a retributive sentencing framework? How should previous convictions enter into the sentencing equation? At what point should prior misconduct cease to count for the purposes of fresh sentencing? Should similar previous convictions count more than convictions unrelated to the current offence? Statutory sentencing regimes around the world incorporate provisions which mandate harsher treatment of repeat offenders. Although there is an extensive literature on the definition and use of criminal history information, the emphasis here, as befits a volume in the series, is on the theoretical and normative aspects of considering previous convictions at sentencing. Several authors explore the theory underlying the practice of mitigating the punishments for first offenders, while others put forth arguments for enhancing sentences for recidivists. The practice of sentencing repeat offenders in two jurisdictions (England and Wales, and Sweden) is also examined in detail.

Studies in Penal Theory and Penal Ethics: Volume 4

Studies in Penal Theory and Penal Ethics

A Series Published for
the Centre for Penal Theory and Penal Ethics
Institute of Criminology, University of Cambridge

GENERAL EDITORS:
ANDREW VON HIRSCH, ANTHONY E BOTTOMS

Ethical and Social Perspectives on Situational Crime Prevention
edited by Andrew von Hirsch, David Garland and
Alison Wakefield

Restorative Justice and Criminal Justice: Competing or Reconcilable Paradigms?
edited by Andrew von Hirsch, Julian Roberts,
Anthony E Bottoms, Kent Roach and Mara Schiff

Incivilities: Regulating Offensive Behaviour
edited by Andrew Simester and Andrew von Hirsch

Previous Convictions at Sentencing

Theoretical and Applied Perspectives

Edited by
Julian V Roberts
and
Andrew von Hirsch

·HART·
PUBLISHING

OXFORD AND PORTLAND, OREGON
2014

Published in the United Kingdom by Hart Publishing Ltd
16C Worcester Place, Oxford, OX1 2JW
Telephone: +44 (0)1865 517530
Fax: +44 (0)1865 510710
E-mail: mail@hartpub.co.uk
Website: http://www.hartpub.co.uk

Published in North America (US and Canada) by
Hart Publishing
c/o International Specialized Book Services
920 NE 58th Avenue, Suite 300
Portland, OR 97213-3786
USA
Tel: +1 503 287 3093 or toll-free: (1) 800 944 6190
Fax: +1 503 280 8832
E-mail: orders@isbs.com
Website: http://www.isbs.com

Hart Publishing is an imprint of Bloomsbury Publishing plc.

British Library Cataloguing in Publication Data
Data Available

ISBN: 978-1-84946-042-2 (Hardback)
ISBN: 978-1-84946-684-4 (Paperback)

Typeset by Forewords, Oxford
Printed and bound in Great Britain by
Lightning Source UK Ltd

Acknowledgements

The chapters of this volume originated in presentations made at two colloquia, one held at Cambridge in May 2008 and the second at Oxford in April 2009. We are very grateful to the Hulme Fund at the University of Oxford, as well as the Yorke Fund and the Centre for Penal Theory and Ethics, University of Cambridge for supporting the first seminar. The second seminar was funded by the Research Support Fund of the Faculty of Law, University of Oxford; the Fell Fund at the University of Oxford; and the Centre for Penal Theory and Ethics, University of Cambridge. Additional funding for both seminars was also provided by the Institute of Crime and Public Policy, University of Minnesota Law School. We would also like to thank the other participants who attended the two seminars for their valuable input into the discussions. Finally, we thank Richard Hart and his team at Hart Publishing in Oxford for supporting publication of this collection of essays as well as George Mawhinney and Maria-Christina Dorado for assistance in preparing the manuscript for publication.

Julian V Roberts
Worcester College, University of Oxford
and
Andrew von Hirsch
Institute of Criminology, University of Cambridge
15 November 2009

Preface

This latest volume in the *Penal Theory and Ethics* series addresses one of the most contested questions in the field of criminal sentencing: should an offender's previous convictions be taken into account in deciding the quantum of sentence? In reality, this single question provokes a series of others: is it possible to justify a discount for first offenders within a retributive sentencing framework? How should previous convictions enter into the sentencing equation? At what point should prior misconduct cease to count for the purposes of sentencing for the current offence? Should similar previous convictions count more than convictions unrelated to the current offence?

Statutory sentencing regimes around the world incorporate provisions which mandate harsher treatment of repeat offenders. The practice of imposing progressively harsher penalties as the offender accumulates more convictions is called the *recidivist sentencing premium* and is the subject of this volume. Although there is a vast literature on the definition and use of criminal history information, the emphasis here, as befits a volume in the series, is on the theoretical and normative aspects of considering previous convictions at sentencing. The focus is upon retributive sentencing perspectives. Utilitarian sentencers justify a recidivist premium on the grounds that harsher penalties are necessary to deter or incapacitate repeat offenders.

The volume begins with three chapters which explore the 'discount theory'—which favours the imposition of mitigated punishments upon first offenders, or offenders with modest criminal records. This theory gives rise to the well-known principle of the *progressive loss of mitigation*. This principle argues that first offenders should receive a discounted sentence. If they reoffend, they should still receive a discount, albeit one of lesser magnitude. Ultimately, after a specified number of reconvictions, their first-offender status expires, and no further discount is offered. The principle has proven very influential in sentencing writings, less so in terms of sentencing practice. Andrew von Hirsch offers an account of the lapse theory and this is followed by two other contributions by Julian Roberts and Jesper Ryberg in which the theory and the principle are discussed at greater length.

Youngjae Lee and Chris Bennett propose retributive justifications for imposing progressively harsher sentences on repeat offenders. Lee argues that repeat offenders may reasonably be considered more culpable for failing to take the necessary remedial steps to prevent reoffending. Chris Bennett also considers repeat offenders to be more blameworthy, but, in contrast to Lee, he locates the justification for a recidivist sentencing premium within a communicative theory of sentencing.

Michael Tonry provides a critique of a number of justifications for criminal-history enhancements, including those proposed in this volume by Lee and Bennett, and elsewhere by Roberts. Richard Frase seeks to identify normative principles and practical rules which may both justify and set limits on the widespread practice of enhancing sentence severity based on prior convictions. In his view the normative principles adopted for this purpose must be capable of generating clear, workable norms, providing guidance to judges and sentencing policymakers on when and why prior-record adjustments are permitted, and also when and why they are excessive.

Repeat offenders are usually defined as people who commit multiple offences over time, with their episodes of offending interrupted by sentencing for each offence. Recidivist statutes are constructed with this profile of offender in mind. However, a significant number of convicted defendants face sentence for multiple offences committed on a single occasion, or over a very short period of time. Sentencing in such cases throws up a raft of problems for the courts. One response to the offender who, for example, commits ten burglaries during the same evening is to impose concurrent sentences. Alternatively, a sentence may be assigned for each conviction; but the overall 'package' of sentences is discounted by the 'totality' principle. This ensures that someone convicted of, say, five burglaries does not receive a sentence that is more severe than an offender convicted of, say, rape. The practical consequence is a paradox, or inconsistency: repeated offences over time may result in a harsher penalty (if a recidivist sentencing premium is adopted), while multiple offences over a single occasion are 'discounted' by another practice (totality). Kevin Reitz explores the complexities surrounding the sentencing of offenders convicted of multiple offences.

In the second part of the volume, we turn from theory to practice. A number of contributors explore the use of previous convictions in three Western jurisdictions. First, Martin Wasik provides a salutary reminder that in practice determining the nature of an offender's record is a far from straightforward exercise. Wasik provides a typical criminal history and works the reader through the practical issues arising from considering previous criminal misconduct. Andrew Ashworth and Estella Baker describe and analyse the law in England and Wales, a jurisdiction in which the role of previous convictions at sentencing has changed significantly within a single decade. In 1991, courts were explicitly directed to ignore an offender's previous convictions. This legislation was subsequently amended in 1993, and in 2003 matters turned full circle. The *Criminal Justice Act* of that year included a provision which requires courts to consider each prior conviction as enhancing the seriousness of the current offence, if this is reasonable.

The chapter by Petter Asp explains the use of previous convictions in jurisdiction which utilises a variant of the principle of progressive loss of mitigation. The volume concludes with a contribution by Lila Kazemian who examines, in the light of recent empirical studies, the assumption that harsher penalties will actually deter or incapacitate recidivists. She notes that the *recidivist sentencing premium*'s promise of lower crime or recidivism rates is remains unfulfilled—at least on the evidence that has accumulated to date.

Contents

Contributing Authors

Andrew Ashworth is the Vinerian Professor of English Law at the University of Oxford, Fellow of All Souls College, Oxford and former Chairman of the Sentencing Advisory Panel in England and Wales.

Petter Asp is Professor of Criminal Law at the University of Stockholm.

Estella Baker is Senior Lecturer in the Faculty of Law, University of Sheffield.

Chris Bennett is Senior Lecturer in the Department of Philosophy, University of Sheffield.

Richard S. Frase is the Benjamin N Berger Professor of Criminal Law at the Faculty of Law, University of Minnesota.

Lila Kazemian is an Assistant Professor at John Jay College of Criminal Justice, New York.

Youngjae Lee is currently Visiting Professor of Law, University of Chicago Law School and Professor of Law, Fordham University School of Law.

Kevin R Reitz is the James Annenberg Levee Professor of Law, University of Minnesota.

Julian V Roberts is Professor of Criminology in the Faculty of Law, University of Oxford and Fellow of Worcester College, Oxford.

Jesper Ryberg is Professor of Ethics and Philosophy of Law, Department of Philosophy and Science Studies, University of Roskilde, Denmark.

Michael Tonry is the Marvin J Sonosky Professor of Law and Public Policy at the Faculty of Law, University of Minnesota and Senior Fellow of the Netherlands Institute for the Study of Crime and Law Enforcement.

Andrew von Hirsch is Honorary Professor of Penal Theory and Penal Law, University of Cambridge; Honorary Fellow, Wolfson College, Cambridge; and Honorary Professor, Law Faculty, Johann Goethe-University, Frankfurt

Martin Wasik is Professor of Law at Keele University, and a former Chairman of the Sentencing Advisory Panel in England and Wales.

Proportionality and Progressive Loss of Mitigation: Further Reflections[1]

ANDREW VON HIRSCH

A. INTRODUCTION

1. The Progressive-Loss-of-Mitigation Model

IN TRADITIONAL DISCRETIONARY sentencing systems, judges generally adjust the sentence to take account of the offender's previous convictions. However, the weight given to the criminal record is uncertain. Should the offender's previous criminal record be the primary determinant of his sentence? Or should the sentence chiefly reflect the seriousness of his current crime, perhaps with modest adjustments made for his prior convictions? Under a discretionary system, different judges answer these questions differently. As jurisdictions move toward more explicit guidance for sentencing decisions, however, it becomes essential to decide how much weight the offender's criminal record should carry, and why.

The significance of the prior record will vary depending on the sentencing rationale relied upon. A rationale emphasising prediction and incapacitation would give the record primary weight. Prediction studies tend to show that the likelihood of someone's reoffending is influenced more by his criminal history than by the seriousness of his current act. What predicts recidivism best (or rather, least badly) is the person's history of previous arrests (for references, see von Hirsch and Ashworth 2005: 149).

For the purposes of the present discussion, however, I am presupposing a sentencing rationale based on proportionality and desert, according

[1] The author wishes to thank Petter Asp, Julian Roberts, Andrew Simester and Natalia Vibla for their advice and comments on this chapter.

to which punishments should be proportionate to the seriousness of the offender's criminal conduct (see generally, ibid: ch 9). On that perspective, what (if any) role should previous convictions play? There has been disagreement on this subject among desert theorists. One school of thought, represented by George Fletcher (1978) and Richard Singer (1979), holds that the prior record should not be considered at all. Another, which includes Martin Wasik (1987), Andrew Ashworth as well as myself (von Hirsch and Ashworth 2005: 148–55; see also von Hirsch 1991), favours a theory of 'progressive loss of mitigation'. A third school of thought, represented by Julian Roberts and Youngjae Lee (chs 2 and 4 of this volume), holds that repetition of the offence should give rise to a *recidivist premium*: the offender should receive additional punishment upon reconviction—for example, because his reoffending shows a greater degree of personal culpability.

I wish, here, to reconsider a 'discount' approach to previous convictions, particularly the progressive-loss-of-mitigation model. This model holds that a reduction in penalty should be provided for first offenders; the discount should gradually diminish over a series of subsequent convictions. Only after the offender has been before the courts on a specified number of occasions should a 'ceiling' be reached, representing the full deserved measure of punishment for the offence. Further repetitions (as far as desert is concerned) should be dealt with by the imposition of the full measure of penalty for the offence. The sentencer would not thereafter be permitted to continue increasing sentence; to practice such cumulative sentencing would give undue weight to persistence, rather than seriousness of crime, and thus sacrifice proportionality.

2. My Previous Account of PLM: The Lapse and 'Limited Tolerance'

Why adopt a discount theory? In previous writings (eg von Hirsch, 1991; see also, von Hirsch and Ashworth, 2005: ch 9), I gave the following account. Our everyday moral judgements, I argued, include the notion of the 'lapse': a transgression (even a fairly serious one) should be judged less stringently when it occurs against a background of prior compliance. The idea is that even an ordinarily well-behaved person can have his or her inhibitions fail in a moment of weakness, wilfulness or aggression. Such a temporary breakdown of self-control is the kind of human frailty for which a degree of understanding should be shown. In sentencing, the relevant lapse is an infringement of the criminal law, rather than a commonplace moral failure, but the logic of the discount remains similar: that of dealing with such lapses somewhat more tolerantly. Such a discount also reflects respect for the process by which persons can attend to, and respond to, censure for their conduct. The offender, after being confronted with censure or blame through his punishment for his first offence, should be capable as a reasoning human being of reflecting on the wrongfulness of what he has done, and of making an extra effort to show greater self-restraint in the future. The aim, in granting the discount, is to show respect for this capacity. With repetitions, however, the discount should diminish, and eventually disappear: the behaviour can less and less plausibly be described as a mere lapse; and repeated reoffending after confrontation with penal censure suggests a failure to make the effort at self-restraint which was the basis for granting the discount.

As a result of the two colloquia which led up to the preparation of the current volume, I am now convinced that in my just-cited account, a number of further questions need to be addressed. Is human frailty a single quality, or something more complex? Should the role of prior offending vary with the institutional context: whether we are speaking of criminal law and criminal sentencing, or some other context—say university disciplinary proceedings? How should other values in sentencing, such as a concern with 'parsimony' in punishment, bear on the argument? Pursuing these lines of thought has convinced me of the need, once again, to try to reformulate my views.

B. PROBLEMATIC STRATEGIES OF ARGUMENT

Before proceeding with the substance of these issues, I think I should call attention to certain strategies of argument that I do not think helpful.

1. Restrictive Taxonomies

One problematic way of arguing is to try to exclude any reliance on previous offending by definition. It is sometimes thus asserted that proportionality of sentence is concerned exclusively with the degree of harmfulness and culpability of the present criminal act. Since conceptions such as 'tolerance' bear upon neither of these elements, they must be ruled out from the outset. Such restrictive taxonomies, however, would rule out by stipulation any debate about how prior criminality could bear upon deserved criminal censure for the conduct. It is necessary, instead, to consider the question of prior convictions in the light of the underlying rationale of proportionality, free of narrow definitional restraints.

2. 'COMMON-SENSE' ARGUMENTS

Another problematic form of argument involves simple appeals to everyday moral judgements. Since in everyday contexts, a discount is expressed by saying the wrongdoer should get a 'second chance', that implies giving him a discount only for the first offence. Alternatively, it is said that treating more than one previous offence as a 'lapse' is inappropriate, because in everyday life only the first misdeed would ordinarily so be described.

Desert judgements in criminal law derive some of their ultimate logic from ordinary moral evaluations. From such everyday contexts, for example, we learn that censure judgements must be retrospectively focused, and should function to recognise the moral agency of the actor (see von Hirsch and Ashworth, 2005, ch 2). The doctrines and principles of the criminal law, however, cannot be extracted *simpliciter* from ordinary moral assessments. This should be evident from the 'lapse' argument concerning prior convictions. Everyday moral discourse does suggest that a general idea of human fallibility should be taken into account in blaming judgements, and should yield some tolerance for lapses. But the criteria of the criminal law may well differ in significant respects from everyday judgements. Judgements concerning criminal wrongdoing, for example, may well have to operate with more (or conceivably, less) 'tolerance' for repeated misbehaviour than ordinary judgements—for reasons discussed below. Criminal sanctions are also different from everyday censuring judgements, in their greater formality and more burdensome character. With such differences may come revised norms for dealing with previous misconduct, for reasons also to be discussed below.

3. Public-acceptability Arguments

It is sometimes asserted that a gradually diminishing discount for previous offending should be rejected, because it does not comport with the public's views. For example, it is said that arguments concerning a limited 'tolerance' for previous offending are out of place because the public would oppose any tolerance for criminal behaviour.

The role of public opinion in the formulation of criminal policy is a large topic, but let me deal with it summarily here. Our present topic is that of delineating principles for a fair system of criminal sentencing, as these relate to sentencing and previous convictions. Questions of fairness, for these purposes, should centrally be concerned with the rights and interests of those punished. The public's view may give little consideration to such questions. The basic fairness questions in criminal law—whether addressed to sentencing principles or procedural justice—should be dealt with by substantive arguments of justice.[2]

Once such principles have been delineated, the question of their application to issues of actual sentencing policy arises. At this stage, it may be legitimate to ask whether and to what extent one might possibly deviate from those principles, to take into account the public's preferences. That should depend on, among other factors, the degree of importance of the fairness principles involved. But such an analysis presupposes formulating the relevant fairness principles first; and *that* cannot be settled merely by appealing what the public might think (see also Tonry, ch 6 below).

C. THE 'RECIDIVIST PREMIUM' AND ITS PROBLEMS

A number of authors—including two contributors to this volume, Julian Roberts and Youngjae Lee—have argued in favour of a recidivist *premium*, instead of a discount theory such as that of progressive loss of mitigation. Before passing on to my own discount model, let me address these first, and suggest briefly why I am sceptical of such premium models.

1. Repeat Offending and Increased Culpability?

Julian Roberts (ch 2 below) has offered a culpability-based argument, in support of a recidivist premium. With each new offence, the offender should receive a sentence increase, subject to certain outer proportionality limits. Reoffending, he argues, shows increased blameworthiness for reasons similar to why premeditation does: it indicates the presence of a more culpable state of mind. Having been convicted before gives, or should give, the actor increased awareness of the wrongfulness of his behaviour when he contemplates committing it again.

This purported analogy to premeditation, however, is questionable. Premeditation concerns a culpable mental state: the offender's planning the offence suggests that he *means* to do the harm. There seems, however, to be no culpable state necessarily linked with reoffending. Indeed, a mark of much recidivism (especially repeat minor offending) is impulsiveness: the repeat shoplifter, for example, may simply see the item and decide to grab it without much thought. It is not easy to discern any typical mental indicia that underlie the heterogeneous motivations for repeat offending.

The recidivist premium also could well lead to significant increases

---

[2] This point becomes obvious when one considers more familiar issues of penal justice, eg the double-jeopardy principle. The public, or significant segments of it, might may not approve of constraints on double jeopardy in criminal trials. That, however, scarcely should settle whether the double-jeopardy constraint should be retained or eliminated.

in penalty levels. In its pure form, the theory could support no penalty reductions for a first offence at all. The offender would thus get the full measure of punishment for the offence upon its first occurrence, with subsequent repetitions calling for yet further increases. Would this be a desirable result? Could it be reconciled with values of parsimony in punishment? In his most recent account, in this volume, Roberts asserts that the first offender should actually get a penalty reduction. But how might such a reduction be justified—other than by resort to a discount theory of the kind that he purportedly rejects? Roberts contends, moreover, that after the first offence, later convictions should be visited by recidivist premiums. Would that not produce a puzzling discontinuity in the penalty structure and its rationale?

A final issue with a recidivist-premium theory is that of establishing limits on penalty increases. If repetition enhances offender culpability, why should further repetitions not enhance culpability still more? It would seem difficult to identify a principle, similar to the discount theory's, for barring further sentence-level changes after a specified number of acts of reoffending. Roberts does assert that his conception, as a species of desert theory, still would accord proportionality the primary role in deciding sentence. To preserve that role, he argues, a limit on sentence increases must eventually be reached. But how could this limit be located and rationalised? And if the upper limit is conceptualised as only a constraint on grossly disproportionate punishments, could that not permit large net increases in penalty levels?

2. Youngjae Lee's 'Omissions' Theory

In his account of previous offending in this volume, Youngjae Lee takes care to avoid simple reliance on everyday moral judgements, and offers a *criminal law*-related account of the role of prior convictions. His account is based on notions of omission in criminal law. On the first offence, he argues, the censure embodied in the sanction should generate an obligation on the defendant to rearrange his life in such a manner as to reduce the temptation to offend. A second or subsequent offence can then be viewed as a culpable omission to take such remedial steps (see Lee, ch 4 below). Novel and interesting as this line of argument is, it raises substantial difficulties. One is uncertainty about what it is that is being omitted. In classical omissions liability, there is an identifiable wrong: with the offence of driving a dangerous vehicle, for example, the omission consists of a culpably negligent failure to ensure that the car is in proper working order before driving it. On Lee's conception, however, no clear duties are prescribed about how the defendant should conduct himself so as to avoid the risk of reoffending. Second, there seems to be no necessary connection between the supposed culpable omission (the offender's not changing his lifestyle) and the conduct triggering the added punishment (his committing another crime). This is because his failure to change his habits would neither be a necessary nor a sufficient condition for imposition of additional punishment. If the defendant successfully avoids tempting situations but offends again anyway, he faces the recidivist premium. If, on the other hand, he makes no such efforts but happens to desist from further criminality anyway, he faces no liability at all. A scheme for inducing the person to alter his habits should operate differently—probation being a ready example. If someone offends and is put on probation, he may be required to undertake various specified tasks designed to make him less inclined to reoffend. Failure to carry out these tasks may have legal consequences—eg probation revocation and reimprisonment—even if he does refrain from actually reoffending.

If the case for a recidivist premium has not been made, what are the alternatives? If a case cannot be made for adjusting the sentence upward, on the basis of previous convictions, then a fallback alternative would be not permitting any prior-record adjustments at all—as George Fletcher (1978) has proposed. There is, however, a further alternative to be considered, before we would be compelled to adopt Fletcher's no-adjustment scheme. That alternative is the one I prefer: a discount scheme. For the remainder of this chapter, I shall address that alternative, and particularly, one of its versions: the progressive-loss-of-mitigation model.

D. WHY PROGRESSIVE LOSS OF MITIGATION? THE MODEL'S RATIONALE RECONSIDERED

If the offender is not necessarily obliged to change his lifestyle, how might previous convictions otherwise bear on the punishment he deserves? And how might such considerations affect the rationale for the discount model?

i. Conception of Offending Underlying the Discount Model

The criminal law declares various acts of wrongdoing to be punishable. Criminal punishment, for reasons elaborated elsewhere (von Hirsch 1993: ch 2; von Hirsch and Ashworth 2005: ch 2), conveys *censure*— ie disapprobation of the offender for his criminal act. Criminalising the behaviour thus expresses an appeal to desist: it signifies that (because the behaviour through its criminalisation has been declared wrongful and blameworthy) persons ought not to engage in it. This appeal, however, applies to all addressees of the prohibition—ie to members of the public generally. How, then, has the convicted offender been given any special reason to make efforts to desist? And efforts of what kind?

When an offender is convicted for the first time, his punishment *confronts* him with the criminal law's censure for the behaviour: he is visited personally with the disapprobation embodied in the sanction. This signifies that the offender has unjustifiably failed to resist the temptation to offend, notwithstanding the conduct's declared wrongfulness. It implies, further, that (in view of the conduct's wrongfulness and his apparent susceptibility to temptation) he should try to comply better in future. What conception of 'trying', however, is involved here?

To answer the latter question, we should recall that desert theory (or at least the version of it on which I am relying) rests on a certain conception of the criminal offender.[3] This is of the offender as a fallible being, but nevertheless as a moral agent. He is fallible in the sense that he reflects the human capacity for infringing moral and legal norms, given certain temptations or provocations. In his case, he has manifested this tendency, by having actually committed and been convicted of a violation of the criminal law. However, he is (or should be deemed to be) a moral agent who is capable of comprehending the disapproval embodied in the sanction, and of responding by trying better to desist in future.

In what manner should he try to refrain from reoffending? Anthony Bottoms has noted that the convicted offender has (at least) two strategies open to him, should he decide to discontinue offending, but nevertheless to believe that in certain circumstances he might be drawn into returning to crime.[4] One strategy, which Bottoms terms 'diachronic', is to restrict certain non-criminal choices for a period of time, namely to eschew lifestyles or behaviour-patterns that are innocuous in themselves but create situations where he might be inclined to reoffend. Requiring an offender to refrain from visiting the pub in order to stay out of fights is an example of this technique. The second, which Bottoms calls 'synchronic', permits an offender to continue his present style of living, but calls upon him to hold firm to his decision to desist when temptations or provocations arise: for example, continuing to visit the pub, but holding to his decision to stay out of fights there. The choice between these strategies may depend on his other priorities, and the context in which offending occurs. What is critical to the effort of will to which I am referring is that, irrespective of which of these two methods he chooses, that he does seriously try to desist.

Who should decide between these two desistance strategies? According to Youngjae Lee (see C.2 above), the state should require the diachronic approach. The offender, on first being convicted, should be called upon to alter his lifestyle so as to make reoffending less likely; and if he does

---

[3] See more fully, Ashworth and von Hirsch (2005: ch 2, esp 22–23)

[4] This sketch of Professor Bottoms's view is based on a lecture by him at the 50th Anniversary Conference of the Institute of Criminology, Cambridge University, 24 September 2009.

reoffend, he should be penalised through a recidivist premium for having ostensibly failed to do so. On the conception of the offender's agency I am adopting here, however, that would be pre-emptive of his proper role as the choosing agent. If one takes the notion of his moral agency seriously, then it should be up to him to decide upon which strategy for desistance to choose. What should matter is his making the effort of will to desist, in one manner or another.

Wherein should this effort of will consist? It is not, as I just noted, necessarily a matter of his changing his habits or life style. The defendant who has been convicted of an assault in a tavern would not have any special duty to stay away from such places in future, or even to refrain from drinking excessively if he goes there (unless, of course, these requirements have been made conditions of probation). He does no wrong if he visits his favourite pub again—so long as he refrains from further assaults.

The effort-of-will should consist, instead, of these three simple elements. (1) The offender's original conviction and punishment should put him on notice that under certain circumstances he may be tempted to offend again. (2) He should make a firm decision to desist in future. (3) He should seek to abide by that decision about his conduct, even when confronted with further tempting or provocative situations.

How should such an obligation, of making an effort of will to desist, bear upon the offender's punishment for his next offence, should he recidivate? The failure to make such an effort cannot in itself be a wrong which the law should penalise. The 'effort of will' has instead a different bearing on punishment: as a basis for the adjustments that the progressive-loss-of-mitigation model envisions. In earlier writings on this subject, I argued that the criminal-history discount reflected not only a certain limited tolerance for 'lapses', but also constituted recognition of a 'respected process' by which the person can attend to the disapprobation visited on him through the punishment (see A.2 above).[5] However, I gave little explanation of what that respected process should consist in. The notion of 'effort of will', discussed here, is designed to help provide such an explanation.

2. Why a Discount?

Why, however, provide the *discount* that the progressive-loss-of-mitigation model envisions? There are several interrelated reasons. The discount provides recognition of the offender as a responsible actor, capable of altering his conduct on the basis of the critical judgement of his behaviour expressed through the previous sentence. It presumes that he will respond

[5] See also von Hirsch (1991), and von Hirsch and Ashworth (2005: 152–54).

as he should, by making an effort of will to desist. It is only when he actually fails to desist that he gradually loses the discount.

The discount thus serves as 'token of recognition', granted in advance. The convicted defendant, on being convicted, is given the benefit of a reduced penal response, in recognition of his assumed capacity to make an effort of will to desist from further offending. Indeed, if any such token of recognition is desired, it can only be through an initially granted discount. When the offender is first convicted, we do not know until after the fact if he will make the requisite effort of will and desist. Were we to attempt to postpone the discount until we can observe whether he has ceased offending, it will be too late. By then, he will have served the full measure of punishment for his first offence, even if he never offends again.

It should be noted that granting the discount does not presuppose that all cases of subsequent desistance by convicted offenders involve the effort of will of which I have just spoken. Desisters will have a variety of reasons for refraining from further crime, including reasons of a non-moral nature: for example, having been intimidated by the prospect of further punishment, having lacked good further criminal opportunities, or having taken up legal pursuits more profitable than offending. However, my suggested approach does not presuppose that desistance must always be for moral reasons. The idea is that through the discount, the person is being treated as a moral agent: he is being given the *opportunity* to exercise self-restraint in this fashion. However, this theory, unlike a penance perspective, is not specifically designed to elicit specified sentiments in the actor (eg penitential attitudes), and there is nothing of which the criminal law should take cognisance should those sentiments fail to materialise—so long as he does indeed desist.[6]

The discount is not, therefore, a matter of gauging individual attitudes. My account takes it for granted that the perspectives of convicted offenders about reoffending will differ: some will consistently feel it a matter of great importance to try to desist, whereas others will respond with varying degrees of commitment or indifference. Because my view is not a penitence theory, these variations of feelings and attitudes should not matter in themselves for the offender's eligibility for the discount: it should not therefore be the sentencers' business to try to plumb such attitudes. What matters, instead, is treating the offender as a moral agent, albeit a fallible one, by giving him the *opportunity* to make the requisite effort of will. He thus should receive the full discount initially, in the expectation that he will respond by desisting. If he does not, he (gradually) loses the discount, depending the frequency of his subsequent reoffending.

[6] For a discussion of a penance perspective and its implications, see Duff (2001: chs 3 and 4); and critically thereto, von Hirsch and Ashworth (2005: ch 7).

Let me also emphasise that the theory is not about the individual offender's degree of personal culpability—eg of his degree of intent, consciousness of wrongdoing, or the like. The underlying conception is a different one: of affording a limited tolerance[7] for human fallibility. And fallibility itself is not a matter of particular psychological characteristics or attitudes: it refers simply to the human tendency to err. People do make mistakes, but also have the capacity to try to pull themselves together and try to avoid repetitions. The discount is designed to recognise this capacity.

3. Multiple Reoffending?

How many repetitions must occur before the discount should disappear? It should be clear that the progressive-loss-of-mitigation discount would not permit deductions to be made indefinitely. If the offender keeps on returning to crime, he eventually should lose the discount entirely, and face the full measure of punishment for the offence.

Among those who do respond and cease offending, there appear to be (at least) two prototypes. One is that of the conventionally behaved individual who errs in an uncharacteristic moment of impulsiveness or unwisdom, and then corrects his behaviour. Here, giving him a single 'second chance'—as Julian Roberts suggests in chapter 2 below—would suffice.

Another kind of response is one familiar to criminologists studying desistance among convicted criminals. It is that of the offender who embarks on a criminal career, but then—after having been punished on a number of occasions—begins to make efforts to desist. The efforts may be halting at first: while he seems to have developed a bona fide desire to stop, he fails initially to implement it well and backslides from time to time. Eventually, however, he does come to cease offending. The pattern is that of a halting, gradual desistance that tends to be linked with the offender's age, his apparent desire to assume a more conventional lifestyle, and his dissatisfaction with living a criminal existence (eg Maruna, 2002). The progressive-loss-of-mitigation model serves to address this second kind of situation. Because the discount is withdrawn gradually, it provides a continuing moral inducement for change in the offender's mode of living over time.

---

[7] Tolerance, as Joseph Raz (1987) has pointed out, does not imply that the conduct is permissible or less serious: one might thus tolerate someone's egotistical behaviour, without denying its wrongfulness; but one cannot tolerate his generosity or decency, because there is no wrong. Granting a partial tolerance, in this context, assumes that the conduct is wrong, but should be treated less severely for various normative reasons—including the reasons discussed in the text.

My previous discussions of the issue of prior offending did not draw sufficient attention to the distinction between these cases. My attempts to provide a rationale for the discount model thus reverted to language which was more suitable to the first kind of case than the second. I spoke of the offender as having had a previous pattern of compliance, of having offended in a moment of weakness or wilfulness, and the like. This mode of discourse makes sense for everyday contexts, where we are chiefly speaking of misconduct among conventionally behaved individuals. A modified vocabulary and way of thinking is needed, however, when speaking of gradual desistance among convicted offenders.

Why this distinction between criminal-law context and other, more everyday settings? A reason concerns whether there are selective entry criteria. One can insist, that is, on more stringent standards, and narrower allowances for acts of misconduct, where (as in choosing a work associate or in appointing someone to an academic or judicial post) one can select only the more promising candidates, and deal with repeat offending through the eventual exclusion of the person from the activity. Criminal sentencing should operate with more generous tolerances for repeated offending, because it cannot have the luxuries of restrictive entry criteria, and exclusion for persistent violators, as we will see next.

4. Multiple Wrongdoing and the Institutional and Social Context

The foregoing point about selective entry criteria can be seen as part of a more general one: that the generosity or stringency of norms concerning repeated wrongdoing should depend on the institutional and legal context. The criminal law should adopt more generous standards concerning repeat wrongdoing, in virtue of the type of enterprise it involves. Other types of enterprise might well adopt more rigorous requirements in their disciplinary standards. Of particular relevance, here, would be (i) the degree of stringency suitable for the system's behavioural norms; (ii) the degree of voluntariness of participation in the enterprise in question, and the ease of exit from it; and (iii) the potential severity of sanctions for violations. On these dimensions, the criminal law differs in important respects from many other forms of activity—and these differences should affect how multiple wrongdoing should be treated. We thus should pay heed (as Lee notes in chapter 4 below) to the institutional context of prior-criminal-record judgements, and to the criminal law's particular role and functions.

Consider, first, a non-criminal form of regulation: a university's disciplinary standards. Given the importance that should be accorded to original scholarship for a university's academic work, a case can be made for strict standards concerning plagiarism. Perhaps, a modest severity-discount might be allowed for lesser first instances of this kind of misconduct.

But repetition of the behaviour (and arguably also, serious first offences) should result in expulsion of the offending faculty member. Thus not much scope for 'lapses' should be allowed. Why not? The three factors, just mentioned, help provide an explanation. Thus (i) a university should hold its academic members to high standards of scholarship and scholarly ethics; (ii) participation in the university's academic enterprise is voluntary—thus those who do not wish to abide by these norms of scholarship, and so face disciplinary action by the university, would still be free to choose some other, less demanding form of activity; (iii) the sanctions the university can levy are of a restricted nature: no loss of liberty, or deprivation of basic civil rights, may be levied as a sanction. Even the ultimate academic penalty—expulsion—eaves the individual free in the community to pursue other forms of work (perhaps advertising or investment banking?) where originality would be less at a premium.

The criminal law should operate with less stringent norms concerning prior misconduct because the character of its enterprise is different, especially in the three respects just mentioned. Thus (i) the criminal law's standards of appropriate behaviour should be less demanding—because those standards should serve to establish the minimum norms of social interaction among citizens. (b) The duty to abide by the criminal law's norms of conduct is not voluntary. Everyone must comply. No person who dislikes obeying the penal law's behavioural standards may quit the enterprise (as the plagiarising academic can), short of emigration or suicide. (c) The criminal law's sanctions are especially burdensome, and include deprivation of liberty. These three factors should call for somewhat more generous norms in criminal law, concerning those relating to repetitive misconduct.

Another feature of criminal recidivism is worth noting here, and militates in favour of having a diminishing discount over several repetitions, until the full measure of punishment is reached. Criminal activity tends to diminish with age, and only a minority of active offenders will remain involved in criminal activity for protracted periods (eg von Hirsch and Kazemian, 2009). The progressive-loss-of-mitigation approach would give offenders several opportunities to respond to penal censure and its moral appeal, before being confronted with the full measure of the penalty. By that time, the offender's propensity for offending might well be diminishing, in any event.

5. An Illustration: Sweden's Treatment of Recidivist Offending

How might such a progressive-loss-of-mitigation model work out in practice? Sweden's scheme for sentencing recidivists provides an illustration (see Asp, ch 11 below). Under that country's sentencing reform statute, which first took effect in 1989, the principle of proportionality is the governing principle, so that the seriousness of the offence of conviction is the primary determinant of penalties' severity. Generally, the statute gives only a limited role to the prior record: serious offenders receive custodial sentences, even if not previously convicted; and lesser offenders are given non-custodial sanctions even for multiple reoffending. Where the defendant has previous convictions, there would be just modest adjustments in the sanctions.

In the middle range of crime-seriousness (eg for burglaries), however, the criminal record does play a significant role—but one that comports with the 'discount' approach. The law prescribes brief periods of imprisonment as the 'standard' sanctions for such middle-range offences. Upon the first and several subsequent convictions, however, the offender is not imprisoned, but instead receives non-custodial sanctions. Imprisonment is imposed only as a last resort, after the offender has accumulated a significant number of previous convictions—as many as four or so. Until that point is reached, there would be a gradation in the degree of onerousness of the non-custodial responses, depending on the number of previous convictions. A first offender would receive as his discounted penalty a unit fine—ie a fine equivalent to a specified number of days' earnings, with that number depending on the seriousness of the offence. Any subsequent conviction would attract a somewhat higher unit-fine or possibly a term of probation involving supervision of the offender in the community. Next, there would be an additional adjustment, eg a stint of community service as a penalty. It is only when the offender keeps on offending that he would face the full deserved sanction, a term of imprisonment.

This illustration from Sweden suggests how a progressive-loss-of-mitigation model can work in practice. It also suggests the model's further attraction, of helping to limit reliance on severe penal interventions. Our Swedish burglar would continue receiving non-custodial sanctions, notwithstanding several reconvictions—albeit ones of somewhat increasing onerousness. It is only with quite frequent reoffending—say, on the fourth reconviction—that he would suffer the 'standard' penalty of a term of imprisonment (albeit still one of comparatively modest duration by English or US standards). The scheme thus helps incorporate a degree of 'parsimony' into standards of deserved punishment.

My espousal of Sweden's approach, however, is normative and desert-oriented; I am not claiming that adopting such a gradually diminishing discount promotes desistance and thus reduces crime. There is no reason to expect that adoption of a Swedish-style discount will actually cause rates of reoffending to diminish. Crime rates generally show little responsiveness to changes in sentencing patterns (eg Bottoms, 2004). Adopting a discount, or making it a gradually diminishing one over several repetitions, is thus unlikely to make much impression on crime rates.

I am also not suggesting that Sweden's norm—of a gradually diminishing discount through about four repetitions—'tracks' actual desistance patterns. Among offenders who do cease offending, desistance patterns will differ. Some will stop committing crimes after the second or third offence—and get the benefit of the remaining portion of the discount. Others will pursue extensive criminal careers before even beginning to making significant efforts to desist. The latter individuals would not be eligible for any discount, because their desistance occurs too late. Sweden's should be seen as normatively based. Its criteria thus should be based on what appears reasonable as implementation of progressive-loss-of-mitigation, taking into account institutional and social context in which the criminal sanction operates.

E. CONCLUDING REMARKS

This chapter returns to a theme I have addressed a number of times previously,[8] namely the bearing of previous convictions on the proportionate sentence. I have retained the basic perspective I developed in earlier writings: one that supports a *discount* approach, and seeks to explain it as a limited tolerance accorded to human tendency to err, but to also the human capacity to make moral efforts at subsequent self-restraint.

This perspective, I am assuming, operates within a proportionality standard that makes seriousness of the offence the principal determinant of a criminal sentence's severity. Any adjustment related to previous offending should therefore have substantially less influence on the severity of the sanction than the judgment of seriousness of the present offence. (I thus am not speaking here, therefore, of a criminal-career-based scheme, where the offender's criminal history would become the primary influence on punishment severity.[9]) The limited tolerance of which I am speaking also does not address the usual determinants of criminal desert relating to crime seriousness, namely the degree of harm and culpability of the instant offence (see B.1 above). It concerns, rather, how much penal censure should attach to conduct of a given degree of seriousness, depending on the criminal history.

My earlier explanations of the rationale of the progressive-loss-of-mitigation suffered, however, from certain deficiencies. First, I relied unduly on inferences from everyday judgements of blameworthiness, without taking adequately into account the special features of the criminal sanction. Second, I failed adequately to take into account the institutional

---

[8] See eg von Hirsch (1981), von Hirsch (1991), and von Hirsch and Ashworth (2005: ch 9).
[9] For a critical discussion of the latter approach, see von Hirsch and Ashworth (2005: 150–55).

and social contexts of desert-judgements: that one might, for example, be chary of granting repeated discounts in certain institutional contexts (eg disciplinary measures for judicial or academic misconduct), while offering more generous prior-offending allowances in other contexts, including that of criminal sentencing. Most notably, my previous discussions failed to elaborate, in detailed terms, the *why* and *how* of the discount: I spoke, for example, of the tolerance as recognition of a 'respected process' by which the actor may attend to the disapprobation visited by previous punishment; but did not specify wherein that respected process consisted.

Here I have tried to provide fuller analysis in these three areas, wherein I felt that my analysis was deficient. Whether my present, revised arguments constitute any more convincing explanation I leave to the reader. Those arguments, however, are still tentative: I am still uncertain whether I have got it even approximately right.[10]

REFERENCES

Bottoms, AE (2004) 'Empirical Research Relevant to Sentencing Frameworks', in AE Bottoms (ed), *Alternatives to Prison: Options for an Insecure Society* (Cullompton, Willan).

Duff, RA (2001) *Punishment, Communication, and Community* (New York, Oxford University Press).

Fletcher, G (1978) *Rethinking Criminal Law* (Boston, Little-Brown).

Maruna, S (2001) *Making Good: How Ex-convicts Reform and Rebuild their Lives* (Washington, DC: American Psychological Association).

Raz, J (1987) 'Autonomy, Tolerance and the Harm Principle', in R Gavison (ed), *Issues in Contemporary Legal Philosophy: The Influence of HLA Hart* (Oxford, Clarendon Press).

Singer, R (1979) *Just Deserts: Sentencing based on Equality and Desert* (Cambridge, MA, Ballinger).

von Hirsch, A (1981) 'Desert and Previous Convictions' 65 *Minnesota Law Review* 591–634.

— — (1993) *Censure and Sanctions* (Oxford, Oxford University Press).

— — (1991) 'Criminal Record Rides Again' 10 *Criminal Justice Ethics* 55–57.

von Hirsch, A and Ashworth, A (2005) *Proportionate Sentencing: Exploring the Principles* (Oxford, Oxford University Press).

von Hirsch, A and Kazemian, L (2009) 'Predictive Sentencing and Selective Incapacitation', in A von Hirsch, A Ashworth and J Roberts (eds), *Principled Sentencing: Readings in Theory and Policy* (Oxford, Oxford University Press).

Wasik, M (1987) 'Guidelines, Guidance and Criminal Record', in M Wasik and K Pease (eds), *Sentencing Reform: Guidance or Guidelines?* (Manchester, Manchester University Press).

[10] Important subsidiary issues also have not been addressed, eg the role of the seriousness of previous offences, and the similarity or difference of previous from current offending; see eg von Hirsch (1981: 620).

2

First-Offender Sentencing Discounts: Exploring the Justifications[1]

JULIAN V ROBERTS

O N WHAT GROUNDS should first-time offenders receive more
lenient treatment than recidivists? Several utilitarian justifications
exist for offering a sentencing discount to novice offenders—
for example, in order to provide an incentive for the offender to return
to a law-abiding lifestyle, or because deterrence may already have been
achieved through the process of conviction, thus rendering imposition of
the full sentence unnecessary. However, justifying the use of a first-offender
sentencing discount within a desert-oriented sentencing framework has
proved more challenging, to say the least.

Retribution is concerned with recognising, in the severity of the
sentence imposed, the crime of conviction and the offender's level of
blameworthiness for the offence. In order for a retributive account to
legitimately incorporate a given factor at sentencing, the factor must
affect either the seriousness of the crime or the offender's level of blameworthiness. Crime seriousness is clearly unaffected by the offender's
criminal antecedents, and blameworthiness is therefore the only route by
which previous convictions may enter the *retributive* equation. Otherwise, a retributively oriented model of sentencing must find room for the
consideration of an offender's previous convictions within a category of
factors relevant to sentencing but external to the model.[2]

---

[1] I am grateful to the other participants at the Oxford and Cambridge seminars for their
feedback, and Estella Baker for comments on an earlier draft of this chapter.

[2] Other legitimate considerations at sentencing are also external to desert, including factors such as assisting the state in other prosecutions, or pleading guilty. Gross (1979: 279)
notes that: 'The punishment deserved for the crime is no less when these things are taken
into consideration, but since what is deserved is not all that matters in deciding what sentence is right, there is good reason for a lighter sentence in spite of that.' von Hirsch and
Ashworth (2005) discuss a number of other factors which are external to desert theory but
which may legitimately be considered at sentencing, including a delay since the commission
of the crime (see von Hirsch and Ashworth 2005: appendix 1).

A number of retributive theorists (eg Fletcher 1978; Singer 1979; Durham 1987; Bagaric 2001) have dismissed any consideration of previous convictions at sentencing, arguing that prior convictions affect neither crime seriousness nor blameworthiness, and therefore should be ignored. More recently, a number of authors have argued that previous convictions enhance an offender's level of blameworthiness, and that they should therefore be considered at sentencing (eg Macpherson 2002; Roberts 2008; Lee 2009[3]). The focus of this chapter is upon a third group of retributivists, those who recognise the limited relevance of previous convictions within the doctrine known as the *progressive loss of mitigation*.

A. OVERVIEW

This chapter explores the justifications for discounting sentences for first-time offenders, or people with modest criminal records. Ultimately I will argue that first offenders deserve—and are therefore entitled to—some leniency at sentencing because we regard most (but by no means all) of them to be less blameworthy as a result of their history of compliance with the law. For a variety of reasons, criminal behaviour should be judged less stringently when considered within a context of prior compliance with the law.

The chapter begins by considering the justifications that have been offered for discounting sentences for first offenders, and then examines in greater detail the tolerance-based concept of the progressive loss of mitigation. Although the *progressive loss of mitigation* model is described in a number of publications (eg von Hirsch 1985, 1998; Wasik and von Hirsch 1994; Ashworth 2005; see also Duff 2001: 167–70), I draw most heavily on von Hirsch and Ashworth (2005) and a recent essay by von Hirsch (2009). I express some criticisms of the concept, both at the theoretical and practical level. I argue that the *progressive loss of mitigation* model is over-broad; it is valid only when applied to minor crimes. Rather than being granted to all offenders (and on repeated occasions), leniency should be offered to some offenders, and usually only once.

Three specific questions are addressed here:[4] (i) Is it justified within a censure-based framework to discount the sentence for first offenders? (ii)

---

[3] It is worth noting that almost 40 years ago the author of the first English sentencing text posed the question '[H]ow can past offences affect the gravity of a current crime?' His response was that 'resort may be had to the retributive theory for an answer' (Cross 1971: 149).

[4] In this chapter I draw attention to difficulties associated with extending tolerance repeatedly for multiple lapses. In his contribution to this volume, Jesper Ryberg discusses other problematic elements of the lapse theory, such as the difficulty in determining whether a given crime is in fact a 'lapse'.

Should this sentencing 'discount' be categorical in nature—extended to *all* first offenders regardless of the nature or seriousness of their current convictions? (iii) Should the discount be offered on multiple occasions—as found under the *progressive loss of mitigation* model—or rather limited only to the first conviction?

B. JUSTIFYING A SENTENCE MITIGATION FOR FIRST-TIME OFFENDERS

1. Offender's Ignorance of the Full Consequences of Crime and Punishment

One justification for leniency towards first offenders involves recognition of their lack of awareness of the consequences of their conduct. Some first offenders may argue, and reasonably in my view, that they were insufficiently aware of the criminal character of their actions or the magnitude of the legal repercussions of that conduct, until they were ultimately convicted and sentenced ('I never thought he would care so much about a mobile phone!').[5] This claim may have validity even if the offender was well aware of the criminal nature of his actions. On this account, first offenders should be considered less blameworthy than offenders who break the law despite the full knowledge of the consequences. Over 20 years ago the Victorian Sentencing Committee noted that:

> In many instances the effects of the crime are far more serious than were contemplated by the offender before or at the time that it was committed. Sometimes this arises from the fact that the offender was immature, failed to exercise any reasonable judgment. . . . If on the material presented to the court, the court accepts that the offender did not think that his or her conduct would cause, or involve the threat of serious injury to any person, then *that person's culpability is greatly reduced*. (1988: 261, emphasis added)

This justification for the first-offender discount should be particularly appealing because awareness of consequences is one of the characteristics which most obviously distinguishes novice from recidivist offenders. A first-time burglar may not be fully aware of the harm inflicted by breaking into someone's home. A repeat burglar who has experienced numerous sentencing hearings and received multiple sentences is under no illusions about the consequences of domestic burglary. This differential awareness

---

[5] Offenders who commit crimes against large companies sometimes justify their behaviour by arguing that 'they can afford the loss' or 'they're insured anyway', and one purpose of the sentencing hearing is to disabuse them of such self-serving beliefs.

distinguishes the two categories of offenders. If an offender does lack awareness of the truly wrongful nature of his conduct, it is reasonable to consider him somewhat less blameworthy than others who commit the same crime fully aware of its consequences.

von Hirsch and Ashworth (2005: 150) reject this 'partial ignorance' justification for leniency. They note the difficulty that 'many of those convicted for the first time may have been perfectly aware of the prohibition and of the wrongfulness of their conduct, but simply committed it anyway'. True enough, but a claim for leniency on the grounds of partial ignorance should be examined on its merits; is it asking too much of a court to consider whether the claim is valid and, where appropriate, to accord some leniency? There are surely many cases, particularly involving younger offenders, where a crime is committed spontaneously or impulsively and where the offender failed to fully consider the consequences of his actions for himself or for others. Offenders sometimes realise the full consequences of their actions only at the stage of sentencing. Indeed, one of the goals of a sentencing 'hearing' is to bring home to the offender the consequences of his actions, for himself and the victim, often through the use of victim impact evidence at sentencing (Roberts 2009).

This justification should not therefore be categorically dismissed or categorically accepted. However, it is relevant only to a one-time (not repetitive) discount—a subject which will be discussed later in this chapter. Nor does this justification have any credibility as a plea for mitigation in cases of serious 'consensus' crimes: one does not need to be sentenced and to listen to a victim impact statement to know the consequences of the more serious forms of assault, for example.

2. Credit for a History of Compliance with the Law

A second justification for leniency as a response to a first offence invokes first-offenders' untarnished life history until this point in time. This notion is also echoed in the 'progressive loss of credit' described by Thomas (1979: 197) by which the offender draws down his credit for a conviction-free life to the point of his first conviction. First-time offenders may advance a moral claim to be spared the full reprobative power of the criminal law. They claim some credit for having led a life of compliance with the law, in the same way that an employee who steals after 30 years of honest labour for his employer is entitled to more leniency than an employee who steals on his first shift at the factory. The context cannot be ignored: what kind of sentencing system would say to the offender, 'Yes, you have been a model employee for 30 years, but sorry, that has no bearing on your theft from your employer'? A history of compliance is particularly relevant if, during this period, the offender has been subject to temptation—but has resisted. For example, the narcotics officer offered bribes for 20 years but who finally succumbs to temptation is surely less blameworthy than one who takes the money at the first opportunity.

Once again the seriousness of the offence plays a role; being a model citizen for years cannot generate credit to mitigate the sentence for rape. This claim is also restricted, presumably, to a single occasion, and loses force when applied to multiple recidivists. An offender convicted of assault for the third time cannot plausibly claim leniency on the basis that the current offence was an isolated island of misconduct set within a sea of compliance with the law.

3. Previous Good Character of the Defendant

A related but independent justification for a repetitive discount for novice offenders is founded on the defendant's previous good character. Here the offender argues: 'That's not me!—I don't know what came over me.' There is a clear appeal to environmental influences upon the offender's behaviour. The defendant adduces evidence of his previous good character as grounds to mitigate the sentence. Character-based justifications are anathema to retributive theories which focus tightly on the offence, and the offender's culpability for the crime, not his general character. Yet the question of character lurks behind several justifications for the mitigation. It may lie at the end of the 'lifetime of compliance' argument, as in 'My lifetime of compliance with the law . . . *proves my good character.*' In practice, good character appeals at sentencing are common.[6] A character-based appeal may also divert a court from certain utilitarian objectives. A punitive sentence imposed to deter the offender from further offending may be seen to be unnecessary in the case of defendants with a good character who are sensitive to the need to comply with the law. Or, people with good characters may be seen to be sufficiently horrified at the consequences of their criminal 'lapse' as to launch themselves on the road to rehabilitation—without the need for state-imposed and potentially intrusive treatment orders.

The danger with this (and the preceding) justification is that the offender may cite a wide range of circumstances to demonstrate his good character, and this may include much that lies beyond the simple fact of a lifetime of compliance with the law. He may invoke his steady employment record, a commitment to raising a family, volunteer work, or contributions to

---

[6] The appeal may also be made on more than a single occasion—it may take several convictions before an offender's claim to have a good character becomes unbelievable. This is particularly the case if he is allowed to place a range of unrelated good works before the court in support of his claim (see below).

charity, a good war record—a spectrum of activities that may be denied or less available to socially disadvantaged defendants. Singer wrote that

> [T]he argument of character clearly raises the specter of bringing into the sentencing process all of that soft data upon which sentencing judges have relied for the last hundred years—the defendant's religion, his past unemployment, his relations with his spouse, his childhood history, whether he loves animals, and so forth. (Singer, 1979: 70)

Indeed, the plea for mitigation becomes in Walker's memorable phrase, a 'leap into a bog with no boundaries' (Walker 1985: 45). For this reason alone, a claim for leniency on the grounds that the offender is of good character is less appealing than the other justifications for the practice.

4. Optimistic and Pessimistic Views of the Offender

Finally, Gross (1979) also proposed a justification for mitigating punishments for novice offenders. His proposal has sunk without trace from writings on the subject, but it is worth noting because it also invokes a relationship between the offender and the state, which is also part of the tolerance-based justification (to which I shall turn shortly). According to Gross, after the offender's first conviction, a court may adopt an optimistic view about his future conduct: the sentence now imposed will be sufficient to recall him to a law-abiding lifestyle.[7] This optimism justifies punishing the offender 'less severely than culpability would warrant' (Gross 1979: 456) and 'it is a matter of giving them the benefit of the doubt as long as there is a reasonable doubt about their intentions' (ibid).

This language is reminiscent of the dialogue between court and offender described by Ashworth (2005: 188). In both cases the state is offering some leniency and is anticipating a positive response from the offender. As additional convictions accumulate, the court's sunny optimism gives way to pessimism about the offender's probable intentions and likely future behaviour. This pessimism justifies the imposition of the full tariff; but the optimism may take some time to evaporate, hence the offender may benefit from repeated discounts. Thereafter, Gross shares with Ashworth and von Hirsch (2005) the view that additional convictions cannot justify the imposition of a harsher sentence. As a justification for a discount, the optimistic–pessimistic dimension seems unconvincing and in any event is not related to retributivism per se.

---

[7] This assumption also has a utilitarian component. As Manson notes: 'It is assumed that the offender will respond positively to the deterrent effects of the process of arrest, charging, finding of guilt, and imposition of sanction. This discounts any need for individual deterrence and suggests that a lenient sentence is in order' (Manson 2001: 131).

To summarise, a number of justifications may be advanced to support a sentencing discount for first offenders, although only the partial ignorance and credit for prior compliance are in my view legitimate grounds for regarding first-time offenders as less blameworthy and therefore entitled to some leniency. One common feature of these two justifications is that they arise from the conduct of the offender; now I turn to the justification which is independent of any claims by the defendant, namely the 'lapse' theory.

B. SOCIETAL TOLERANCE AND THE PROGRESSIVE LOSS OF MITIGATION: THE LAPSE THEORY

1. Definition and Ambit

Since being formally articulated in the 1980s[8] (see von Hirsch 1985), the *progressive loss of mitigation* model of previous convictions has proved influential. It is repeatedly cited in the case-law, the appellate jurisprudence of all common law countries and sentencing texts (eg Piper and Easton 2008: 86–88; Ashworth 2005: 188). In addition, the doctrine has influenced statutory sentencing provisions in a number of jurisdictions, most notably England and Wales, and Western Australia.[9] Despite the proliferation of the doctrine, few publications have explored its consequences or subjected its justifications and essential features to critical scrutiny.[10]

The concept of the progressive loss of mitigation is straightforward: impose a discounted sentence upon first offenders, and then progressively reduce the magnitude of the discount as the offender accumulates addi-

---

[8] An earlier description of the concept of a repetitive, but diminishing, leniency can be found in Thomas (1979: 197–99) who discusses the essential elements of the practice of offering a limited sentencing discount. References to a first-offender sentencing discount go back much further. More than a century ago Cox noted that: '[F]or he who has had so emphatic a warning as a trial, a conviction and a punishment can plead none of the excuses which may be properly urged in behalf of first offenders' (Cox 1877: 146–47).

[9] The 1991 Criminal Justice Act in England and Wales placed relatively strict limits on the ability of a court to consider previous convictions at sentencing. It was subsequently amended by the 1993 Act. S 7(2) of the Sentencing Act 1995 (Western Australia) which prevents courts from aggravating the sentence on the basis of the offender's criminal record. These are the only statutes of which I am aware that restrict the use of previous convictions at sentencing in a way consistent with a progressive loss of mitigation or a 'purely' retributive analysis.

[10] One exception is Bagaric (2001: 238–45) who provides a critical analysis of the progressive loss of mitigation. Walker (1985: 91) criticised the first-offender discount on the basis that it constitutes sentencing on character. See also the contribution by Ryberg to this volume, and Ryberg (2004: 81).

tional convictions; eventually a point is reached at which the offender receives the 'normal' or deserved sentence. Thus once the discount is exhausted, further convictions have no impact on the severity of sentence imposed. This consideration of an offender's record creates an asymmetry of application: the absence of prior convictions may be used to mitigate the sentence, but an accumulation of convictions may not aggravate.

Advocates of the *progressive loss of mitigation* doctrine make it clear that the progressively diminishing discounts are available across the spectrum of offending: 'The discount should be available to *every* first offender—and continues (at diminishing levels) until he has accumulated the requisite number of convictions to lose it' (von Hirsch and Ashworth (2005: 154, emphasis in original; see also von Hirsch 1985: 84). The discount applies even to offenders being sentenced for serious crimes and who have prior convictions—as long as it is the offender's first *serious* offence.[11] Thus:

> Suppose someone has committed a serious intentional wrong, and wants to claim that he act is uncharacteristic of his past behaviour. Suppose he has previously been censured for other wrongs, but of a much less serious character. He might still plausibly claim that it was uncharacteristic of him to commit wrongs of this magnitude. (von Hirsch and Ashworth 2005: 154)

In practice, as Ashworth (2005: 191) notes, courts subvert this conceptualisation of the doctrine by denying the discount to offenders convicted of the more serious forms of offending—a finding which itself might give us pause to question a theoretical model with such a broad application.[12]

2. How Many Lapses Should Be Allowed?

Opinions vary regarding the number of times that an offender may expect a mitigated punishment, but it is clear that an offender may accumulate multiple convictions before the mitigation is fully exhausted. For example,

---

[11] The relevance of the doctrine for more than trivial offences was confirmed more recently by von Hirsch (2009), who argued that 'In the middle range of crime seriousness . . . the previous record plays a quite significant role' (182).

[12] Academic writings on the progressive loss of mitigation explore the principle at the conceptual level but it is worth considering an actual offence. Consider the case of three men who are convicted of assault. Coming out of a pub, they follow the victim down an alley where he is punched and kicked several times. The offenders are ultimately convicted—for the first time. According to the definitive guidelines of the Sentencing Guidelines Council, with at least two aggravating factors, this case has passed the custodial threshold. An appropriate sentence may be 90 days—reduced, say, to 45 days for a first offender. Imagine a subsequent conviction on the same fact pattern, and a sentence now stepped down from 90 to 60 days for the second offence. Imagine further a court noting that the sentence is more lenient than it would otherwise be because the offender has only a single previous offence. The court displays, on behalf of the state, tolerance towards the offender to mark his limited engagement in criminality. These decrements in severity will mean little to the offender.

Wasik (1987: 118) suggested up to five convictions might be necessary to exhaust all the mitigation. Ashworth (2005: 188) states that the offender should be fully censured on the third conviction, limiting the 'second chances' offered offenders to two, a position also adopted by Duff (2001: 169). Most recently, von Hirsch (2009: 183) has suggested four convictions might be result in mitigated punishments before the offender receives the full, deserved sentence. At the end of the day, Thomas (1979: 199) and von Hirsch (1985: 87) are probably correct when they note that there is no hard and fast rule governing the number of discounted sentences, but that the nature and timing of the fresh convictions would determine how rapidly the mitigation was lost. Adhering to a rigid number of mitigations would be as mechanistic as the approach taken by cumulative sentencers whereby each additional conviction automatically triggers an escalation in severity. For present purposes, the important point is that according to the *progressive loss of mitigation* approach, mitigation is offered on multiple occasions.

C. JUSTIFYING THE PROGRESSIVE LOSS OF MITIGATION

1. Tolerance for a 'Lapse'

von Hirsch and Ashworth (2005) explain the tolerance-based justification for the progressive loss of mitigation in the following terms: 'humans are not angels . . . a certain tolerance seems appropriate' (151). Despite its counter-intuitive nature, a link to everyday moral judgments is rapidly made: 'Our everyday moral judgments include the notion of a *lapse* . . . some understanding should be shown' (152). Human fallibility, they argue

> calls for a limited tolerance of failure, expressed through some diminution of the initial penal response. The respected process . . . is that by which a person can attend the disapproval visited upon him and *alter his course accordingly*. In viewing the person as a moral agent, we initially assume him capable of such a response and thus give him a 'second chance' (153, emphasis added)

Several comments may be offered with respect to this key passage. First, it implies a series of exchanges between the court and the offender: the former mitigates the punishment (out of tolerance) and awaits the response of the defendant. Ashworth (2005: 188) elaborates on the justification for the declining mitigation in terms of a dialogue between the state and the offender:

> The justification for the gradual losing of that mitigation on second and subsequent convictions is that the 'second chance' has been given and not taken; the offender has forfeited the tolerance, and its associated discount, because the

subsequent criminal choices show insufficient response to the public censure. In principle then the second offence deserves greater censure than the first.

But why does the second offence deserve more censure than the first, and the third more than the second, yet the fourth no more than the third. And when the offender's 'response' consists of further offending, wherefore the additional leniency?[13]

The 'second chance' logic does not sustain a repetitive, declining degree of mitigation. Consider an offender convicted of a crime for which the usual sentence is a term of custody in the 12-month range. Reducing the sentence to 6 months in recognition that the offender is a first- or second-time offender is hardly giving him a second (or third) chance—it is a rather a question of simply mitigating his punishment. The logic of providing a second (or third) chance may, however, justify the imposition of a suspended sentence. Indeed, sentencing statutes in many jurisdictions employ first-offender provisions which require the court to suspend a sentence in the case of an offender convicted for the first time.

When applied to offences insufficiently serious to warrant a lengthy period of custody, these provisions make a lot of sense; they provide the offender with a chance to avoid imprisonment. In everyday life, the concept of a second chance has great appeal—but a third, and a fourth chance? How are these additional 'chances' justified? How much tolerance should we, as a society, be required to display? Tolerance is a virtue, but not if it is carried to excess, otherwise the tolerant society becomes the unjustifiably permissive society. Mercy is subject to the same kind of limits; it is a virtue to be merciful, but not repetitively, without any positive response from the offender or for all manner of transgressions—at least not in a secular society, although some religions may endorse a concept of recidivist forgiveness. Mercy should be exercised with prudence, not profligacy.

Finally, it is also worth noting that by detaching the leniency extended to first offenders from any notion of diminished blameworthiness, the tolerance justification deprives these offenders of any *claim* to leniency. The first-time offender claims some consideration to reflect his law-abiding life to this point, and to distinguish himself from multiple recidivists. According to the lapse theory, this claim is rejected by the benign state, which acts graciously by tolerating the weaknesses of the human condition. Offenders convicted for the first time may take issue with this approach which denies them agency in this way. They may prefer to affirm that their lifetime of compliance prior to their offence entitles them to more consideration

---

[13] In practice, courts never communicate a message of partial, repetitive tolerance of criminal conduct. Imagine a court addressing the first offender: 'You deserve a harsher sentence, but I am going to be tolerant of your offending on this occasion, and somewhat less tolerant as you reappear for sentencing, but ultimately my tolerance will reach its limits.'

than would be accorded a multiple recidivist.[14] First-time offenders may feel that they *deserve* a mitigated punishment. Their entitlement in this regard is denied by the lapse account.

The consequence of the policy is counter-intuitive, to say the least. Consider the *progressive loss of mitigation* logic in the context of a specific offence: drunk driving. The first-time impaired driver makes an appeal for leniency, and since it is his first 'lapse', he is accorded a mitigated punishment. Upon re-conviction, he excuses himself again ('I don't know what came over me—yet again') and receives another, slightly less mitigated punishment. On the third occasion, yet *another* discount, albeit more modest, is offered and so on. What possible penal logic underpins this sequence of mitigated punishments?

Represented graphically the principle of *progressive loss of mitigation* has two phases or zones. First, there is the mitigation stage at which leniency is progressively withdrawn and the punishment becomes increasingly harsher. If the leniency is continuous rather than dichotomous, then offenders must be arrayed on a dimension of some kind. Risk-based or culpability-based justifications of a recidivist premium create a dimension (of risk, or moral blameworthiness, along which offenders may be arrayed). But what quality do first offenders possess in greater degree than second offenders, who in turn possess to a greater extent than third-time offenders and so on? There is no answer to this question because the justification is located not with some attribute of the offender but the tolerant state that offers the iteratively (but declining) mitigation. According to this model we should tolerate the fifth-time offender slightly less than the fourth-time offender, the fourth-time offender slightly less than the third time offender and so on down the line. The dimension, then, is tolerance: societal tolerance for criminal wrongdoing.

The second phase is the 'flat line' which reveals no increment in severity despite the possibly endless repetition of criminal conduct. Consider offenders falling within this phase of the model. Imagine an individual convicted of dangerous driving for the tenth time. Should he receive the same sentence as the offender convicted for the third time? Both have exhausted their lapse-based leniency, yet is it reasonable to treat the pair in the same way?

2. Justifying a Repetitive Discount

The concept of offering wrongdoers a second chance is undoubtedly founded in everyday conceptions of wrongdoing and punishment. Most

---

[14] See Green (2008) for a discussion of the resentment that toleration engenders in the individuals on whose behalf it is exercised.

people are willing to withhold full judgment—to offer a 'discount' in response to a first transgression. Where the principle of the *progressive loss of mitigation* departs from everyday moral judgements—and becomes implausible—is in its repetitive nature, and its application to serious crimes.[15]

Let us deal with the first of these departures. von Hirsch (2009) has recently proposed that the more serious wrongs (proscribed by the criminal law and punished at sentencing) should be met with a *greater* degree of tolerance than the less serious, even trivial transgressions of everyday life. His justification is threefold: (i) in non-criminal regulatory contexts (such as a university) there should be less tolerance for lapses from acceptable conduct because participation in the society is voluntary. A faculty member who is censured for misconduct may resign from her post, while offenders cannot depart from open society so readily; (ii) the standards set are higher in such a restricted context, and the degree of tolerance should therefore be less generous; (iii) criminal sanctions are potentially so severe that the state should exercise great restraint, and this may be interpreted to mean more tolerance for conduct giving rise to such sanctions.

3. Justifying Less Tolerance in the Criminal Law than in Everyday Life

Against these justifications a number of objections may be made which suggest that the criminal law should be less, not more, tolerant. The behaviours proscribed by the criminal law should be, and generally are, more serious than the conduct proscribed by non-penal regimes—Oxbridge college statutes for example. This obvious fact has two consequences. First, rule-breaking in a *non*-criminal context is, and should be, tolerated with greater leniency than in the criminal justice system. The predicate conduct is less serious, and leniency is always easier to justify for minor than major transgressions. We have more tolerance for minor transgressions ('I can forgive pretty well anything, but not *that* . . .'). It will be recalled that, in practice, first-offender mitigation is denied offenders convicted of the most serious crimes. This speaks to the distinction between everyday moral judgments and the criminal law: the more serious infractions of the latter should elicit a response of low tolerance.

Second, it is generally[16] harder to violate the criminal law inadvert-

[15] The fact that repetitive discounting violates intuitive responses to offending does not invalidate the principle of *progressive loss of mitigation*, but it does suggest that the principal requires additional justification.

[16] Like so much in the field of sentencing, this is a generalisation to which there are many exceptions.

ently, without full awareness of so doing, or without fully appreciating the consequences of one's actions—one of the principal justifications for extending some mitigation to first offenders.[17] College rules such as the wearing of academic gowns on specified occasions may (and in practice are) broken relatively easily—violations should accordingly be treated with some leniency, even when repeated (the absent-minded professor). However, if the predicate conduct is serious, lapses should surely be treated with *more*, not less severity. If someone steps on your toes more than once, the second occasion will probably be met with a more rigorous response, although forgiveness is still likely; someone who punches you in the face twice cannot expect this same level of indulgence from his victim.[18]

Third, infringements of the criminal law usually affect the rights of third parties. Crimes are prosecuted on behalf of the state, but often involve an individual victim. Repetitive leniency towards rule-breaking in an Oxbridge college has few implications for other members of the college. If I repeatedly flout the rule requiring me to wear a gown at official college meetings, the interests of others are largely unaffected. The college can afford to respond to my recalcitrance with repeated warnings which may get increasingly more threatening. However, if I steal from, or worse, assault my colleagues, their interests are affected by the state's response to my transgression. Victims in this case may not see the merit of repetitive tolerance and their interests need to be considered (see later sections of this chapter).

Fifth, in private clubs, Oxbridge colleges, football teams and other such micro-societies, a 'thick' relationship develops between members, and between the association itself and the membership. The *social distance* between members of a community determines the degree to which tolerance will be justified; levels of tolerance are inversely correlated with the social distance between members. One consequence of this is that members may expect some consideration beyond that which exists outside the college or society. Even if the interests of others are affected by rule-breaking, members will exercise more tolerance of incivilities and transgressions of various kinds when the transgressor is a fellow member. Of course, the ultimate in-group is the family, where repetitive tolerance is the norm, not the exception. Uncle Tony's annual drunkenness during Christmas dinner is likely to be tolerated ('He *is* family, after all'). No such relationship exists between an individual citizen and the impersonal state in modern society, or between anonymous citizens, one of whom transgresses against another. Strangers do not owe each other a duty of

---

[17] This second point is related to the first; it is generally harder to commit serious transgressions through inadvertence or negligence; they usually require effort and commitment.

[18] Bagaric agrees that 'The less serious the violation, the more likely it is that forgiveness will be forthcoming' (2001: 238).

repetitive, mutual tolerance—at least not in Western industrialised societies.

Sixth, with respect to the argument that the more punitive sanctions of the criminal law justify greater tolerance, it may be said that a one-time first-offender discount spares the offender the full brunt of punishment. In addition, all common law sentencing regimes incorporate features to ensure that the offender is spared the more punitive sanctions unless and until it becomes absolutely necessary, particularly with respect to the use of imprisonment.[19] These mechanisms should achieve the 'liberal norm for prior offending' which von Hirsch (2009: 182) sees as justifying a scheme of repetitive mitigation.

Finally, von Hirsch (2009: 160) has argued that a lapse-based, *progressive loss of mitigation* model is appropriate because offenders in time grow out of offending as a result of the 'age–crime' curve. Desistance will ultimately ensue as a result of maturation; the deserved sanction is therefore being mitigated because in all probability the offender will, a year down the road, desist anyway. While this may be true, it represents a utilitarian intrusion into a deontological model of sentencing. Moreover, the argument also invites sentencers to deny mitigation or even to sentence more punitively if the offender is at the start of the age–crime curve, with a relatively high probability of reoffending in the short-term, even if ultimately he will cease to reoffend.

4. Perspective of the Crime Victim

The view of the crime victim is an overlooked issue in the literature on previous convictions. von Hirsch (1993: 10) noted that a censure-based account of sentencing recognises the interests of the crime victim. The message of censure conveyed in open court carries recognition that the victim has been wronged and not simply suffered harm by accident. Two aspects of the *progressive loss of mitigation* will trouble many crime victims. First, there is the asymmetry that the absence of priors (or the existence of few priors) may mitigate while a lengthy record cannot aggravate the sentence imposed. From the victim's perspective the asymmetry is likely to exist in the opposite direction. A victim of a violent crime is likely to oppose first-offender mitigation, arguing that the injuries he sustained are unaffected by the criminal history of the transgressor. On the other hand, learning that the offender in their case has previous, related convictions is likely to provoke a punitive reaction from the victim on the grounds that state should have imposed a more severe (and potentially effective)

---

[19] Most countries have placed the principle of restraint regarding the use of custody on a statutory footing (see Roberts and Baker 2007). In addition, in many countries first offenders are eligible to have their first term of custody suspended.

sentence at earlier sentencing hearings. Previous convictions will be seen as grounds for aggravation; the absence of priors will not be seen as justifying leniency.

Second, victims of the more serious cases will be particularly unsympathetic when mitigation is extended to offenders convicted of serious crimes. The practice of repetitive discounting of the sentence may be very troubling for these victims. The problem for the *progressive loss of mitigation* therefore arises as the offence becomes more serious. Having been subjected to an assault, a crime victim may have difficulty in seeing the logic in imposing a mitigated punishment because it was the first time that the offender had been convicted of an offence of this gravity. If it is the offender's third offence, and he still benefits from some leniency, the victim will be further alienated from the sentencing process. This example is comparable to the objection made to the exercise of mercy in cases of serious personal violence; mercy should not come at the expense of the victim's interests. At the very least, when imposing a more lenient sentence to reflect the absence of previous convictions, a court should articulate the rationale justifying this practice for the benefit of the victim.

D. RESTRICTING THE AMBIT OF MITIGATION

To summarise, the lapse theory has many deficiencies which can be can be remedied by circumscribing the leniency extended to novice offenders. The *progressive loss of mitigation* model makes sense only for crimes of relatively low seriousness. Offenders convicted of these crimes should be spared the full degree of condemnation for two reasons. First, there is a high probability that they have slipped into offending as a result of environmental factors—eg as a result of peer pressure or substance abuse. You do not slip into a career in armed robbery quite so easily. Second, the criminal justice system will want to avoid drawing such offenders into an escalating cycle of offending. These considerations justify the staggered pattern of severity characteristic of phase one of the *progressive loss of mitigation* model. The low serious nature of their crimes explains the second (flat line) phase of the *progressive loss of mitigation* graph: why escalate severity when the crime is relatively trivial? However, once we move out of the zone of low seriousness the model becomes less credible.[20]

---

[20] Ashworth (2005: 191) notes that at common law, little or no mitigation is afforded first offenders convicted of a serious crime such as rape. Ashworth suggests that the concession to human frailty should taper off at a crime with a starting point of five years' custody. In my view, this threshold seems too high: it still leaves a wide range of very serious conduct that may result in a mitigated punishment for first-, second- and possibly third-time offenders.

E. ONE-TIME FIRST-OFFENDER DISCOUNTS

If repetition is at the heart of the problem, is there a merit in a *single* discount? Whatever the advantages and disadvantages of a progressively declining reduction in severity, there is a reason to treat *most* first-time offenders differently from recidivists. The 'first-offender discount' differs from a *progressive loss of mitigation* principle at sentencing. The former is dichotomous rather than continuous in nature: first offenders receive a discount but there is no notion of something being progressively withdrawn according to a smooth gradient of declining leniency. Does one approach make more sense than another?

'One-off' sentencing discounts are appealing from a number of perspectives, retributive as well as utilitarian. All sentencing theories would endorse a policy of offering a discount for first offenders, although there will be disagreement over the magnitude of the reduction. Returning to the justifications for discounting sentencing, first-time offenders may: (i) point to a lifetime of law-abiding conduct to contexualise their current lapse; (ii) argue (with varying degrees of plausibility) that they had failed to fully appreciate the wrongfulness of their conduct until they were convicted and censured; (iii) present a better prospect for rehabilitation, and hence need little further hard treatment; (iv) be deterred by the process of arrest, trial and conviction without the need for the full severity of the deserved sentence.

The first-offender discount is unlike some other 'discounts' such as the reduction for a guilty plea. All offenders who plead guilty should be rewarded with a discount—whether convicted of rape or drunk driving—for having spared the state the expense and trouble of a prosecution, the victim from having to testify and so forth. But as with *progressive loss of mitigation*, the first-offender discount runs into difficulty when applied to more serious forms of offending. The relevance of the discount is highly dependent on the seriousness and nature of the predicate conduct.

For less serious offences, the offender may plead for leniency on the grounds that the crime was a criminal act which may occur as a result of a relatively minor departure from law-abiding conduct. Examples include: driving after having a second drink when restricting consumption to one pint would have kept the motorist within legal blood alcohol limits; or declaring, for the purposes of taxation, slightly less income than was actually earned. However, the claims made above on behalf of the first offender have little plausibility when advanced by those who have committed serious, 'consensus' offences, where the line between legitimate and illegitimate conduct is blindingly bright. Offenders convicted of armed robbery, major fraud, serious assault and other such crimes cannot plausibly appeal for a first-offender discount, and in practice do not benefit from one. Duff (2001: 169) makes the same point: 'The more serious the crime, the more obvious its utter wrongfulness ought to have been to anyone with even a modest regard for the rights and interests of others, the less room there is for this kind of mitigation of a first offense.'

Although 'lapse'-based accounts of the discount do not discuss the issue, that perspective should also deny the discount to serious or well-planned offending. A lapse is by definition transitory. A lapse of attention during a seminar is excusable; a lapse that lasts the duration of the class is harder to justify, and so it is with criminal behaviour. The first-offender discount is exactly that: a discount for *first-time* offenders, [21] but it is much harder to justify for a second, third or fourth occasion.

i. Summary

To summarise, in my view the lapse-based, *progressive loss of mitigation* doctrine should be jettisoned in favour of a more circumscribed first-offender discount which recognises first offenders' legitimate claim to some leniency at sentencing. I happily leave for another day the trickier question of the grounds for distinguishing between recidivists—those offenders who in the language of the *progressive loss of mitigation* have lost all mitigation arising from the tolerance of the state.[22] Is it desirable to distinguish among these individuals, or as all retributive theorists suggest, to treat recidivists alike, regardless of their criminal histories?[23]

F. CONCLUSION

The search for a single, unitary justification for imposing sentences of variable severity to reflect differences in criminal history has proved fruitless; there are multiple considerations that justify more lenient treatment for first offenders. So, let us return to answer the three questions raised at the outset of this chapter. First, several legitimate justifications exist for discounting the severity of sentences imposed on first offenders. Second, while most offenders in practice will benefit from a stepped-down penalty for their first conviction, some will not: the discount will become decreasingly likely as the seriousness of the offence increases. Novice offenders convicted of the most serious crimes should receive no discount because none of the justifications for the practice may be plausibly invoked in

---

[21] There may be some discussion around the definition of a 'first offender'—the phrase should be interpreted to the benefit of the defendant, meaning that an official caution should not count as the first contact with the criminal justice system.

[22] See discussion in Lee in this volume, as well as MacPherson (2002) and Roberts (2008).

[23] The two groups of retributivists agree with respect to repeat offenders who have exhausted their mitigation: further convictions should not aggravate the sentence imposed.

their case. Third, the discount should not normally be repeated. Having been charged, tried, convicted and punished, offenders need no additional moral education about the consequences of offending.

Finally, a last word about community reaction is in order. Desert-based approaches to sentencing, with their emphasis on proportionality and restraint, as well as their rejection of utilitarianism as the principal reason for imposing punishment, represent our best hope for a humane and liberal sentencing process. However, they need to resonate—or at least not clash—with fundamental community values. The progressive loss of mitigation runs contrary to intuitive conceptions of how often indulgence should be extended to 'first offenders' and by doing so undermines community support for a proportionality-based model. It needs rethinking.

REFERENCES

Ashworth, A (2005) *Sentencing and Criminal Justice*, 4th edn (Cambridge, Cambridge University Press).
Bagaric, M (2001) *Punishment and Sentencing: A Rational Approach* (Sydney, Cavendish Publishing).
Cox, E (1877) *The Principles of Punishment as Applied in the Administration of Criminal Law, by Judges and Magistrates* (London, Garland Publishing).
Cross, R (1971) *The English Sentencing System* (London, Butterworths).
Duff, RA (2001) *Punishment, Communication, and Community* (Oxford, Oxford University Press).
Durham, A (1987) 'Justice in Sentencing. The Role of Prior Record of Criminal Involvement' 78 *Journal of Criminal Law and Criminology* 614–43.
Fletcher, G (1978) *Rethinking Criminal Law* (Boston, Little, Brown).
Green, L (2008) 'Tolerance and Understanding', in M Kramer et al (eds), *The Legacy of HLA Hart* (Oxford, Oxford University Press).
Gross, H (1979) *A Theory of Criminal Justice* (New York, Oxford University Press).
Lee, Y (2009) 'Recidivism as Omission: A Relational Account' 87 *Texas Law Review* 571–622.
MacPherson, D (2002) 'The Relevance of Prior Record in the Criminal Law: A Response to the Theory of Professor von Hirsch' 28 *Queen's Law Journal* 177–219.
Manson, A (2001) *The Law of Sentencing* (Toronto, Irwin Law).
Piper, S and Easton, C (2008) *Sentencing and Punishment. The Quest for Justice* (Oxford, Oxford University Press).
Roberts, JV (2008) *Punishing Persistent Offenders. Community and Offender Perspectives* (Oxford, Oxford University Press).
—— (2009) 'Listening to Crime Victims: Evaluating Victim Input into Sentencing and Parole' in M Tonry (ed), *Crime and Justice* (Chicago, University of Chicago Press).

Roberts, JV and Baker, E (2007) 'Sentencing in Common Law Jurisdictions' in S Shoham, M Kett and O Beck (eds), *International Comparative Handbook of Penology and Criminal Justice* (New York, Taylor & Francis).

Ryberg, J (2004) *The Ethics of Proportionate Punishment. A Critical Investigation* (Dordrecht, Kluwer).

Singer, R (1979) *Just Deserts: Sentencing Based on Equality and Desert* (Cambridge, Ballinger).

Thomas, D (1979) *Principles of Sentencing*, 2nd edn (London, Heinemann).

Victorian Sentencing Committee Report (1988), *Sentencing. The Report of the Victorian Sentencing Committee* (Melbourne, Victorian Attorney-General's Department).

von Hirsch, A (1985) *Past or Future Crimes* (Rutgers, Rutgers University Press).

—— (1993) *Censure and Sanctions* (Oxford, Clarendon Press).

—— (1998) 'Desert and Previous Convictions' in A von Hirsch and A Ashworth (eds), *Principled Sentencing*, 2nd ednn (Oxford, Hart Publishing).

—— (2009) 'The Discount Approach: Progressive Loss of Mitigation' in A von Hirsch, A Ashworth and JV Roberts (eds), *Principled Sentencing*, 3rd edn (Oxford, Hart Publishing).

Walker, N (1985) *Sentencing. Theory, Law and Practice* (London, Butterworths).

Wasik, M, and von Hirsch, A (1994) 'Section 29 Revised: Previous Convictions in Sentencing' [June] *Criminal Law Review* 409–18.

3

Recidivism, Retributivism and the Lapse Model of Previous Convictions

JESPER RYBERG

EVEN THOUGH THE theory of punishment is today dominated by retributivism—the perspective that punishment is justified on the ground of desert—there is still wide disagreement amongst retributivists with regard to what the basic idea of just deserts more precisely amounts to, and how one should deal with the more detailed challenges that arise within the field of penal theory. This is certainly the case if we turn to the subject of this chapter, namely how one should punish offenders with a criminal record.

Theorists within the retributivist camp divide into three positions: firstly, that first-time offenders and recidivists should not be punished differently if they have committed the same crime, ie sentencing should not be influenced by the offender's prior record (this position is usually referred to as 'flat-rate sentencing'); secondly, that there should be a recidivist premium implying that one should ceteris paribus impose progressively more severe punishments for each new crime a person has committed; and finally, that first-time criminals should receive a discount which, in the case of reoffending, is gradually lost until a point is reached at which it is entirely exhausted (this is the principle of the progressive loss of mitigation).[1]

The purpose of this chapter is not to engage in considerations of whatever retributivist arguments might be presented in support of each of the three approaches to recidivism. Rather, I limit myself to focusing on the last approach, the principle of the progressive loss of mitigation. More

---

[1] Adherents of the first position include Fletcher (1978) and Singer (1979). Versions of the second position—based on the idea of an enhanced culpability of recidivists—have been proposed by MacPherson (2002), Roberts (2008) and Lee (2009). While the third position, as we shall see, is defended by von Hirsch (this volume) and von Hirsch and Ashworth (2005). For an outline of the different models, see Ashworth (2005) or Roberts (2008). Whether any of the positions are consistent with a consequentialist point of view is an empirical question which I shall not pursue in this chapter.

precisely, I shall assess the claim that a progressive loss of mitigation can be justified on the grounds of consideration of human frailty and the notion of a 'lapse'. There are both intuitive and theoretical reasons in favour of this choice of focus.

As Julian Roberts notes in his recent book on the punishment of persistent offenders, the fact that an offender has had a hitherto spotless reputation may be something which a judge may take into account by offering some degree of first-timer leniency. If an employee is convicted for the first time of defrauding and if her employer asks a sentencing court for a 'second chance', on the intuitive grounds that the crime was only a temporary slip in a normally law-abiding life, then it would—as Roberts points out—'be a severe judge indeed who would deny some mitigation in response to such an appeal' (Roberts 2008: 57). This way of reacting carries some intuitive appeal. Moreover (and more importantly), a number of theorists have defended the lapse model; first and foremost Andrew von Hirsch, in several writings, as well as Andrew Ashworth and Martin Wasik.[2] Thus, there are reasons to consider the plausibility of this proposal more thoroughly.

The idea behind the lapse model is that human beings should be seen, on the one hand, as capable of moral deliberation and, on the other, as vulnerable to temptation (see von Hirsch and Ashworth 2005: 23). Together, these two sides of our psychological make-up imply that we should be regarded not as angels, but rather as fallible beings. What we should do—according to von Hirsch and Ashworth—is incorporate some tolerance for the imperfections of human nature, which is precisely what is done in our everyday notion of a lapse. A transgression is judged less stringently when it occurs against a background of prior compliance. However, if transgressions are repeated, they can no longer be regarded as aberrational failures of moral inhibition, ie they can less and less plausibly be characterised as lapses (von Hirsch and Ashworth 2005: 153). Thus, repetitions no longer call for some immediate leniency. Now, this idea of human fallibility and a lapse is what von Hirsch and Ashworth believe should be incorporated in the way the criminal justice system deals with offenders. A concession to human frailty is shown by giving the first-time offender a limited discount. However, in cases of recidivism this discount should diminish and eventually disappear. In this way, the idea of human frailty and of a lapse is held to provide a justification for the principle of a progressive loss of mitigation in sentencing.[3]

---

[2] See eg von Hirsch (1981, 1991), von Hirsch and Ashworth (2005), Ashworth (2005), Wasik and von Hirsch (1994a).

[3] von Hirsch and Ashworth also sustain the idea of a first-timer discount by reference to a 'person's capacity' to attend to censure in punishment. It is not absolutely clear to me how the capacity argument relates to the lapse argument. In this chapter I shall restrict the discussion to the latter argument. As I have argued elsewhere, the capacity argument is vulnerable to several objections (see Ryberg 2004: chs 2 and 3). Moreover, it is clearly

Before engaging in a closer scrutiny of this justification, two minor comments should be made. Firstly, retributivists such as von Hirsch contend that the severity of a punishment should be proportionate to the gravity of the crime, where crime gravity is determined by harm and culpability. However, lapse-based tolerance is not a result of reduced harm or reduced culpability. In other words, paying respect to human frailty and the notion of a lapse in one sense is a way of overruling the demands of strict proportionality. Obviously this does not in itself constitute a problem. However, by weakening the demand that proportionality should be scrupulously observed, it may become more difficult to explain why other factors—which might also have some intuitive appeal when it comes to the question of sentencing decisions—should not taken into account as well, even if this would violate strict proportionality.[4] However, I shall not pursue this point any further here.

Secondly, the lapse model provides only a limited degree of guidance. Ideally, a justification of the principle of progressive loss of mitigation should provide us with answers to the following questions: (i) How large should a discount be? (ii) How precisely should a discount be reduced in cases of reoffending? And in this connection, (iii) when are discounts fully exhausted? (iv) How does the seriousness of an earlier crime affect the size of the discount of the punishment for the present crime? (For example, does it make any difference whether the crime for which one has previously been punished is murder or pick-pocketing?) And, finally (v) what precisely is the significance of the temporal span between the present and earlier crimes? The lapse theory has little to offer in response to these questions.

Adherents of the theory maintain that with regard to the size of the discount, fallibility calls for a 'limited tolerance', thereby indicating that the non-recidivist discount should be modest. But why is this so? If we take seriously the idea of a lapse, why not hold that the sentence of the first-time offender should be significantly reduced? With regard to the question as to how many repetitions must occur before the discount is exhausted, von Hirsch suggests that the discount is lost after three prior convictions. Wasik, for his part, proposes five as the appropriate number. However, it seems clear that these numbers are highly intuitive, ie they are certainly not in any strict sense deduced from the overall theory of a lapse.[5] When it comes to the answers to the other questions, even less is

the lapse argument that plays the main role in the authors' most recent exposition of their view on the role of criminal records.

[4] To hold that gravity should be determined by harm, culpability and criminal record, and that considerations of criminal record are therefore part of the proportionate punishment for a certain crime is a mere linguistic move that does not change anything. The question could just be rephrased by asking whether other factors might also be taken into account in the determination of proportionality.

[5] von Hirsch and Ashworth clearly admit this when they say that 'there are no magical

said. Thus, it seems that more could have been wished for with regard to the capability of the theory in terms of action guidance. This being the case, let us now turn to the main question concerning the overall plausibility of the lapse theory.

A. WHAT DOES A LAPSE IMPLY?

In order to assess the proposal, it is first necessary to take a closer look at what the idea of a lapse implies. Our everyday concept of a lapse is not very precise. Moreover, linguistics is not the arbiter in philosophy. Thus, we need to spell out what the notion of a lapse implies according to the proponents of the lapse model. More precisely, there are three aspects to the idea of a lapse which should be highlighted in order to evaluate the proposal.

The first thing worth noting is that a present act presupposes a certain background in order to be characterised as a lapse. In more precise terms, a lapse seems to presuppose a preceding series of cases in which a person has abstained from performing the type of act that constitutes the lapse.[6] To hold that a person's first act constituted a lapse makes no sense. And not only does it not make sense, adherents of the lapse model are also explicit in the way they underline the existence of a certain foregoing behavioural pattern as a precondition for characterising a present act as a lapse. However, the fact that a present act deviates from a behavioural pattern consisting of a series of omissions is not sufficient to qualify the act as a lapse. If a person has previously abstained from doing act A for the simple reason that she has never *wanted* to do A, then carrying out A one day, when she suddenly feels like it, does not constitute a lapse. Thus, the second point that should be underlined is that a lapse somehow presupposes that one has previously omitted acting in a certain way *despite one's temptations*. However, even if this is the case, it is not yet sufficient to turn a present act which deviates from a foregoing set of omissions into a lapse. If a person has previously abstained from giving in to her temptations to do A because she regards A as a wrong, but now decides to do A because she has discovered that A is actually the right thing to do, then obviously this present act does not constitute a lapse. A lapse is not just a change of conviction but rather an act performed out of temptation. Thus, the third condition for an act to count as a lapse

---

numbers' with regard to when the discount should be lost (see von Hirsch and Ashworth 2005: 155). However, obviously it would be desirable if a theory was able to provide us with more precise guidance than this.

[6] Obviously, a lapse may also consist in an omission taking place against a background of a series of acts of a certain type. However, this does not change the fact that a lapse presupposes a certain pattern in a person's previous behaviour.

is that the act deviates from a previous behavioural pattern of omissions because a person suddenly gives in to her inclinations. von Hirsch and Ashworth are clear about this aspect of the notion of a lapse when they say that 'The idea is that even an ordinarily well-behaved person can have his moral inhibitions fail in a moment of weakness or wilfulness' (von Hirsch and Ashworth 2005: 152), or when they characterise frailty and a lapse as 'a loss of self-discipline' or 'a temporary breakdown of self-control' (Wasik and von Hirsch 1994a: 410).

Thus, in sum, a lapse presupposes: (i) a series of omissions of the type of act presently performed (constituting the lapse); (ii) that these omissions have been performed in accordance with one's moral inhibitions, ie despite one's temptations; and (iii) that the present act (the lapse) is performed as a result of having failed to control one's temptations. This exposition of the idea of human frailty seems to capture the conception of a lapse which adherents of the lapse model have in mind. However, as we shall now see, each of the three conditions gives rise to challenges when the notion of a lapse is applied to our cardinal question of how one should punish first-time offenders and recidivists.

B. A PREVIOUS SERIES OF OMISSIONS

Consider first the claim that a lapse presupposes a preceding series of omissions of the type of act presently constituting the lapse. The obvious question which this proposition gives rise to is: when can omissions and the present act properly be said to be of the same type? Surely the preceding series of cases cannot include any possible omissions. The answer given by von Hirsch and Ashworth is that 'the prior compliance in question is that of not having committed and been convicted for a criminal offence' (von Hirsch and Ashworth 2005: 152). Apparently they believe that the fact that one has previously omitted committing illegal acts is sufficient to count a present crime as a lapse. However, firstly they do not present an argument as to why it is only preceding omissions of criminal acts that count in the proper series of foregoing omissions. Secondly, and more importantly, to consider all earlier omissions of criminal acts as belonging to the series of omissions on the ground of which a present act constitutes a lapse seems to limit this series much too widely. To hold that a present case of embezzlement does not fully count as a lapse because last year I drove my car having had a few too many glasses of wine does not seem very plausible. Nor, I believe, is it plausible to contend that the present killing of my wife out of jealousy is less of a lapse if last year I committed perjury. In both cases the acts involved—despite their both being illegal—simply seem too different to count as the same type in the proper sense.[7]

The obvious reply to this would be to affirm that, in order to characterise a present act as a lapse, the foregoing series of omitted acts must be of the same type in a much more narrow sense. Suppose that, as an employee in a shop, it is my job to bring the daily turnover from the shop to the bank. I have done so every evening for two years, but one evening I succumb to the temptation of stealing the money. In this case, it seems much more plausible to claim that my previous behaviour in the last two years constitutes a proper background for judging my present theft as a lapse. The acts I have abstained from doing in this period are not just illegal but belong in a much more narrow sense to the same type. They are the same acts. However, if this is what is required with regard to the series of omissions on the ground of which a present act is considered a lapse, then this gives rise to an obvious problem: in some cases a crime may be carried out the first time it presents itself as a possibility for the offender. That is, a present crime need not be committed against a background of a series of omissions of the same type of act. For instance, if I commit perjury it may happen the first time I get the opportunity to do so, for the simple reason that I may never have been in court before. If I buy a car, and have not previously had one, then my driving too fast may happen the first time I get the chance to do so. If the security code to another person's safe is by mistake revealed to me, and I subsequently steal what is in the box, then this may be the first time I have had a chance like this. In neither case is it correct to assert that the criminal act happened against a background of a preceding series of omissions of the very same act. Obviously, many such examples can be presented.

Thus, in sum, the problem that confronts the adherent of the lapse model is to specify what constitutes the proper behavioural pattern on the ground of which a crime constitutes a lapse. If the series of preceding acts or omissions is specified broadly it becomes, as we have seen, more dubious. If it is specified narrowly—ie if it is only precisely the same sort of acts that counts—then this seems more plausible; however, this implies that there may be various cases where a crime is committed the first time a person has the opportunity which means that the crime of the first-time offender cannot be characterised as a lapse. Thus, the first challenge that arises is to specify what constitutes the proper behavioural

[7] Moreover, the answer given by von Hirsch and Ashworth implies that, if two persons have each previously abstained from performing act A but now both succumb to the temptation of doing A, where the only difference is that A was illegal when the first person abstained from doing A and when she later did A, while A used to be legal but was made illegal just before the second person did A, then it would only be the act of the first person that would constitute a lapse. And this would be so even had the two persons acted in precisely the same way and even if they had done so with precisely the same motivational background. This—I suggest—does not seem plausible.

pattern of omissions in such a way that this is consistent with the claim that first-time offenders should have a discount because their crimes are lapses. As indicated, this is by no means a simple task.

However, there is also another challenge that relates to the presupposition that a lapse is preceded by a series of omissions. When the focus is on the commission of a crime it is not necessarily the case that a present crime occurs against a background of prior compliance. A first-time offender may have committed several crimes without detection prior to the present. It is a well-known fact from victimisation surveys that, with regard to many crimes, there is a great difference between the actual number of crimes and the number of crimes that result in the imposition of a sentence. And empirical research suggests that, for every previous crime for which offenders are punished, many admit to having committed several unpunished crimes (von Hirsch and Ashworth 2005: 152). But if a first-time offender has already committed a number of crimes prior to the present, then obviously the present crime does not constitute a lapse. Thus, what does this mean with regard to the justification of first-timer discounts?

von Hirsch and Ashworth are aware of this possibility, but do not consider it to constitute a problem. What they contend is that '[I]t would be unjust—and in some cases inaccurate—to impute prior criminality to a defendant facing his first conviction, on the basis of such statistical information about the behaviour of many offenders' (von Hirsch and Ashworth 2005: 152). In their view, denying first-offender status is only justified on the ground of proof of guilt, which means that the person has been convicted for prior crimes. This answer is hardly satisfactory. It may well be correct that it is unjust to deny a particular first-time offender a discount on the basis of the statistical behaviour of many offenders. However, it is also unjust to give a discount to a particular apparent first-time offender who has got away with several crimes prior to the present. The latter offender simply does not get the punishment she deserves. Recall that von Hirsch and Ashworth are advocating a version of *positive* retributivism, according to which it is wrong to punish a criminal too severely but also wrong to punish the criminal too leniently.[8] The criminal who is treated too leniently is not appropriately censured. Thus, it is unjust to punish the genuine first-timer too severely, but also unjust to punish the apparent first-timer who has committed other crimes too leniently. To object that we cannot *know* that it is actually the case that a particular apparent first-time offender has already got away with a number of crimes is of no help: neither do we know that a particular offender is a genuine first-timer. One might of course hold that, in the absence of knowledge,

---

[8] This problem would not occur if one favours a *negative* version of proportionalism according to which the proportionate punishment is regarded only as an upper limit that should not be transgressed. See eg Ryberg (2004: 193).

all we can rely on is whether a criminal has or has not been convicted in court. But what if statistical evidence showed that 99.9 per cent of all first-time offenders had already committed three unpunished offences? The only plausible way, I believe, to ascertain that we can trust the claim that the transgression of a first-timer actually occurs against a background of prior compliance is to introduce statistical data on the matter. But, as already indicated, this route is not simple. It leads directly to the above-mentioned challenge of specifying which of a person's foregoing omissions should be included in the set of omissions that are required in order to justify the claim that a present crime constitutes a lapse.

C. OMISSIONS DESPITE ONE'S TEMPTATIONS

Let us now proceed to the second of the presuppositions that relate to the notion of a lapse. As has been mentioned, in order for a certain act to count as a lapse, it is not sufficient that it constitutes a deviation from a foregoing series of cases where the person has not committed this type of act. If every morning I used to choose the fastest route to my work rather than the more scenic road, but then suddenly one morning I decide to take the latter one then, despite the deviation, this does not itself turn my present act into a lapse. A simple change of mind is not a lapse. Something more is required. What is missing—at least in the interpretation provided by von Hirsch and Ashworth—is that I have previously abstained from choosing the beautiful route despite the temptation to use that road. In more general terms, a lapse presupposes a series of foregoing cases where a person has omitted a certain act by resisting her temptation to perform this act. von Hirsch and Ashworth are pretty explicit about this presupposition when they characterise a lapse as a 'failure of moral inhibition' or talk about human frailty as a 'loss of self-discipline'.[9] However, is it plausible to hold that a first-time offender—in contrast to the recidivist—has hitherto succeeded in resisting the temptation to perform the type of act for which she is presently being sentenced?

Consider again the example of the person who, every evening for two years, has brought the daily cash from a shop to the bank but who one evening suddenly decides to steal the money. Are we justified in claiming that this person has previously succeeded in resisting this temptation? The answer is obviously in the negative. It might well be the case that the person was not at all thus tempted. She might have been very proud of performing the trusted job of delivering the money, without ever having dreamt of stealing it. The fact that she nevertheless ends up committing

---

[9] Thereby indicating that the omissions preceding the present act constitute cases where one has succeeded in exercising self-discipline: von Hirsch and Ashworth (2005: 152).

the crime may be explained by changes in this person's life. For instance, she may suddenly find herself in a totally new situation in which she is in desperate need of money. Various explanations for why this could happen can of course be imagined. Put in more general terms, even though a first-time offender has not previously committed crimes this compliance need not be—and in many cases is probably not—a result of a previous exercise of self-discipline or control of one's desires. Of course compliance may sometimes be explained in this way. But the important thing is that there may well be cases where there is an alternate explanation. And if that is the case, then the condition for characterising a first-time offence as a lapse—and thus for giving the offender a discount—is not satisfied.

Once again these considerations raise the question as to which omissions should be included in the set of foregoing omissions in order to turn a present action into a lapse. If the set is broadly defined, then clearly it sounds more plausible to claim that one may have been tempted (eg even if the employee had not previously been tempted to steal the turnover there may well have been other actions which she found tempting but nevertheless resisted by exercising sufficient self-control). However, as we have seen, a broad definition of the set of omissions is quite dubious. If, on the other hand, the set is more narrowly defined, ie if it consists only of omissions of the very same acts as the one presently performed, then—as the employee example illustrates—it becomes much less likely that the self-control condition is satisfied. This clearly highlights the importance of the delimitation challenge.

D. GIVING IN TO INCLINATIONS

The idea of a lapse not only presupposes a set of foregoing cases where a person has been tempted to perform a certain act but has nevertheless abstained from performing it. As has been mentioned, the idea also presupposes that the present act—the lapse—constitutes a case where a person fails to resist temptation. What it means to succumb to temptation is made more precise by von Hirsch and Ashworth when they say that a well-behaved person can have his moral inhibitions fail 'in a moment of weakness or wilfulness'. Or when they talk of an act performed 'in a moment of unwisdom' (von Hirsch and Ashworth 2005: 152). However, even though this image of a lapse as some sort of momentary slip of self-control accords well—at least so I believe—with our ordinary notions of a lapse, it does not provide a plausible description of several of the types of crimes which a first-timer might have performed. For instance, a carefully planned economic crime or a terrorist attack planned in every detail cannot plausibly be held to constitute crimes committed in a moment of failing self-discipline. More generally, all crimes which involve long-term planning and deliberation, or which simply cannot be performed on the spur of the moment seem to fall outside the scope of the suggested concept of a lapse (see also Roberts 2008: 56). But, if that is correct, then the lapse model cannot explain why first-time offenders in general should receive a discount. All it explains (at best) is why some first-timers should be treated more leniently.

Moreover, the idea of succumbing to temptation calls for a final comment. Suppose we accept the basic idea of the lapse model, namely that some understanding should be shown for human frailty and thus for the fact that we all sometimes succumb to temptation. Would it then not seem natural to contend that our understanding to some extent depends on the strength of the temptation that is put in a person's way? To my mind, it is easier to understand if a person has committed a wrongful act out of a strong temptation than if committed in response to a minor temptation. For instance, it calls for more understanding and perhaps tolerance if a person has committed a burglary because of a desperate need for money than if it was committed simply for fun (assuming that the temptation in the former case is much stronger). In other words, the intuition to which exponents of the lapse model appeal seems to imply more than is contained in their proposal, namely that different degrees of temptation may call for varying degrees in the understanding shown to those who fail to resist the temptation. But, if that is correct, then it has significant implications. Even if two first-time offenders have committed the very same crime, then, if different degrees of tolerance should be shown to different degrees of temptation, it does not follow that they should receive the same discount. However, if this is correct, then it constitutes a serious drawback for the model. It leads the lapse model into the very kind of individualisation which retributivists have eagerly tried to avoid and which, in this case, may render the theory practically inapplicable.[10] Thus, what is required from adherents of the model is a good explanation as to why the understanding and tolerance which should be shown to those who fail to resist their temptations should not—and in contradiction of the basic intuition—pay respect to differences in the strength of the involved temptations. Merely to respond that this would lead to problems of application will hardly suffice. We cannot without any supporting arguments just redefine what counts in some practically convenient but morally arbitrary way. Thus, as is the case with regard to the former conditions, the third condition gives rise to challenges of its own.

---

[10] Clearly it is in most cases impossible to estimate the strength of a present temptation, to which a person has succumbed, with any applicable degree of precision.

E. CONCLUSION

The time has come to summarise and draw some conclusions. As initially indicated, one might question whether it is at all plausible to regard human frailty and fallibility as morally significant and, further, whether it is plausible for the retributivist to accept that tolerance of failure justifies deviations from what strict proportionality prescribes. However, these questions have not constituted the focus of this chapter. Rather, what has been considered is what a lapse theory—if from the outset it is taken for granted—implies with regard to the sentencing of first-time offenders and recidivists.

What has been argued is firstly, that it is not every type of crime which, when committed for the first time, can properly be characterised as a lapse. And, secondly, that even if we consider a crime which could in principle constitute a lapse, it is not necessarily the case that, for a present crime, there exists the proper set of foregoing omissions which a lapse presupposes; and that even if such a set of omissions exists it is, in contrast to what a lapse presupposes, not necessarily the case that the former compliance is due to the resistance of temptation. Moreover, it is not necessarily the case that the first conviction is for the first crime an offender has actually committed. Finally, it is unclear why the strength of temptation—which might of course vary interpersonally—should not be taken into consideration if one accepts a lapse model in the first place. All in all, if these considerations are correct what we can conclude is that there might be some cases where it is justified to provide a first-time discount, and there may be many other cases where a person has committed exactly the same crime where a discount is not justified. Furthermore, considering the content of the three outlined conditions, it is obvious that in individual cases it will most likely not be possible to investigate whether these conditions are actually satisfied. Thus, it is simply not correct when von Hirsch and Ashworth contend that the 'discount should be available to *every* first offender' (von Hirsch and Ashworth 2005: 154), nor when it is held that the lapse model provides a justification for a general application of the principle of progressive loss of mitigation in sentencing.

REFERENCES

Ashworth, A (2005) *Sentencing and Criminal Justice* (Cambridge, Cambridge University Press).

Bagaric, M (2000) 'Double Punishment and Punishing Character: The Unfairness of Prior Convictions' 10 *Criminal Justice Ethics* 10–28.

—— (2001) *Punishment & Sentencing* (Great Britain, Cavendish Publishing).

Durham AM, III (1987) 'Justice in Sentencing: The Role of Prior Record of Criminal Involvement' 78 *The Journal of Criminal Law and Criminology* 614–43.

Fletcher, G (1978) *Rethinking Criminal Law* (Boston, Little Brown).
— — (1982) 'The Recidivist Premium' 1 *Criminal Justice Ethics* 54–59.
Lee, Y (2009) 'Recidivism as Omission: A Relational Account' 87 *Texas Law Review* 571–622.
MacPherson, D (2002) 'The Relevance of Prior Record in the Criminal law: A Response to the Theory of Professor von Hirsch' 28 *Queen's Law Journal* 177–219.
Roberts, JV (2008) *Punishing Persistent Offenders* (Oxford, Oxford University Press).
Ryberg, J (2001) 'Recidivism, Multiple Offending, and Legal Justice' 36 *Danish Yearbook of Philosophy* 69–94.
— — (2005) 'Retributivism and Multiple Offending' 11 *Res Publica: Journal of Legal and Social Philosophy* 213–33
— — (2004) *The Ethics of Proportionate Punishment. A Critical Investigation* (Dordrecht, Kluwer).
Singer, R (1979) *Just Deserts* (Cambridge, Ballinger).
von Hirsch, A (1981) 'Desert and Previous Convictions in Sentencing' 65 *Minnesota Law Review* 591–634.
— — (1991) 'Criminal Record Rides Again' 11 *Criminal Justice Ethics* 54–56.
— — (1993) *Censure and Sanctions* (Oxford, Clarendon Press).
von Hirsch, A, Ashworth, A and Roberts, JV (eds) (2009) *Principled Sentencing*, 3rd edn (Oxford, Hart Publishing).
von Hirsch, A and Ashworth, A (2005) *Proportionate Sentencing* (Oxford, Oxford University Press).
Wasik, M and von Hirsch, A (1994a), 'Section 29 Revised: Previous Convictions in Sentencing' [June] *Criminal Law Review* 409–18.
— — (1994b) 'Guidance, Guidelines, and Criminal Record' in M Wasik and K Pease (eds), *Sentencing Reform: Guidance or Guidelines?* (Manchester, Manchester University Press) 105–25.

4

Repeat Offenders and the Question of Desert

YOUNGJAE LEE

ARE REPEAT OFFENDERS more culpable than first-time offenders?[1] It is commonly, and casually, assumed that repeat offenders deserve more punishment than first-time offenders. The US Federal Sentencing Guidelines, for instance, justify their heavy reliance on criminal history partly on the argument that '[a] defendant with a record of prior criminal behavior is more *culpable* than a first offender and thus *deserving* of greater punishment'.[2] The political rhetoric surrounding California's 'three-strikes' law[3] frequently included the language of desert and retribution, with some people saying that repeat offenders deserve draconian prison sentences for being recidivists. Public perceptions of a crime's seriousness vary according to the criminal record of the offender as well (Roberts 2008b: 172–74).

While the belief that repeat offenders are deserving of greater punishment is thus widespread, there is no satisfactory retributivist defence of that prevailing view, as desert theorists have been generally critical of sentencing enhancements based on the offender's criminal history (see eg Fletcher 1978: 462–66; see also Roberts 2008a: 468, 469). The seriousness of a crime does not change, the objection typically goes, depending

---

[1] This essay uses the terms 'repeat offender', 'recidivist', 'offender with prior record' and 'offender with criminal history' interchangeably and as a way of describing only those who reoffend after being convicted for previous offences. While this is the most common understanding of the terms, it is not the only way to define them. For example, if a person commits multiple crimes but is sentenced separately for them, that person may be sentenced as a 'repeat offender' in every sentencing that follows the first one. That is, if an offender is sentenced in the morning for a crime and then sentenced in the afternoon for the second crime, it is possible for the second sentence to be enhanced on the basis that the offender accumulated a 'criminal record' that morning. This essay is not about those with 'criminal records' in this latter sense, although arguments discussed in this essay have implications for such cases as well.

[2] US Sentencing Commission, US Sentencing Guidelines Manual (2008) § 4A, introductory comment (emphasis added).

[3] Cal Penal Code Ann. § 667(b)–(i) (West Supp 2006).

on the criminal history of the person committing it. A robbery is a robbery, whether it is committed by a first-time offender or a repeat offender; therefore, there should be no difference in the way the state responds to repeat offenders and first-time offenders who commit the same crime (see eg Singer 1979: 67–74).

This chapter argues against the prevailing view among desert theorists and defends the view that repeat offenders are more culpable and that sentencing enhancements for prior convictions are justifiable on retributivist grounds.[4] The fact that desert theorists have failed to come up with a persuasive account of the recidivist premium does not mean that there are no strong desert-like intuitions about the justifiability of the premium, and sections A and B discuss such intuitions. Section A focuses on character-based accounts of making the punishment fit not the crime but *the person*. Section B examines notice- or defiance-based accounts that provide that an offender's *past* criminal history makes a *current* offence somehow *worse* than an equivalent crime committed by a first-time offender.

Section C advances a new theory of the recidivist premium. It argues that we should think of the recidivist premium as stemming not from repeat offenders' bad characters, enhanced knowledge or allegedly defiant attitudes, but from what the repeat offenders have failed to do between the time of the previous conviction and the time of the new offence. I call this justification for the recidivist premium 'recidivism as omission'. Section C argues that punishments for such omissions are justified as a matter of desert because the relationship between an offender and the state is altered when the first conviction and punishment occur. The offender then has an obligation to organise his life in a way that reduces the risk of his reoffending, and it is the failure to fulfil that obligation that justifies the additional punishment. Section C further points out that the relationship between the offender and the state is a two-way street, in the sense that offenders' obligations to organise their lives in a way that steers clear of criminality coexist with the state's corollary obligation not to interfere with their returns to normal lives.

The purpose of this chapter is not to advocate that we punish repeat offenders more harshly than first-time offenders. For one thing, it should be kept in mind that an articulation of a retributivist basis can serve both as an affirmative basis for increasing a repeat offender's punishment *and* as a negative constraint that limits permissible amounts of punishment. The goal here is to offer a retributivist account of the recidivist premium that is congruent with the common belief that repeat offenders deserve more punishment and also to explore what the preferred account suggests about when and why it may be appropriate to either cancel or mitigate

---

[4] The recidivist premium may be justified on other penological grounds such as deterrence, rehabilitation and incapacitation. This chapter focuses on the question of desert only.

the recidivist premium in individual circumstances. In other words, this chapter offers a framework to think through the culpability of repeat offenders, which is not at all the same as counselling that repeat offenders be punished more harshly.

A. PUNISHING BAD CHARACTER

The practice of punishing repeat offenders and first-time offenders differently is often justified on the basis that different punishments reflect the different 'characters' of the offenders.[5] What does that mean? For instance, if a person is convicted of robbery once, is punished for it and then commits another robbery, what inferences can we draw about this person that warrant a harsher punishment? To isolate the effects of criminal history, let us assume that the first robbery and the second robbery are identical in every relevant way except for the existence of criminal record in the second instance.

There are two possibilities. The first possibility is the idea of lapse or acts that are 'out of character'. The reason the offender (O_1) should be dealt with more harshly after the second time (t_2) the crime was committed than after the first time (t_1) is that, at t_1, it is possible that O_1 acted in a way that was out of character, whereas any inference that O_1's act was out of character at t_2 would no longer be warranted. The second possibility is as follows. Say at t_1 there are two offenders, O_1 and O_2, who commit identical crimes. And after they are convicted and punished, O_2 never commits another crime, whereas O_1 does, at t_2. Why should O_1 be punished more harshly at t_2 than he was at t_1? The answer is that O_1 was in fact a worse person than O_2 at t_1—something that we did not know at t_1, but we do know now. The relevant comparison is, then, between O_1 and O_2. We know that O_1 has continued to offend, whereas O_2 has stopped, which can give rise to the inference that O_1 is worse than O_2, which in turn justifies the recidivist premium. (Another possibility is that O_1 has in fact turned into a worse person between t_1 and t_2, but this scenario can be treated the same as the second since the idea still is that O_1 is a worse person than O_2.)

---

[5] While the 'character' theory of culpability is controversial, it seems to me that character theorists are correct when they argue that criminal law punishes persons for their actions only when those actions reflect badly on the actors in the sense that the actions display their character defects. For a discussion leading up to this conclusion, see Lee (2009: 571, 578–83); see also generally Tadros (2005).

1. First-Time Offences as Acts 'Out of Character'

The first, 'out of character', account is a theory of 'first-offence discount',
as opposed to 'recidivist premium', and it is a combination of two ideas:
mercy and epistemic limitations of the criminal justice system.

In a series of writings, Andrew von Hirsch has defended a version of the
first-offence discount (see eg von Hirsch 1986: 81–91). Von Hirsch points
out that even well-intentioned, law-abiding citizens may at times come
across opportunities to commit crimes and may give in to the temptation
at moments of weakness. The first-time discount is given in acknowledge-
ment of that fact and in the spirit of tolerance and recognition of human
frailty. This is the 'mercy' aspect of the first-offence discount. The discount is then gradually taken away as one's criminal record grows, since
a record of repeat offending starts to become inconsistent with the idea
that the given individual's criminal activity should be characterised as a
'lapse'. In other words, as a person accumulates a history of offences,
any claim that the person's acts are somehow 'out of character' becomes
no longer credible. This is the epistemic-limitation aspect of the first-time
discount. The idea is that the criminal justice system is not able to tell
whether first-time offenders have acted 'out of character', in the sense
of having a one-time slip, or whether they actually have permanent, bad
character traits that are manifested in their offences. Since the criminal
justice system is not good at distinguishing those who lapsed and those
who are fundamentally criminals, it should err on the side of giving a
first-time discount and then take away the discount when someone with
a criminal history commits a crime, because at that point we know that
the offender *is a criminal*, not a law-abiding citizen who 'slipped' in a
moment of weakness.

The first-offence discount idea, however, has some problems as a defence
of the recidivist premium. First, the idea of 'human frailty' is more suited
to the ideas of forgiveness and mercy than to the idea of desert. To the
extent that the first-offence discount is a theory of mercy as opposed to
desert, it dissolves the problem of the argument for the recidivist premium
on the basis of desert by denying the problem's existence. This account
explains and justifies *some* differential treatment between first-time offenders and offenders with criminal records, but it cannot explain the intuition
that the difference is due to the fact that repeat offenders are somehow
deserving of *more* punishment—an intuition that is indicated by people's
increased sense of resentment at recidivists.

Second, some people who are convicted for the first time did not have
a lapse that led to their first crime; rather, they simply did not get caught
the first time. The lapse theory does not apply to those whose first crimes
did not end in conviction. A criminal history is not a history of how
many crimes one has committed, but a history of how many times one

has been convicted, and the lapse theory has trouble explaining why convictions, rather than multiple offences, are significant. This is a specific manifestation of a broader problem. If one's criminal record serves only the evidentiary function of revealing one's true character, then the significance of conviction and punishment becomes merely incidental. In other words, if there were a better way of getting at the question of offenders' characters, then we would not need to pay attention to criminal records at all. And there is no reason to think that a conviction record is a better measure of character traits than, say, family background, education, work history and relationship to community.

2. Second-Time Offences as Marks of 'Bad Character'

The first problem of the first-offence discount argument can be solved only at the cost of exacerbating the second problem. This approach would take into account the intuition that repeat offenders are deserving of more punishment, as opposed to merely that first-time offenders are deserving of less punishment, by explaining the recidivist premium as reflecting the state's increased knowledge over time of an offender as a criminal. In other words, the epistemic-limitation aspect of the first-offence discount argument can be used to generate an argument in favour of the recidivist premium, as opposed to an argument in favour of the first-offence discount. This revision, however, worsens the second problem because what we infer from offenders' criminal records is not merely the conclusion that their offences are not acts out of character, but also that they in fact have character traits that are worthy of the extra punishment.

And what would those character traits be? It would depend on their offences, but some possibilities may be as follows: cruelty, malice, abusiveness, arrogance (manifesting in the belief that rules of the society do not apply to them), callousness, dishonesty (if the crimes involve fraud), greed, hatred (if the crimes are motivated by hateful feelings), indifference (to human suffering), lack of discipline (if the crimes result from an inability to stick to a law-abiding path), weakness of will (if the crimes result from an inability to resist temptations), insensitivity, irresponsibility or ruthlessness.

Now, these kinds of character traits may be relevant at the guilt stage, depending on how a crime is defined. For instance, a person who is found to be guilty of murder for driving drunk and killing may be found by the jury to have manifested some of these character traits. If so, what does one's criminal record add in terms of character assessment once a person has been convicted of a crime? We might conclude that a repeat conviction demonstrates that such bad character traits are deeply ingrained. The conclusion is warranted by the fact that the first conviction and punishment apparently have not brought about a reform, when we may assume that those who have not reoffended were able to change their ways. And unlike other character approaches outlined thus far, it ties the enhanced culpability of repeat offenders to the process of conviction and punishment by positing, as a key step in the analysis, the assumption that those who do not respond to punishment have character traits that are deeply ingrained.

An account like this may be the best and most plausible theoretical approach to the recidivist premium that focuses on the character of the offender. However, there are some problems. First, notice that the list of character traits mentioned above shows that these traits, even if all are considered vices, cannot all be considered criminal by themselves. The character traits themselves do not come with clear labels 'criminal' and 'non-criminal'. Perhaps a criminal, in committing a crime, demonstrates some of these vices, and perhaps society's condemnatory response to the criminal is rightly limited only to situations where the criminal acts can be connected to the bad character traits. But these character traits cannot themselves be targets of criminal law. The traits can be expressed in both criminal and non-criminal ways, and focusing on the traits themselves as opposed to the criminal acts obscures the extent to which *how* these traits are expressed makes all the difference in the world for the legal system. This problem, it seems to me, is a symptom of a broader problem with theories of culpability that focus on character traits.[6]

Second, there remains the issue that the same conduct may reflect different defects in character, and it is not clear whether we can infer which character traits people have by looking at their behaviours. For instance, we may have several people who steal once, get caught and punished, and then after their punishments steal again. One thing that these thieves may have in common is that they desire goods and they are willing to steal from other people to satisfy such desires. But they may steal for different reasons. One person may steal because he has no respect for other people's claims to their property or the legal system that protects people's property rights. Another may, on the contrary, recognise that others have valid, legally protected claims to their things, but steal because she has trouble resisting the temptation of getting something for nothing. Yet another may steal because he is jobless, and stealing is the simplest and quickest way for him to feed himself. Yet another may steal in order not just to feed herself but to feed her children. And so on. It seems prima facie sensible to take some of these differences into account in sentencing; however, it is not then clear how informative the idea of 'repeating' offences can be in assessing people's character, compared to all other factors that may be

---

[6] For related criticisms of the character theory of culpability, see eg Horder (1993: 193, 206).

relevant. There is no clear reason to privilege one's criminal history as particularly informative of an offender's character.

Third, the idea that certain character traits are deeply ingrained in recidivists and *that* is what justifies the additional punishment has the unattractive consequence of treating a large number of people as permanently irremediable. This is not to assert that it makes no sense to treat character traits as permanent. At the same time, asserting that certain people have deeply ingrained bad character traits that they can never rid themselves of could lead society to give up on them and feel justified in permanently excluding these people from society. We should be wary of a way of thinking that seems eager to draw a line between insiders and outsiders and seeks to segregate 'outsiders', perhaps permanently, from the rest of the society.

While these concerns do not 'refute' the character theory of the recidivist premium, they are serious weaknesses nevertheless. The next section examines efforts that focus on the increased badness of a repeat offence as the justification for the recidivist premium.

B. PUNISHING BAD ACTS

Another approach to the recidivist premium is to focus not on offender characteristics, but on whether offences committed by those with criminal records are worse than offences committed by those without. Here I consider two arguments, one having to do with notice, the other with defiance.

1. Notice

The 'notice' argument for the recidivist premium is that a person is more aware of the wrongness of a criminal activity after being convicted and punished for it. The same way that we draw a distinction in culpability between 'knowingly' and 'unknowingly' in standard *mens rea* analysis, one might argue that a greater awareness that what one has done is wrong contributes to a greater level of culpability the second time around, which in turn justifies a greater amount of punishment. For instance, persons who are unaware that blowing one's nose at the dinner table is considered rude by the host may be forgiven the first time they do the offensive deed, but it would not be as forgivable if they do it again after having been told that hosts consider such behaviour rude and unacceptable.

There are several problems with the notice argument. First, it seems to imply that the recidivist premium must be limited to situations where a person is committing the same crime for which that person has previously been convicted and punished. The idea may be that a person commit-ting a robbery is potentially unaware that robbery is prohibited but that the person becomes aware of it after being convicted. But if that is the case, there would be no reason to presume that his conviction for rob-bery would put him on notice that rape is prohibited as well. In other words, under the notice theory, persons with prior convictions for robbery should not receive sentencing enhancements for their criminal records if they are later convicted for rape. Perhaps it is fruitful to determine the relationship between an offender's current offence and past offence when judging how large of an increase on the basis of one's criminal record is appropriate, but the concept of 'notice' is much too crude to do that kind of work.

Second, the argument seems to depend on the patently implausible assumption that most people who are convicted of crimes for the first time are unaware, until the time of apprehension, of the illegality of what-ever they were doing that led to their conviction. If a person is convicted of shoplifting and, after having been punished for it, does it again, it is unclear in what sense the person is more aware of wrongness of stealing the second time unless one assumes that it is unreasonable to expect people to know that stealing is a crime without first having been convicted for it. The absurdity and unacceptability (both as a factual and a normative matter) of defences such as 'I didn't know rape was illegal', or 'I didn't know stealing was illegal', is, at its core, what is right about the maxim that ignorance of the law is no excuse.

Some might respond to my objection to the notice argument by focus-ing on the meaning of the term 'notice'. It may be the case that everyone 'knows' that stealing is wrong in the abstract, but once a person is appre-hended for stealing, convicted and then punished, then he *really knows* that stealing is wrong. That is, there may be a difference in quality between knowledge based on direct experience and knowledge based on indirect experience. A repeat offender's knowledge—the knowledge that the offence was wrong, caused real harm to real people and deserved soci-ety's condemnation—should be held not just in some intellectual sense, but also in a deeper, experiential, affective sense. Furthermore, the argument might go, it is *that* deeper, more personal, individualised sort of knowl-edge—perhaps analogous to the phenomenon of 'muscle memory'—that is missing in the case of the first-time offenders.

This suggestion is plausible, but it cannot carry the weight of justifying the recidivist premium. First, there is no good reason to focus on criminal record to get at this—or any other—kind of notice. Say a person grows up in a household of criminals. He experiences firsthand what crimes look like, and what law enforcement looks like when crimes take place. Even if he never commits the crimes himself, he may be close enough to the experience that he ends up with the kind of advanced knowledge about the effects of crimes that those who learn about crime only secondhand—from books, television, films and various other media outlets—lack. The implication of the notice argument seems to be that persons with this kind of advanced knowledge when they commit a crime are more culpable than persons who lack such knowledge. And this seems odd.

Even if we set aside the oddness of this implication, it seems that a more direct way of getting at the question of how familiar offenders are with the wrongfulness and the harmfulness of their crimes would be to do a background check on all people convicted of crime to see how much they knew about how bad crimes can be when they committed the crimes for which they are now being punished. There would be little reason to give criminal records much weight, which would draw a sharp distinction between first-time offenders and repeat offenders, because many first-time offenders know, in both the superficial sense (from reading books, watching television, etc) and the deep sense (from direct experience), what is wrong with what they are doing when they commit crimes.

2. Punishing Disobedience[7]

Another argument that is frequently mentioned as a justification for punishing repeat offenders more is that repeat offenders should be punished extra for defiance or disobedience. Commentators tend to reject this argument. Antony Duff, for instance, has argued that 'a liberal polity . . . should not punish "disrespect" as a wrong distinct from or additional to the particular substantive crimes' (Duff 2001: 168). Andrew von Hirsch has objected that '[t]reating defiance as an evil in itself that warrants substantial extra punishment presupposes authoritarian assumptions about the state, the community and the criminal law' (von Hirsch 2002: 443, 445). George Fletcher similarly writes that 'in a liberal society, defiance should not constitute a wrong that justifiably enhances the punishment a recidivist deserves' (Fletcher 1982: 54, 57). The critics are correct to reject defiance- or disobedience-based arguments in favour of the recidivist premium, but not for the reasons they cite.

We in fact do punish disobedience in certain situations, and they are not all problematic. The crime of contempt prohibits disobedience of courts' orders. Disobedience is punished also when people disobey commands given by law-enforcement officers dealing with, say, emergencies. Such provisions criminalise disobedience and punish people for their failures to obey commands by legal authorities in certain situations; the fact that one did not do what one was told to do is precisely at the heart of

---

[7] For a more detailed treatment of the question of disobedience, what it is, when it is just or unjust to punish disobedience, and an argument that 'disregard' is a culpability-enhancer, see Lee (2009: 592–605).

this type of criminality (*cf* Feinberg 1987: 19–21). If it were truly the case that punishing disobedience is illiberal, authoritarian, and thus impermissible, then these laws would all be problematic as well, but they are not.

Here is one possible reason why such punishments are morally permissible: the legal system needs to employ coercive devices to ensure compliance with the law, because otherwise the rule of law, presumably a valuable thing, could not become reality. The problem with this rationale, however, is that the fact that the legal system needs the ability to punish people for disobedience in order to administer justice is insufficient to show that those who disobey the law in these contexts are blameworthy. An argument that appeals to the system's need to punish is a consequentialist argument, and a consequentialist argument in favour of a punishment by itself is insufficient to demonstrate that the punishment is justified—no matter how valuable the rule of law might be.

At the same time, the observation that the legal system crucially depends on the co-operation of those who are subject to it in order to function as a legal system can serve as the basis for a moral obligation on the part of the citizens. That is, a failure to obey government officials in certain situations interferes with the government's ability to carry out the functions of a legitimate state. Punishment of disobedience is justified in these instances because persons have a moral duty not to interfere with workings of a legitimate and reasonably just legal system (Edmundson 1998: 48–70; Waldron 1993: 3, 9–10),[8] and those who violate such duties by disobeying authoritative directives in these specified conditions are morally culpable for that reason.

This conclusion—that punishment of disobedience is sometimes justified—of course does not show that the recidivist premium is justified. The question remains as to whether the recidivist premium is one of the justifiable instances of punishing disobedience. Assuming, then, that disobedience (or defiance) can be culpable, does it make sense to punish recidivists more for their disobedience?

The answer is no. The obstruction-of-justice provisions are not analogous because they criminalise failures to obey particular directives that were individually created for particular persons. When a court issues an order to a particular individual to testify at a trial proceeding, the normative relationship between that individual and the court changes at the moment the court issues the order. Before a court issues an order, no duty to testify exists. But when a court issues the order, the recipient of the

---

[8] It should of course be kept in mind that the duty to obey legal officials is not an absolute duty but a prima facie duty. There will be cases in which the prima facie duty to obey is overridden by a competing consideration, if the reasons to disobey are of correct kinds and of sufficient strength. But for our purposes, the fact that there exists a prima facie duty to obey the orders of government officials who are administering justice is enough to show that punishment of disobedience in a liberal society can be permissible.

order has a new obligation to the court. It is unclear how this idea applies in the context of recidivism. When a person is convicted and punished, is it the case that the person is now facing a special order not to commit a crime that did not exist before? A person who has been convicted of stealing was a recipient of the message that stealing is prohibited before he committed the crime, after he committed the crime, during the legal process and after the punishment. A special order for the convict that he should not commit a crime does not change the content of the prohibition itself. His duty not to break the law against stealing remains the same before, during and after his contact with the legal process.

In other words, in the obstruction-of-justice context, those subject to official orders have duties created by those orders, and those not subject to those official orders do not have the same duties. There is no such difference between recidivists and first-time offenders. The only new command or knowledge gained by an offender, it appears, has to do with the fact that particular legal actors bothered to deliver an individually tailored condemnation on the offender. But because the 'additional' command or awareness is essentially redundant, it is hard to see what new normative significance it generates. Without a new normative significance, the additional command or awareness cannot carry the weight of justifying the recidivist premium. Further, attempts to justify the recidivist premium on such a thin rationale simply confirm the suspicion that the recidivist premium is merely a loud cry by an authoritarian figure demanding obedience or else, which is hardly an attractive picture.

In short, even if it is the case that disobedience can be culpable, it is unclear whether we can justify punishing repeat offenders more than first-time offenders on the basis that repeat offenders are disobedient and first-time offenders are not.

C. RECIDIVISM AS OMISSION

1. The Basic Idea

I have considered various arguments for the recidivist premium above, and although they all differ theoretically, they essentially fail for one reason. It is difficult to make a good argument as to why repeat offenders are, in principle, different from first-time offenders when we focus on the badness of their characters or badness of their acts. The fault of these arguments, I would argue, is twofold. First, the arguments take a snapshot of the offenders' character traits or bad acts at the moment of their reoffending. This is a mistake. The key to understanding the recidivist premium lies in seeing that a person can influence how he or she will behave in the future by making decisions in the present. Second, the theories approach the question of individual culpability by focusing on the individuals in question in isolation, and by focusing on their acts or character traits. This, too, is a mistake. The key to the recidivist premium lies not just in evaluating an individual's act of reoffending or bad character traits. Rather, the focus should be on the ongoing *relationship* between the offender and the state.

One of the conceptual difficulties of the recidivist premium is that if we focus on the moment of offending, the offence does not look, at least at first, any different no matter who commits it—whether it was a repeat offender or a first-time offender. The first step out of this conundrum is to see that criminal offences—like many acts that we undertake in life—do not happen in isolation. A series of events and circumstances can combine to produce a moment ripe for a crime to take place. This in turn means that well before individuals end up committing crimes, they can steer their lives in different directions in order to minimise the risk of finding themselves in a position in which committing a criminal offence becomes a compelling—or at least appealing—option.

Generally speaking, what a person does at one moment can powerfully shape the choices that the he or she faces in the future. To use a mundane example, a person on a diet might decide to travel out of the way to avoid passing next to a fast-food joint later that day. A person who has a tendency to overspend at grocery stores might eat in advance to avoid grocery shopping on an empty stomach. Obviously, how one finds oneself in situations that tempt or induce one to commit a crime is a far more complicated matter. But a person who thinks that she has a tendency to give in to peer pressure to commit criminal acts may stay away from those who are likely to encourage her to engage in criminal activities. If a person understands that having no source of income may lead him down the path of a life of a criminal, he could try to find a job to support himself and his family. If a person's drug addiction leads her to look for quick bucks through burglary, then perhaps combating the drug addiction could lead to a life away from crime. If a person is tempted to molest children whenever he is around them, he can organise his life in a way that minimises his contact with children. The point is that for every crime that a person commits, we can point at other decisions that led to the moment the crime was committed.

So what does this have to do with the recidivist premium? I am suggesting that the recidivist premium is not about what an offender does or reveals at the moment a crime is committed; rather, the recidivist premium is additional punishment directed at the previous steps taken by him that *enabled* the later crime to be committed. The recidivist premium does not punish disobedience or bad character; rather, it punishes an ex-offender's omission—the omission being his failure to take steps to prevent himself from committing another crime.

Do we not demand that *all* persons organise their lives so that they steer clear of criminality? Why is it not the case that when first-time offenders are being punished, they are being punished not only for committing the crimes with which they are charged, but also for their failures to live life in a way that would have allowed them to steer clear of criminality? The answer is that there is a difference between a first-time offender and a repeat offender because a repeat offender has gone through the process of conviction and punishment and a first-time offender has not. When a person is convicted and punished for a crime, one thing we can say with confidence is that the relationship between that person and the state has changed in a way that makes that person different from others who have not had that kind of encounter with the state. It is *this* change in relationship that changes the normative positions of persons with regard to the state. In other words, the recidivist premium should be thought of as grounded on the idea of associative obligation.

Associative obligations are, generally speaking, obligations that one has by virtue of one's membership of some group.[9] Such obligations may be voluntarily undertaken (say, by joining a fraternity) but need not be. For instance, family is often given as a paradigmatic example of an association that gives rise to obligations despite the fact that it is not—or at least not fully—voluntary. Sometimes, such as in friendships, associative obligations can gradually come into existence over time without anyone doing anything like signing up for a list of obligations. In addition, the content of such obligations tends to be defined by not abstract moral ideas but by particular conventions that shape the relevant practice. Often there is no basis other than convention to ground these obligations; the only thing one can do is identify and describe the relevant social practice and point.

In the punishment context, even though phrases like 'paying one's debt to society' imply that once individuals have been punished, they start with a clean slate, the idea that punishment puts people back to where they were before flies in the face of our everyday experiences. One's life cannot be thought of as simply one event after another, one encounter after another, each of which is discrete and disconnected from the others. 'After all we have been through', a phrase that typically precedes a normative statement, is not an idle phrase; it is a way of emphasising the different normative expectations that arise as a result of what 'we have been through'. What we expect of one another is shaped by what we have been through, and different relationships people enter into can inject new, morally significant elements into their lives.

---

[9] For a discussion of common features of associative obligations, see Simmons (1996: 106, 247, 247–52).

What kinds of morally significant duties or obligations exist as a result of the existence of a relationship depend on the nature of the relationship itself. Obviously, merely spending time with someone does not give rise to obligations. If a person beats me up every day for several days and later I notice that the person who assaulted me is drowning, there may or may not be a duty for me to rescue my assailant, depending on a number of factors. However, it would be absurd for anyone to argue that I have a duty to rescue him *because* we have had a relationship. Everything about the argument being advanced here thus turns on the nature of the relationship between an offender and the state.

The nature of the offender–state relationship is as follows. The institution of punishment has a communicative, expressive dimension. When the state punishes, it condemns what the offender has done as blameworthy and it communicates to the offender that what he has done is wrong. Implicit in that message, of course, is that the offender is being punished for what he has done, and after his punishment is complete, he shall not offend again. This is one way in which punishments that carry stigma are different from, say, receiving a parking ticket. The message that people experience when they receive a parking ticket is not, 'Do not park illegally again', but, 'If you park illegally and you are caught, you have to pay.' By contrast, when a person is convicted of rape, the message given is, 'What you did was wrong, and you cannot do it again', not, 'If you rape again and you are caught, you have to serve time.' The possibility of committing the crime again should not even be contemplated, as the whole point of criminal prohibition is that some things just should not be done.

Now, if the process of conviction and punishment communicates the message that what the offenders have done is wrong and they should not do it again, the process also should prompt a period of reflection on the part of offenders to determine how they ended up committing the prohibited act. This kind of self-diagnosis, aided by the institution of punishment, should identify what has gone wrong in an offender's life. People may end up committing crimes for different kinds of reasons, and those reasons differ for different types of offences. Such diagnoses should lead to appropriate prescriptions for each offender, and each offender should follow those prescriptions while and after serving a sentence. A repeat offence by someone who has or should have gone through this process of reflection, diagnosis and prescription justifies the inference that, for whatever reason, the prescription was not followed, and the offender failed to prevent herself from reoffending by failing to organise her life in a way that steers clear of criminality.

Some may still object that none of this is unique to repeat offenders. Those without criminal histories have the ability to know themselves and to understand the kinds of factors that lead people into situations in which they end up committing a crime. First-time offenders may have taken each step leading to their crimes knowing exactly what they were doing and understanding that each step was leading them closer to the commission of a crime. Also, as mentioned above, those who are convicted of a crime for the first time are not necessarily those who have committed only one crime in their lives. Some may already have an impressive criminal background without ever having been caught. If my argument holds, and that those who are convicted of crimes know themselves well enough to know what kinds of things lead them down the path of the criminal, then that argument should apply to those first-time offenders who have good understandings of such factors as well. And if that is the case, then my argument ceases to become an argument in favour of singling out an offender's criminal history as a significant aggravating factor.

However, this objection misses the point that the crucial difference between first-time offenders and repeat offenders is that the repeat offender has *gone through a process with the state that has created a relationship with the state, and the point of that relationship was to ensure that whatever led the offender to the status of being a convict should be avoided in the future.* It is *that history* of having had *that relationship* that first-time offenders lack. And once a person enters into a thick relationship with the state through the process of conviction and punishment, it is appropriate for the state to attribute blame to how a person has increased the risks of criminal wrongdoing over time.[10]

Why should the state not apply the same kind of scrutiny to first-time offenders? The answer is that we have a society that respects individual autonomy. We provide space for people to feel free to move about as long as they do not cross certain boundaries. And if a person crosses a boundary, it is likely that the person's wrongdoing was not only in doing the prohibited act, but also in taking the steps leading up to the prohibited act. But such steps leading up to the prohibited act should not be what the state concerns itself with; they are none of the state's business. However, it all becomes the state's business once the offender and the state enter into a relationship the sole point of which is to recognise that what the offender did was wrong and should not be done again.

At the same time, this proposal does not require the institution of punishment to seek a transformation of an offender's character or soul. The message is, 'We are making you go through the process of conviction and punishment because you crossed certain lines, and we don't want you to cross those lines again.' This is very different from the message, 'We are

---

[10] Michael Tonry believes that my analysis fails because 'it does not explain where the offender's obligation comes from'. See ch 6 in this volume. In evaluating the force of this criticism, it should be kept in mind that the nature of associative obligations generally is such that it is difficult to ground the obligations on something other than the existence and nature of the relevant relationship itself.

making you go through the process of conviction and punishment because
you are a bad person, and we want you to come out of the process a
good person.' Perhaps some of these people have desires to hurt others
that they never rid themselves of. But if that is the case, they must find
ways to weaken or suppress those desires, or to organise their lives in
ways that help them avoid situations in which those desires are triggered
and avoid opportunities to act on such desires. But what is not required
of them is to transform themselves into people with different traits, preferences and attitudes.

It is important to be clear here that I am not suggesting a new command during the process of conviction and punishment that states that
offenders must now 'get their acts together' and that the recidivist premium is for offenders' violations of that command. There would be several
problems with positing that kind of command in explaining the recidivist premium. First, it is not likely that such a command is actually part
of the meaning of the process of conviction and punishment, whereas it
seems incontrovertible that the process of conviction and punishment carries the message that the offender should not reoffend. Second, a regime
of such commands already exists in the form of probation, parole and
supervised release. A command-centred account would then have two sets
of parallel commands—explicit commands and implicit commands—and it
is unclear why the explicit commands would not simply 'occupy the field'
and become an exclusive set of commands. The account advanced here
avoids this problem by focusing instead on the nature of the offender–
state relationship, and the kinds of normative expectations that are raised
once the offender enters into that relationship.

I should also make clear that by arguing that we should think of the
recidivist premium as punishment for 'omission', I am only making an
argument for interpreting the idea of imposing additional punishment for
repeat offenders. I am not advocating a creation of the new crimes of
'failure to fix your own life' or of 'aiding and abetting your future self to
commit another crime'. In other words, the idea is not to create a situation where individuals are punished for failing to reform even though they
never reoffend. Say a person commits a crime and is convicted, and once
he completes his sentence, he goes back to his old way of living. Despite
the fact that he—call him an 'unrepentant law-abider'—never shows any
sign that he has rearranged his life in order to steer clear of criminality,
he miraculously never commits a crime. My argument thus far does not
imply that the unrepentant law-abider should be punished because, after
all, he is a law-abider. A prior offender's act of offending again should
give rise to an inference that the offender helped himself commit another
crime, and it is on the basis of that inference that we can justify imposing additional punishment. However, that does not mean that the failure
to prevent oneself from committing another crime need be criminalised

by itself; it can simply be a culpability enhancer, the same way in which racial hatred is not a crime but is a culpability enhancer for racially motivated crimes.

On the flip side, some may wonder whether an inference that there was a failure to reform is always justified when assessing reoffenders. It is easy to imagine a 'repentant law-breaker', a mirror image to the unrepentant law-abider. It is possible for a person to be convicted and punished, and then, once she completes her sentence, to act like a model citizen. She cleans up her act, finds a job, avoids her criminal friends and so on, but, for whatever reason, she finds herself back in court for committing some crime. Or, even worse, she attempts to clean up her act, find a job and avoid her criminal friends, but she finds that her options post-incarceration are few and far between, and all her attempts to rearrange her life fail. It seems unfair to punish such a person for failure to reform when they reoffend.

How to deal with situations like these is not easy to determine, and would depend on individual situations. For the purposes of this paper, I can say only the following. First, it seems that the repentant-law-breaker scenario is the kind of situation where repeat offenders might say things like 'I couldn't help it', and 'I could not do otherwise', because they might have tried to do everything possible to set their lives straight but failed anyway. But such excuses are codified in the criminal law as formal defences such as duress or insanity, and if a repeat offender's repeat offence can somehow fall into one of those categories, then there can be a genuine defence against the recidivist premium—or even against the conviction for the reoffence itself. Second, the inference of the offender's failure to reform need not be absolute, meaning that it may be rebutted by the offender.[11] One could accordingly imagine allowing partial or full excuses for one's failure to reform. Although details as to how to design a system

---

[11] Some might wonder here why the burden of proving that there was a failure to reform is not on the government and why the burden of proving that there was an attempt to reform is on the defendant. The reason for this is that the state is, ultimately, too far removed from individuals to know how they ought to reform their lives. The state can listen to individuals' stories as to how they have tried to reform and understand them, but how a particular individual is to avoid a life of crime is not information that the state has access to, given the individual variations and opacity of the internal lives of individuals. There are many ways of living a law-abiding life, and they cannot and should not be specified by the state. A broader point here is that it is inappropriate to have an absolute rule barring presumptions that go against criminal defendants just because we are in the criminal context; a more general articulation of the proper relationship between citizens and the state must come first. For a discussion of some of the general issues involved in determining when legal presumptions are appropriate, see Duff (2005: 137–43). It is true that through probation and parole conditions and so on, the state does keep an eye on how ex-offenders return to a life of normalcy. But that does not show that the state has any special insight as to how to live a law-abiding life; such post-release conditions are more about the state's maintaining a tight control over each individual—in a way privileging one state-chosen way of staying out of trouble—and less about the state knowing what is good for each individual.

of full and partial rebuttals and excuses cannot be worked out here, it seems to me that repeat offenders ought to be able to present the ways in which they have tried to steer clear of criminality and, depending on the reasonableness and sincerity of their attempts, receive a reduction in the recidivist premium.[12]

2. Advantages over Competing Accounts

My account has several advantages over competing accounts of the recidivist premium. First, it explains and justifies the extra resentment felt against repeat offenders. Given that the point of the punishment system is to express and communicate blameworthiness of criminal conduct, another offence by someone who has been punished can be an indication that the person has failed to rearrange his life in a way that ensures that he does not offend again. The special kind of resentment that people may feel about a repeat offender stems from the feeling that we have all been through this before. The purpose of the institution of punishment is to forcefully drive home the point that what the offender did was wrong and should not be done again, not just the point that what the offender did carries a price. Once offenders have gone through that kind of process, the expectation is for them to change their ways of life, and the extra resentment arises from *that* expectation. Arguments against the recidivist premium or arguments for a sentencing differential that is solely based on first-time offender mitigations have trouble explaining and justifying this intuition.

Second, recidivism as omission does not suffer from the problems that plague obedience- or character-based accounts of the recidivist premium. Both obedience and character arguments have the same weakness; it is not clear why one's criminal record—reflecting not necessarily the number of times one has committed a crime, but the number of times one has been caught and punished—should be privileged as a way of getting at a person's bad character or disobedience. First-time offenders can have bad character traits or can act in rebellion against the state, just as repeat offenders can repeat without having permanent 'criminal' traits or rebelling against authority. By tying the recidivist premium to additional obligations that arise from the relationship that an offender and the state enter into with each other, my account avoids such problems.

Third, by specifying exactly what the wrongdoing consists of, my proposal gives more guidance as to what amount of extra punishment is appropriate. When one encounters habitual-offender statutes, two reactions are common: (i) some kind of additional punishment is appropriate;

---

[12] For a similar suggestion, see Roberts (2008b: 220–22).

(ii) the additional punishment should not be 'too much'. Accounts that focus on disobedience or bad character traits have trouble placing a principled limitation on the size of the recidivist premium. If an offender has bad character traits that are deeply ingrained and irremediable, how much additional punishment is appropriate? If an offender has rejected the idea of playing by the rules, how much additional punishment is appropriate? It is unclear whether any principled limitation can be placed on the size of the recidivist premium. In fact, arguments based on character or defiance have a tendency to recommend large increases in punishment without encountering any meaningful resistance, simply because what justifies the additional punishment is an abstract 'harm' of being a 'bad person' or 'defying authority'.

By contrast, my account of the recidivist premium takes into account the belief that some additional punishment is appropriate, but places a ceiling on it because the wrongdoing does not consist of being defiant of authority, rejecting society's norms or being a heinous human being. Rather, the wrongdoing we are concerned with has to do with living one's life in a way that is insufficiently far away from criminal activity. And given that the recidivist premium punishes for increasing the risk of a criminal activity, as opposed to punishing for engaging in the criminal activity itself, the premium should not be more than the punishment for the subsequent offence.

3. Government as a Responsible Party?

Finally, the account advanced here opens up a new line of inquiry that, in my view, should always be part of the recidivist-premium calculus: the idea of assigning to the state at least partial blame for an offender's recidivism. As I have been stressing, the engine that drives the recidivist premium is the relationship between the state and the offender, the point of which is to acknowledge that what the offender has done is wrong. And implicit in that relationship is a commitment on the part of the offender to organise his life in a way that steers clear of criminality so that he does not reoffend. Like most relationships, this is a relationship that places obligations on all parties involved. In the same way that the relationship between an offender and the state allows the state to take a closer look at how an offender carries out his life, the state also has a heightened responsibility towards the offender, namely to help him get back to a life of normalcy or at least to not interfere with an offender's effort to become a law-abiding citizen. In other words, if the recidivist premium is imposed for one's failure to set his life straight post-conviction, if what justifies the recidivist premium is the relationship between the individual and the state, and if the moral logic of the relationship necessitates the parties' commitment that the offender should organise his life in order to prevent another offence, then it seems to follow that the state has a role to play in helping the offender live a life away from crime as well.

This last implication is especially significant for the recidivism issue because there are serious and legitimate concerns that the increasing punitiveness of the US criminal justice system in the past few decades has had the perverse effect of driving up the rate of recidivism. Many offenders who are released from prison frequently face daunting prospects as they try to get their lives back in order. First, they will find that, because of their felony convictions, they are excluded from public housing. Second, they will find that they not only are excluded from housing, but also are excluded from a source of income because their felony convictions make them ineligible for welfare. Third, if they seek to get education to improve their lots, they will find another stumbling block if they were convicted of a drug-related offence, as Congress has made such people ineligible for student loans. Fourth, they will find that they may not be able to find jobs as teachers or childcare workers due to various laws regarding the eligibility of individuals with criminal records. Fifth, even if they somehow find jobs, they will find that they cannot drive there because of laws that revoke or suspend their driver's licenses because of their felony backgrounds.[13]

In short, as the recidivist premium has increased in the past few decades, various government policies have simultaneously made it difficult for ex-offenders to pursue normal lives by denying them housing, welfare, education, certain jobs and the ability to drive to work. On top of all of this, ex-offenders are hit with the ultimate symbol of exclusion: denial of the right to vote. The connection between the lack of the right to vote and recidivism may be a bit more tenuous than the connection between recidivism and the lack of basic needs such as food, housing and education. However, those who commit crimes tend to be those who feel alienated from the mainstream society and who do not have a faith in the democratic process to reflect their interests; such a lack of faith in turn can lead them to lose respect for the law. Taking away offenders' right to vote would naturally exacerbate such attitudes, and it is difficult to deny that the state's reinforcement of their feelings of alienation from the rest of the society and other citizens would have a detrimental impact on rehabilitative efforts (Manza and Uggen 2006: 137–64).

These types of social exclusionist policies are inconsistent with the system's demand that offenders set their lives straight after going through the process of conviction and punishment. Our consideration of the recidivist premium should take into account the government's role in making

---

[13] For more detailed discussions of these restrictions, see Mauer and Chesney-Lind (2002: 37, 40–43).

recidivism a comparatively appealing option for ex-offenders. But in what way? If the government is a complicit party in the recidivist's reoffending, the theoretically consistent thing to do seems to be to impose some kind of a penalty on the government as a complicit actor contributing to the reoffending. However, the most effective way of communicating the government's responsibility in contributing to the reoffending may instead be to reduce the offender's recidivist premium—even though there is something theoretically odd about one's criminal culpability being reduced just because there is another blameworthy subject. The difficult question, of course, is how all this would be done, and the proposal raises many questions. For the purposes of this essay, the only propositions that I would like to advance are that the recidivist premium can be justified on the basis of the relationship offenders enter into with the state; that *this* relationship places an obligation not only on the offenders, but also on the state; and that the size of the recidivist premium should reflect the ways in which each party to that relationship has failed.

D. CONCLUSION

This chapter has argued that the recidivist premium should be thought of not as punishment for a defiant attitude or a bad character trait, but as punishment for an omission. The culpable omission that justifies the recidivist premium is the repeat offender's failure, after conviction, to arrange his life in a way that ensures a life free of further criminality. Although how individuals conduct their lives as a general matter is not properly the business of the state, once offenders are convicted of a crime, they enter into a thick relationship with the state, and that relationship gives rise to an obligation for the offenders to rearrange their lives in order to steer clear of criminal wrongdoing. This chapter has also argued that obligations between the state and offenders run in both directions, and that we should recognise the ways in which the state may be a responsible actor that should share the blame for recidivists' reoffending. Needless to say, many questions remain as to how to implement a theory like this, and which aspects of our current practices would remain and which would change.

In addition, there are two broader normative questions that this chapter has not addressed. First, given appropriate retributivist limitations, is it ever nevertheless justifiable for the state to 'punish' those who are likely to reoffend beyond the level allowed by the just-deserts constraints for deterrence or incapacitation purposes? This is a question that this chapter must leave untouched.[14] Second, can the recidivist premium be based

---

[14] For a general discussion of the question of 'selective incapacitation' of dangerous offend-

on some idea of forfeiture or loss of citizenship? There are times when
the rhetoric surrounding habitual-offender statutes sounds like an argument in favour of *excluding* certain people from the rest of the society,
as opposed to *punishing* them. It is beyond the scope of this chapter to
fully evaluate this argument. I would only say that in debating the recidivist premium, we must identify the moment at which the discourse of just
deserts turns into an argument based on the idea of forfeiture. Habitual-
offender statutes sometimes seem as if they are ways of taking away
people's citizenship and banishing them outside the community's territory.
There is a difference between giving people what they deserve and strip-
ping them of their citizenship, and we must always be on the lookout for
the moment at which a person who is a full member of the community,
but whose acts nonetheless call for condemnation, starts being treated as
a person who should not be part of the community at all.

REFERENCES

Ashworth, A (2005) *Sentencing and Criminal Justice*, 4th edn (Cambridge, Cambridge University Press).
Cal Penal Code Ann (2006) § 667(b)–(i) (West Supp).
Duff, R (2001) *Punishment, Communication, and Community* (Oxford, Oxford
   University Press).
— — (2005) 'Strict Liability, Legal Presumptions, and the Presumption of Inno-
   cence' in AP Simester (ed), *Appraising Strict Liability* (Oxford, Oxford Uni-
   versity Press) 137–43.
Edmundson, WA (1998) *Three Anarchical Fallacies: An Essay on Political Author-
   ity* (Cambridge, Cambridge University Press).
Feinberg, J (1987) *Harm to Others* (Oxford, Oxford University Press).
Fletcher, G (1978) *Rethinking Criminal Law* (Boston, Little Brown).
— — (1982) 'The Recidivist Premium' 1 *Criminal Justice Ethics* 54–59.
Horder, J (1993) 'Criminal Culpability: The Possibility of a General Theory' 12
   Law & Philosophy 193–215.
Lee, Y (2009) 'Recidivism as Omission: A Relational Account' 87 *Texas Law
   Review* 571–622.
Manza J and Uggen, C (2006) *Locked Out: Felon Disenfranchisement and Ameri-
   can Democracy* (New York, Oxford University Press).
Mauer, M and Chesney-Lind, M (2002) *Invisible Punishment: The Collateral Con-
   sequences of Mass Imprisonment* (New York, New Press).
Roberts, JV (2008a), 'Punishing Persistence: Explaining the Enduring Appeal of
   the Recidivist Sentencing Premium' 48 *British Journal of Criminology* 468–81.
— — (2008b) *Punishing Persistent Offenders: Exploring Community and Offender
   Perspectives* (Oxford, Oxford University Press).
Simmons, JA (1996) 'Associative Political Obligations' 106 *Ethics* 247–73.

ers, see eg Ashworth (2005: 206–17).

Singer, R (1979) *Just Deserts: Sentencing Based on Equality and Desert* (Cambridge, MA, Ballinger).

Tadros, V (2005) *Criminal Responsibility* (Oxford, Oxford University Press).

US Sentencing Commission (2008) *US Sentencing Guidelines Manual* (Washington, DC).

von Hirsch, A (1986) *Past or Future Crimes: Deservedness and Dangerousness in the Sentencing of Criminals* (New Brunswick, Rutgers University Press).

—— (2002) 'Record-enhanced Sentencing in England and Wales' 4 *Punishment & Society* 443–57.

Waldron, J (1993) 'Special Ties and Natural Duties' 22 *Philosophy & Public Affairs* 3–30.

5

'More to Apologise For': Can a Basis for the Recidivist Premium Be Found within a Communicative Theory of Punishment?[1]

CHRISTOPHER BENNETT

A. THE INTUITIVE BASIS OF THE RECIDIVIST PREMIUM IN EVERYDAY MORAL PRACTICE

SHOULD WE PUNISH repeat offenders more simply because they are repeat offenders? In this chapter I discuss the problem of the 'recidivist premium' from within the perspective of a communicative theory of punishment.[2] The communicative theory takes it that the fundamental purpose of punishment is to express due condemnation of an offender for an offence, and on the face of it this looks incompatible with the recidivist premium. On the communicative theory, the condemnation is of the offender *for* a particular offence. The punishment ought to fit the crime. So how can the fact that she had previous convictions make the present crime any more serious?[3]

Nevertheless, the idea that repeat offenders ought to be dealt with more harshly seems to be firmly grounded in our moral practice in everyday, non-legal life. Imagine, for instance, that one of my student e-mails me to make an appointment for the next day. It sounds quite urgent and concerns an upcoming essay. I had been planning to work at home that day, but agree to come in anyway in order to see him. The allotted time

[1] I would like to express my gratitude to the organisers of this project on prior convictions for inviting me to participate. I have learned a lot from the discussions. I am also very grateful to the participants at the workshops for helpful discussion of this chapter.
[2] For some sources of this view, see Feinberg (1965); Duff (1986) and von Hirsch (1993).
[3] Indeed, we might conclude that the recidivist premium cannot be justified according to any rationalisation of penal practice: see eg Dubber (1995).

comes and goes—no sign of the student. I begin to feel a bit taken advantage of, and cross that I gave up my day working at home in an act of faith to this person who has not repaid that faith. Some hours later, an apologetic e-mail arrives. The author does not claim to have any cast-iron excuse, but claims to have been disorganised, and to have 'had a lot on his plate'. I, perhaps slightly grudgingly, accept the apology and we arrange another time for a meeting that the student continues to claim is important to him. Nevertheless (inevitably given the point of the example . . .) the time for this second meeting also comes and goes with no sign of the student.

My sense is that in this situation some resentment on my part at the student's behaviour will be quite justified, and that it will be greater than the resentment I would be justified in feeling towards him on the basis of the first failure to attend. Furthermore, this greater resentment does not simply reflect the fact that I am the one who has been messed about in this situation. Rather my resentment can be understood as showing the degree of condemnation that I think is justified. This is reflected in the fact that, in the absence of a valid excuse the student will have *more to apologise for* because this is the second time that he has done this to me. He will have more to apologise for, not simply because of the psychological fact that I happen to be more grumpy with him second time round, but because—it seems natural to say—of the greater gravity of what he has done, this being a repeat offence. Of course *in one sense* there is nothing more serious that he has done to me this time than he did the last time. But that is only a perspective that we can adopt if we deliberately and artificially leave out the previous events. In reality I have a relationship with the student that includes both wrongs. It is the events affecting this relationship that I am responding to when I frame my resentment and set my demands for an apology. This suggests that the student who repeats his offence deserves greater resentment, blame or condemnation than the student who offends only once. And if, as in the communicative theory, the deployment of the criminal sanction should be based in some way on the (justifiable) operation of our reactions of blame, resentment, etc, in moral life, it suggests, at least on the face of it, that we ought to be able to find some justification for the recidivist premium in the terms of the communicative theory.

In this chapter I follow Lee in discussing two main strategies that those attempting to answer this question have adopted (see Lee 2009, and this volume): (i) that condemnation of crime is not merely condemnation of *acts* but of *character*, and that repeat offenders display worse character; and (ii) that repeat offenders are guilty of worse acts. As I suggested earlier, the second strategy might be thought implausible because of the implausibility of saying that the repeat offender has committed any *extra* crime that the first-time offender has not. Despite this, I will put forward arguments in favour of Lee's conclusion that it is the second option that is more plausible. I will argue that it is less plausible to claim that repeat offenders are guilty of no other offence than first-time offenders when we are thinking about cases like my student than it might appear if we are only thinking in terms of the law. We will then need to look at whether we can use the same grounds for justifying the recidivist premium in law. This will take us into a discussion of whether some continuity between state condemnation of crime and condemnation in everyday non-legal contexts is necessary in order for state punishment to be properly meaningful as condemnation. Before we get on to this, however, we need to look at the character view.

B. CONDEMNATION FOR CHARACTER

1. Roberts on Culpability as Blameworthiness

As a representative of the character view we can take Julian Roberts's recent defence of the recidivist premium on the grounds that repeat offenders show a greater degree of culpability or *blameworthiness* than first-time offenders (see Roberts 2008a, 2008b: ch 4). For Roberts, blameworthiness is determined, not just by the seriousness of the act, but by (at least an aspect of) the offender's character. Roberts explains his view through a rejection of Fletcher's view that culpability is an all-or-nothing matter rather than a continuum. There is such a thing as criminal *responsibility*, which Roberts thinks *is* an all-or-nothing matter. Either you have committed the offence or you have not (ie with some threshold level of responsibility, perhaps signified by the lack of an exculpating condition). This is roughly what Duff calls having a case to answer (Duff 2007). You either have a case for which the state can call you to answer, or you do not. But Roberts calls attention to the fact that there is another sort of judgment that informs our evaluations of a person's blameworthiness. This is a judgment, we might say, about *how bad the action shows the person to be*. And this judgment of (an aspect of) character is a matter of degree rather than a black and white decision. Thus Roberts proposes that we distinguish between responsibility (or having to answer) and culpability (or blameworthiness) and allow a broader range of factors to inform our judgments of culpability—factors that will include 'the offender's state of mind before and conduct after the offence', evidenced by such things as relevantly similar prior convictions and remorseful reactions to the offence. This then gives Roberts an explanation of why we should punish repeat offenders more severely: repeat offences will typically show a deeper disregard for the values that the criminal law serves to defend than a first-time offence.

Roberts defends his view by the occasionally utilitarian-sounding consideration that the criminal justice system must coincide with public opinion if it is to maintain those perceptions of legitimacy that enable it to exact our compliance. However, although the public perception of the criminal justice system is an important consideration, I do not think that it is necessary to this consideration in order to give at least an initial justification of Roberts's view. Rather I think that the need to take Roberts's 'enhanced blameworthiness' into account can be established simply by looking at what punishment must be like if it is to have a properly condemnatory function. If punishment is to be condemnation of *the offender for* the offence, then one might think that Roberts is quite right about what the object of condemnation ought to be. It should be a reaction to the wrongful attitudes of the offender as manifested in the offence. Given that (i) the criminal law sets morally important limits on how citizens can act; (ii) those limits are set for reasons that relate to important values; and (we are assuming) (iii) the point of having the criminal sanction is to condemn conduct that transgresses those limits, it is hard to see how the censure theorist can resist saying that the offender should be censured for the attitudes expressed in the criminal act where those attitudes are contrary to the values that provide the point of the criminal law. For by this hypothesis the criminal act represents some disregard of the importance of these limits, and it is in order to express the importance of these limits that, on the censure account, the criminal sanction exists. Hence the offender should be condemned for the extent of her disregard of the values for which the criminal law stands. If we condemn repeat offenders more, then should it not be because (and insofar as) by repeating her offence she shows herself to be more vicious, more lacking in the basic moral sensitivity that, as a political community, we expect of one another?

2. Why the Character View Cannot Justify the Recidivist Premium

However, the view that character is the object of condemnation in punishment faces a number of problems. Roberts himself is sensitive to the possibility that his view might be taken to imply punishment for character, in the sense that sentencing might be allowed to be determined by evidence of character such as 'the defendant's religion, his past unemployment, his relations with his spouse, his childhood history, whether he loves animals, and so forth'.[4] However, he rightly points out that his view has no such implication. The criminal law ought to be interested in dealing out punishment that expresses condemnation of (and hence is proportionate to) the wrongful attitudes manifested in the offence. It would corrupt

---

[4] R Singer, quoted in Roberts (2008a: 475).

this aim if the sentence were to be informed by extraneous factors, however much these may be part of the offender's bad character. The state can have a concern with offender's reasons for acting, the attitudes that are expressed in action, and this is all the conception of character that a theorist like Roberts needs.

However, although I think that Roberts may provide an account of culpability or blameworthiness that fits well with some versions of the condemnatory view of punishment, I deny that his is the account we are looking for in this chapter to justify the recidivist sentencing premium. The thought behind the character account, as I originally introduced it, was that, if it could be shown that punishment was for character, we would be able to see why punishment should be greater for repeat offenders, since we would be able to see that repeat offenders were worse people, having repeatedly committed some type of criminal act. To flesh out the picture a bit more, we might say that, if the degree of condemnation should match the degree of bad character, repeat offenders deserve greater condemnation since their repeat offending shows that the tendency to offend, the insensitivity to whatever reasons speak in favour of not offending, is more deeply embedded in their character, a more profound or stubborn failing than was obvious at first. The problem is that, although plausible for some repeat offenders, this is not plausible for all—and hence the character view cannot explain the attractiveness of a blanket increase in punishment for repeat offenders.

The character view is therefore a combination of a number of thoughts. First of all, there is the view of the *object of condemnation* that we have just been looking at: what is to be condemned is not simply the act but rather (or also) the character-traits or attitudes that the act manifests—this is necessary in order to vary the condemnation from first-time to repeat offences, when the same offence is committed each time. Secondly, there is an *epistemic limitation*: when the offender commits the first offence we must be unsure what traits of character or attitudes the offence really manifests. Is it a momentary lapse of proper concern, or a giving way to temptation, or is it a more profoundly rooted contempt for persons and property? The thought is then that it becomes clearer which traits are really operative as there are more offences: each offence provides further evidence that can be taken into account, and will tend to point to traits at the worse end of the scale. Thirdly, there is a principle of *charity* in the interpretation of the offender's motives: we must have a duty, in the first instance, in the face of such uncertainty, to give the offender the benefit of the doubt and not to assume the worst.

Now the epistemic limitation principle and the principle of charity must operate in tandem: neither would get us to the recidivist premium in the absence of the other. The principle of charity would have no discretion to work within if our knowledge was perfect (as long as condemnation

is meant to track character); while if there is epistemic limitation but
we do not adopt a principle of charity then we would have no reason
not to assume the worst, or not to take action in which every way was
operationally most effective according to other criteria. However, if this
is correct, then the character view considered here will fail. And this is
because the argument can *only* justify the premium in cases in which there
is uncertainty about the offender's motivations. The recidivist premium,
however, operates *regardless* of such uncertainty: intuitively, it is a *blanket* tendency to think that the repeat offender deserves more punishment.[5]
Say, for instance, that someone is convicted of an offence that, although
a first-time offence, has been meticulously planned over a number of
years (and we have compelling evidence to that effect). Furthermore, the
offender has boasted of it to his intimates before and after carrying it out.
This first-time offender gives us no doubt about his motives. So imagine now that after release he commits another relevantly similar crime
(or two, or three). If you have the intuition that repeat offenders ought
to be punished more harshly, then I suspect you will have it in this case
too. But in this case it cannot be that we are discounting a principle of
charity. Because the offender's motives were abundantly clear in the first
offence, no principle of charity was operative there. Thus if our intuition
in favour of the recidivist premium has any rationality, then it has not
yet been discovered.

These remarks can also be applied to Andrew von Hirsch's defence of
the recidivist premium in *Past or Future Crimes* (von Hirsch 1985: 2002).
On the basis that his view involves taking a charitable view in the first
instance, which charity is then withheld in later offences, von Hirsch calls
it 'progressive loss of mitigation' rather than a recidivist premium. On von
Hirsch's view there is a reasonably clear equivalence between crime and
punishment, but there is a band of possible punishments for any crime.
At sentencing we consider mitigating (and perhaps aggravating) factors: a
first-time offence, on his view, ought to be considered a mitigating factor.
Furthermore, von Hirsch fleshes out our reasons for believing in the principle of charity, which he thinks is justified for the following reasons of
sympathy and solidarity for inevitable human weakness:

> Although it would be wonderful if people's moral inhibitions were strong
> enough to keep them from wrongdoing at all times, we know that even the
> self-control of those who ordinarily refrain from misconduct may fail in a
> moment of weakness or wilfulness. We wish to condemn the person for his act
> but accord him some respect for the fact that his inhibitions against wrongdoing
> have functioned on previous occasions, and show some sympathy for the all-

---

[5] This is not to rule out the exercise of discretion in sentencing. Pillsbury (2002) claims
that recidivist statutes deliberately leave no room for discretion. But this applies only to
the 'three-strikes' approach that dictates a mandatory sentence; what we are arguing about
here is at best a mandatory premium.

too-human frailty that can lead someone to such a lapse. This we do by showing a reduced disapproval of him for his first misdeed (von Hirsch 1985: 83–84).

von Hirsch's view takes it that the first offence can be viewed as a lapse. Censure, for von Hirsch, is directed not just at the act but at the agent for the act. At least to some extent he acknowledges a concern for the agent's character and motivation. He imagines the possibility of a first-time offender making a plea that this was a first mis-step and out of keeping with his habitual practice: in other words that it does not show his character in such a bad light as it might seem. For this plea to be acceptable we would either require evidence that it was a lapse, or at least be in a position of uncertainty in which we could give the offender the benefit of the doubt. However, as I have pointed out, we can imagine cases in which there would be no uncertainty but in which we would still think the recidivist premium ought to operate for a second offence. Hence von Hirsch, and the other proponents of the character view, have not explained the basis of the recidivist premium.

C. REPEAT OFFENCES AS MORALLY WORSE THAN FIRST-TIME OFFENCES

1. Disobedience

As we saw above, a second broad strategy for justifying the recidivist premium is by claiming that a repeat offence is in some way morally worse than a first-time offence, perhaps because there is a further wrong, or a further crime, that is committed by the recidivist that is not committed by the first-time offender. As I said, this view is often rejected out of hand because it seems hard to see how there could be a crime that is committed in the second case that is not committed in the first. Nevertheless it might be said, in the case of my student, that there is clearly a sense in which I can feel more aggrieved by his failure to turn up second time around. This grievance is more than just an evaluation of the student's character: it is a reaction to some way in which he has wronged me through his failure to treat me as he has a duty to treat me, to give me some basic consideration that he owes me. Thus we might think that the character explanation does not fully capture the logic of our reactions.

I may have an added grievance against my errant student, but what about the criminal case: is there some analogous party that can have a further grievance against an offender because that offender reoffends? In order for the recidivist premium to operate as a blanket premium on all repeat offenders, the party holding the grievance would have to be the state: after all, only in a few cases will the repeat offender have reoffended against the same specifiable individual. Thus the question for the rest of this paper is: why should the state have an extra grievance against the *repeat* offender? One way in which we might answer this question (an answer which will form the topic of this section) is through the claim that the repeat offender is guilty of a certain kind of disobedience or defiance that the first-time offender is not.[6] For any offence there are moral reasons that count against performing the criminal action which apply equally to the first-time offender as to the repeat offender. However, the repeat offender has been told explicitly that this action is criminalised and that certain sanctions will attend its performance. In that case, if the offender goes on to reoffend it might be argued that he will have shown himself to be disobedient, or defiant, or contemptuous of, the law to a greater degree than the first-time offender. Therefore it is perhaps not so implausible after all that the repeat offence can involve the commission of an extra offence: that there might be aspects of the repeat offence that are relevant to further criminalisation.

Nevertheless, there has been opposition to this perceived 'criminalisation of disobedience'. For some writers there is something authoritarian in punishing people, not just for their crimes, but for the element of disobedience of state authority that they represent. It might be thought that making disobedience a crime is incompatible with giving citizens the kinds of freedoms they ought to have in liberal society.

Whatever one thinks about this claim of illiberalism, the claim that punishment for disobedience explains the recidivist premium is subject to two further compelling objections. The first is that it assumes a narrow model of offences.[7] The claim that there is greater disobedience in the repeat offence assumes a mitigating factor of something like ignorance of law in the first offence, which factor cannot be said to be present in the repeat offence since the offender was told the nature of the law at conviction. For instance, if a small employer is prosecuted for failing to pay the proper national insurance payments for her employees, the complexity of the regulations and her lack of time for mastering them might be regarded as mitigating her culpability. But if she does it again she cannot give the same excuse. However, while this strategy might explain more severe punishment for repeat perpetrators of some *regulatory* offences, it will not work for the central *mala in se* of murder, assault, battery, rape and theft. Ignorance of the criminality of these actions would be more like an aggravating than a mitigating factor. Yet the recidivist premium accords with intuition in *mala in se* cases as well.

The second objection to the disobedience strategy is that it does not explain the recidivist premium in terms that are continuous with the expla-

---

[6] My argument of this section owes a lot to that of Lee (2009); see also von Hirsch (2002).
[7] See Lee's discussion of examples of differing degrees of culpability for ignorance of law (2009: 602–04).

nation of my reaction to my student. Of course, it *might* be the case that what explains my reaction to my student is that I have *commanded* him to make sure that he turns up for the rearranged meeting, and that in failing to turn up he contemptuously rejects my authority, thus culpably disobeying me. However, this is not the way I described the example, and this description of it does not seem necessary to explain why I should resent his failure more second time around. At best it will explain why greater resentment might be appropriate in a small minority of cases. As long as we are justified in thinking that there ought to be some continuity between the reasons for condemnation that operate in everyday moral life and in the criminal justice system, this counts against the disobedience view.

2. Omission, or Failure to Take Steps to Reform

Lee argues that the reason theorists have failed so far to give a satisfactory account of the recidivist premium is that they have been looking at offences as isolated acts. Lee's claim is that the recidivist is guilty of a further offence of omission that the first-time offender is not. But he thinks that we need to look at the context of the act in order to see how this could be so (see Lee 2009: 608, and this volume). He thinks, firstly, that to understand the wrong that a repeat offence is we need to see it, not just as the same type of crime as before, but also as a *failure to prevent reoffending*—given that agents can take steps to influence what they later do; and, secondly, that we need to understand that the relationship that exists between the state and the repeat offender is different from that that exists between the state and the first-time offender. So Lee's claim is that in the repeat offence there is always an extra offence, that of failure to prevent reoffending (Lee 2009: 610).

There is a problem facing Lee's account—a problem he recognises. It is true that a repeat offender can generally be taken to be capable of taking steps to organise her life and behaviour so as to avoid a repeat of criminal behaviour. Nevertheless this point is not sufficient on its own to explain the existence of the recidivist premium since *all* citizens, previous offenders or not, are required to organise their behaviour so as to avoid criminality. In the case of first-time offenders this failure to organise their behaviour to avoid criminality is not taken to be a further crime. Lee needs to explain why it *is* a further crime—of omission—for repeat offenders but not for first-time offenders (Lee 2009: 611). What Lee must argue is that repeat offenders are under *a further specific obligation* to take steps to organise their behaviour to refrain from the kind of criminality that characterised the previous offence, and can thus be further condemned should they fail to do so. The obvious strategy here, as Lee recognises, is to claim that it is through the process of conviction that the previous offender incurs such an obligation. But it is not clear that Lee fully explains why we should take the process of conviction to confer on the offender such an obligation. The argument that Lee gives for this point refers to the communicative function of punishment:

> Now, if the process of conviction and punishment communicates the message that what the convicted has done is wrong and that he should not do it again, the process should prompt a period of reflection on the part of the offender to determine how he ended up committing the prohibited act. . . . Such diagnoses should lead to appropriate prescriptions for each offender, and each offender should follow these prescriptions after they complete their sentences. A repeat offence by someone who has gone through this type of process of reflection, diagnosis, and prescription justifies the inference that, for whatever reason, the prescription was not followed, and he failed to prevent himself from reoffending by failing to organise his life in a way that steers clear of criminality (Lee 2009: 613).

This argument appeals to the idea that punishment is not merely communicative but that there is—ideally—something penitential about punishment (see eg Duff 1986). Nevertheless this characterisation of the ideally successful case of communicative punishment is not enough by itself to show why *every* previous offender should be taken to have an obligation to prevent herself from reoffending. It explains how, ideally, an offender ought to react, and that an offender who reacts as she ought to will form a determination to refrain from such conduct in the future; but it does not explain why every convicted offender should be thought to have undertaken an obligation to desist from further relevantly similar crimes, an obligation that, should she fail to meet it, will bring further condemnation on her. Is Lee claiming that each offender has an obligation to enter this 'period of reflection' and then to act accordingly—ie to follow the prescription to avoid such behaviour? But it seems implausible to think that there could be an obligation to undergo such reflection, at any rate an obligation that is enforceable by the state. And it is also not plausible that in all cases such reflection will be followed by a determination to reform. What Lee describes is the ideal case. But then we are still left with the question of how obligation enters the picture.

Nevertheless I think that Lee's insight *can* be developed into a full explanation of the recidivist premium. What we need to do is to explain why the process of conviction confers a legally binding obligation to take some steps to reform, something that can mandate greater condemnation for reoffending. In order to do this we need some explanation of how the ideal case that Lee describes is relevant to the obligations we think offenders have, and what they can be required to do on pain of further sanction. I want to suggest that the obligation we need is to be found in our practice of *apologising*. In apologising for some wrong one accepts an obligation to take steps not to do it again. An apology which did not contain some such understanding would be quite empty. Of course, offenders do not actually apologise, or not often. So this suggestion might seem a bit of a dead end. But I would like to suggest, not that *actual* apology is necessary to punishment, but rather that the *form* of ideal apology should be the basis for working out how (and how much) to punish. The reason for thinking this is that it is only in being tied to symbols drawn from intuitive moral practice that state condemnation of crime can be meaningful. Therefore, I argue, the way in which the state expresses condemnation of the offender through punishment should be based on the practice of apology. In imposing punishment or amends on the offender the state communicates to the offender how much he has to apologise for and hence how serious the offence was. If this view is correct—and I say more to defend it in the next section—then where there is more to apologise for we should expect to find a more severe punishment needed to express the higher degree of due condemnation. If it turns out that repeat offenders do have more to apologise for—if a greater amount of amends would be necessary to 'make up' for the offence, simply because it is a repeat offence—then, on this view, the state should punish more.

3. The Recidivist Premium in the Apology Ritual Account of Punishment

Let us return to the case of my student. Is it plausible that the reason that we think that greater resentment towards the student is justified, and the reason that we think that the student has more to apologise for the second time around, is that he has failed in an obligation to refrain from further offending? I think that this is quite plausible. For as I described the situation, the student issued an *apology* for failing to turn up the first time, and if we look at what is going on in apologising, we will see that issuing an apology involves implicitly undertaking an obligation to amend one's conduct in the future.[8] When one apologises for something that one acknowledges as wrong and for which one accepts that one is fully responsible, one presents one's apology as an expression of remorse, of guilt even, which is to say one presents it as an expression of one's painful recognition of the wrongness of what one did. It is only if one expresses this recognition that the apology is likely to be accepted as sincere. However, if one really accepts the wrongness of what one does and experiences the pain of having done something one rejects as wrong, one will be determined not to do that in the future. Therefore a

---

[8] For more on this, and further references, see my article 'The Varieties of Retributive Experience' (Bennett, 2002).

test of the sincerity of an apology is whether the person's future actions back it up. (Imagine that this was not the case: 'I'm very sorry, but I see no reason not to do it again'!) So in presenting the apology as sincere the student is undertaking an obligation not to do it again: issuing the apology is a complex act, but this aspect of it is a bit like undertaking a promise. When the student wrongs me *again*, not only has he wasted my time *again*, I also have an *extra* grievance towards him which is that he has broken (something like) a promise he made to me in apologising. He made (something like) a promise to organise his behaviour so that he would not wrong me again, and yet he wronged me again.

Does this observation about the workings of apologising shed any light on our discussion of repeat offenders? Lee's position would make sense if, instead of communicative punishment merely ideally evoking a penitent attitude, offenders actively apologised and thereby undertook an obligation to refrain. That obligation would fit Lee's desiderata perfectly: it would be something that singled repeat offenders out from first-time offenders, and would explain why repeat offenders have a different relationship to the state from that of first-time offenders. It would explain why all and only repeat offenders deserve to be condemned more than first-time offenders. However, this observation in fact does not help Lee: rather it allows us to sharpen our objection to his position. For offenders *do not* normally apologise and undertake an obligation to desist as part of their punishment. They do not typically promise to the state that they will refrain from relevantly similar criminal behaviour in the future. Indeed such a promise could only create an obligation if it were undertaken freely and voluntarily. And punishment is coercively imposed.

For this reason Lee's line of thought might sound like a non-starter. Nevertheless I want to see whether there might be some mileage in it. I will proceed in two steps. First of all I will argue that the obligation to reform should *not* be seen as like a promise in the sense that only those who voluntarily undertake it are under it: crucially, *all* past offenders should be thought of as under an obligation to reform, whether they have explicitly apologised or not. And secondly, I will argue that, if punishment is to express meaningful condemnation of an offence, then it should use symbols that resonate with our deepest intuitive understanding of having done wrong: in short it should seek to symbolise *what an offender should be sorry for* by imposing an amount of amends on the offender of the level that he or she would spontaneously be willing to undertake were he properly sorry. If we put these two points together, we can say that repeat offenders have more to be sorry for on the grounds that—whether they explicitly undertook it or not—they have failed to meet an obligation they were under by virtue of their first offence; and that secondly, the punishment of repeat offenders, if it seeks to capture how much a person might be motivated to do to make up for their offence, should be greater where this extra obligation is in play. Our conclusion ought to be that punishment of repeat offenders would not be adequate to their culpability if it did not include some premium that recognised that they were in a special moral position by virtue of their repeat offence. The arguments for both of these points will of course have to be brief.

Let us take the point about promising first. As the parentheses ('(something like) a promise') that I used above indicate, we should not be distracted by the analogy between the obligation to take steps to refrain from such offences in the future and promissory obligation. The obligation I am interested in is *like* a promise in the sense that in making a sincere apology the wrongdoer *undertakes* to take steps to refrain from such conduct in the future. But it is *unlike* a promise in that the content of a promise only becomes obligatory by virtue of being undertaken. Promissory obligation is in this sense arbitrary: it is not binding until voluntarily assumed. It is central to apologising that, in undertaking to reform one's conduct[9] one does not do so in this merely arbitrary spirit. One does not make this undertaking as a special favour; rather one makes it in the spirit of *recognising an obligation that one has* by virtue of having committed the wrong in the first place. Although this obligation is, in a sincere apology, explicitly undertaken, it does not depend on this undertaking for its force as an obligation. This point is important because it shows that even offenders who do not apologise should be thought of as being under such an obligation.

Let us now move on to the second point about the expressive or communicative dimension of punishment. Punishment, on the view we are assuming here, expresses a certain kind of condemnation of the offender for the offence. However, in order to say what it needs to say, punishment needs to be symbolically adequate. Just as a malformed sentence can fail to convey the intended meaning, so a punishment that does not use appropriate symbols cannot convey the appropriate (degree of) condemnation. This is not just an instrumental question of how best to communicate to a certain audience: rather the thought is that if the wrong symbols are used, then the expression will simply fail to be meaningful. So what are the symbols that will give punishment the meaning it needs to have? It is natural to think that these symbols should be drawn from our moral practices and the emotional reactions with which they are entangled. A suggestion that I have made previously (see Bennett 2008) is that punishment can communicate condemnation most meaningfully if it symbolises how sorry the offender ought to be for the offence; and that we can do this by requiring the offender to undertake conduct that she would undertake spontaneously were she genuinely sorry as she ought to be. I have

---

[9] Instead of talking about an 'obligation to reform', I should more strictly talk about previous offenders having a duty to take *reasonable* steps to overcome habits of offending, or to organise their lives so as to avoid criminal behaviour.

called this view the 'Apology Ritual' since, although we do not make the offender literally verbally apologise for the offence, the kind of behaviour in which she is required to engage is modelled on the practice of apology. Thus she might be asked to make restitution and penitential amends of the sort that she *would be* moved to make were she properly sorry. The point of this ritual is not teleological: it is not that it is an effective way of *making* offenders more penitent. Rather the view is that, by imposing a determinate amount of amends on an offender, we symbolise how sorry the offender ought to be; and that this provides us with a meaningful way of expressing a determinate degree of condemnation.

If the argument for the above points is accepted, then we can say that offenders who have been through the Apology Ritual have thereby an extra obligation to reform—an obligation to the state, to whom their 'apology' was directed—that those who have not yet been convicted do not. If successful, it would explain the piece of Lee's picture that was missing: the difference between first-time and previous offenders.

At this point, however, the reader might be concerned about someone who is by law a first-time offender but who is actually a repeat offender. In other words this is someone who has committed the same sort of offence a number of times but has only been caught and convicted for the latest offence. This person, should he become genuinely sorry for what he does, ought to be sorry, as we have said, not just for the offence for which he has been convicted, but also for his failure to reform from previous offences. Therefore he has more to feel sorry for than he would have as a genuine first-time offender. However, when the state comes to sentence him, it will treat him as a first-time offender. Should it not treat the two offenders differently, according to the Apology Ritual theory of punishment? In fact, no. Punishment, on this view, does not express how sorry the offender ought to be in terms of all that is going on in his life but rather how sorry he ought to be given the offences that are relevant to his relationship with the state. The offences that are relevant to his relationship with the state are those for which he has been convicted and punished. Punishing for suspected—or even known—offences for which there has been no conviction would, as our intuitions tell us, be an abuse of due process.

The other objection that I would like to consider is to Lee's idea—which, up to now, I have been seeking to defend—that repeat offenders can be thought of as committing an extra offence. What I have attempted to explain is why, morally speaking, the offender has an obligation to the state to take steps to reform, and hence why the state would be right to punish him more if it is interested in issuing due condemnation of what he has done. On Lee's view, this need for extra punishment arises through the commission of an extra offence, and he defends the idea that there could be such an offence by appeal to omissions liability. However, one might worry that this is a strange sort of offence that stretches omissions liability wider than the criminal law of Western democracies should really tolerate.[10] If this criticism of Lee's account is valid, does it make my argument vulnerable also? I don't think so. At the start of this section, I suggested that there are two strategies for justifying the recidivist premium that focus on act rather than character: one would either have to show that repeat offending involves an extra offence, *or* one would have to show that the repeat offence is somehow a worse act. Say we think that it is implausible to say that there is an extra offence. Could my view be read instead as an explanation of why repeat offending should be seen as making the offence itself morally worse? At the moment I do not see why not. If my explanation is plausible, the gravity of a repeat offence is greater than that of an identical first-time offence because, in addition to violating those obligations that are relevant to the offence itself, the offender has also violated obligations to reform. Assuming that we have no reason to think that the latter obligations are merely a private matter, irrelevant to the state, then the state ought also to condemn this further aspect to the wrongdoing. If we would not want to formalise it as a specific further offence, then perhaps the obvious alternative would be to deploy prior convictions as an aggravating factor at sentencing. After all, the idea that mitigating and aggravating factors at sentencing allow a system of criminal justice to reflect variations in the gravity of instances of a single offence is not entirely alien to a communicative conception of punishment.

E. CONCLUSION

In this chapter I have tried to explain the rationale behind the common practice of sentencing offenders with previous convictions more harshly than first-time offenders. I have argued that an analogue of this practice is also common in everyday moral life. The very fact that an offence is a repeat offence *seems* to call for greater condemnation. If we take the view that the central function of punishment is to provide proportionate condemnation of offenders for their offences, then we might think that there should be some continuity between the explanation for our reaction in the everyday moral case and the criminal case. I considered attempts to explain the 'recidivist premium' (i) as showing worse character, and (ii) as incorporating the extra offence of disobedience. However, these accounts were inadequate, either because they did not capture the reasoning behind everyday non-criminal cases, or because they could not explain

---

[10] See the chapter by Michael Tonry in this volume. I am also grateful for discussion on this point with Antony Duff.

why repeat offending by itself should call for greater condemnation. A better account is that suggested by Lee: that repeat offending should be taken as violating an obligation, conferred on the offender by previous conviction, to take reasonable steps to organise her behaviour to avoid further such offences. But Lee has difficulty accounting for why repeat offenders are under such an obligation while first-time offenders are not. I concluded the chapter by attempting to explain how we could account for this obligation if (i) we see punishment as seeking to express proportionate condemnation by symbolising how sorry the offender ought to be for the offence; and (ii) we draw the appropriate symbols from the practice of apologising, where a person apologising undertakes an obligation to reform. If this account is right, we should doubt the symbolic adequacy of any expression of condemnation that does not include the implication that an offender would be subjected to greater condemnation for repeat offending. After all, how can an act of condemnation fully express that an act is wrong if it does not also say that the person who does it has an obligation not to do it again?

REFERENCES

Bennett, C (2002) 'The Varieties of Retributive Experience' 52 *Philosophical Quarterly* 145–163.
—— (2008) *The Apology Ritual: A Philosophical Theory of Punishment* (Cambridge, Cambridge University Press).
Dubber, D (1995) 'Recidivist Statutes as Arational Punishment' 43 *Buffalo Law Review* 689–724.
Duff, RA (1986) *Trials and Punishments* (Cambridge, Cambridge University Press).
—— (2001) *Punishment, Communication and Community* (Oxford, Oxford University Press).
—— (2007) *Answering For Crime* (Oxford, Hart Publishing).
Feinberg, J (1965) 'The Expressive Function of Punishment' 49 *The Monist* 397–423.
Lee, Y (2009) 'Recidivism as Omission: A Relational Account' 87 *University of Texas Law Review* 571–622.
Lee, Y, 'Repeat Offenders and the Question of Desert', this volume, ch 4.
Pillsbury, S (2002) 'A Problem in Emotive Due Process: California's Three Strikes Law' 6 *Buffalo Criminal Law Review* 483–524.
Roberts, JV (2008a) 'Punishing Persistence: Explaining the Enduring Appeal of the Recidivist Sentencing Premium' 48 *British Journal of Criminology* 468–481.
—— (2008b) *Punishing Persistent Offenders: Exploring Community and Offender Perspectives* (Oxford: Oxford University Press).
Tonry, M, 'The Questionable Relevance of Previous Convictions to Punishments for Later Crime', this volume, ch 6.
von Hirsch, A (1985) *Past or Future Crimes: Deservingness and Dangerousness in the Sentencing of Criminals* (Manchester, Manchester University Press).

—— (1993) *Censure and Sanctions* (Oxford, Oxford University Press).

—— (2002) 'Record-enhanced Sentencing in England and Wales: Reflections on the Halliday Report's Proposed Treatment of Prior Convictions' in S Rex and M Tonry (eds), *Reform and Punishment* (Cullompton, Willan).

6

The Questionable Relevance of Previous Convictions to Punishments for Later Crimes

MICHAEL TONRY

I T IS CURIOUS that the problem of punishment in respect of previous convictions has received little attention in the United States during the retributivist ascendancy that began in the mid-1970s. Before that, during the century-long utilitarian ascendancy,[1] previous convictions were but one among many considerations that might be germane to individualisation of punishment in a particular case. When intellectual fashions changed, much scholarly writing focused on what HLA Hart called the justification of punishment (eg Morris 1966; Kleinig 1973; Murphy 1973). In the earliest days only Norval Morris (1974) and Andrew von Hirsch (1976, 1985) wrestled with distributive questions of how much an offender should be punished under a retributive punishment regime. For other early retributivist writers who discussed the distribution of punishment, such as George Fletcher (1978) and Richard Singer (1979), the rationale for individual punishments was entailed by the general retributive justification of punishment. The inference they drew was that previous convictions are irrelevant to sentencing new crimes and cannot justly be taken into account.

Four positions soon emerged:

---

[1] In 1920s–1940s America, a distinction was commonly drawn between 'utilitarian' (ie Benthamite, primarily deterrent) and 'positivist' (primarily rehabilitative and incapacitative, commonly associated with Enrico Ferri) ideas (Michael and Wechsler 1937: 1262). US indeterminate sentencing embraced those aims and others (with at most a nod to retribution), as evidenced by the purposes clauses of the Model Penal Code which mention deterrence, reformation and incapacitation but give no role to retribution except in setting upper limits (American Law Institute 1962: section 1.02(2): 'The general purposes of the provisions governing the sentencing and treatment of offenders are: . . . (c) to safeguard offenders against excessive, disproportionate or arbitrary punishments'). Although 'consequentialist' might better describe the theoretical undercarriage of indeterminate sentencing, I follow the usage of that earlier period by describing a multiple-purpose preventive set of aims as 'utilitarian.'

1. Previous convictions should be given no weight in sentencing later crimes. The deserved punishment for the previous conviction has been suffered; the debt to society has been paid. Any increment to punishment for a subsequent crime that is attributable to a previous conviction is unjust (Fletcher 1978; Singer 1979).
2. Previous convictions justify incremental additions to later punishments because their existence makes an offender more culpable (von Hirsch 1976).
3. Previous convictions do not justify increments to later punishments. First offenders, however, should be given a discount from the deserved punishment because the offence may have been out of character; the discount should gradually disappear with subsequent offences. This is sometimes referred to as 'progressive loss of mitigation' (von Hirsch 1985). After the discount disappears, addition of increments based on previous convictions is unjust.
4. Punishments for particular crimes must be set within a range of 'not undeserved' punishments, and normally at the low end. Previous convictions are among a number of considerations that may justify more severe sentences up to but not above the upper limit of the range, assuming various empirical or policy tests are satisfied (Morris 1974).[2]

The subject of previous convictions received relatively little further development. Among people who write about sentencing theory, the first-offender discount and progressive-loss-of-mitigation analyses were prominent. I have always thought them unpersuasive, unconvincing rationalisations that acknowledge widely shared intuitions and try not to offend or contradict them. In this they resemble arguments by utilitarians that punishment of innocents can never be justified because news will inevitably slip out at untold costs in legitimacy and public confidence. Both seem to me strained efforts to avoid being impolitic or controversial. There is something to be said for saying what you believe—as George Fletcher and Richard Singer did about previous convictions or as Oliver Wendell Holmes (1881) did about what he saw as the defensible inevitability of executing innocent people—even if others disagree.

There in any case, as a theoretical matter, the subject rested until Julian Roberts (1997, 2008) reinvigorated it. Policymakers and practitioners in the United States merrily set and applied policies that extended

---

[2] Morris occasionally waffled. Some of his writings (eg Morris 1974, 1982) imply that previous punishments 'contumaciously ignored' might justify harsher later punishments, as might the 'greater wickedness' or 'contempt of law' expressed by subsequent offending. I believe his considered view to be that expressed in the text. He mostly wrote about punishment before the development of sentencing guidelines provided a mechanism for specifying upper and lower bounds of deserved punishment. Once that framework was available, his writings assumed that justified increments would occur within established bounds (eg Morris and Miller 1985).

punishments on the basis of prior convictions. At least in some English-speaking countries, judges routinely increased the severity of punishments on account of prior convictions, legislatures enacted laws requiring severer punishments for recidivists, and sentencing commissions promulgated guidelines that prescribed successively harsher sentences as the number of previous convictions increased.

In the United States, most sentencing commissions made criminal history one axis of a grid that set out presumptive or advisory sentence ranges; so far as I know (I worked with seven commissions), none of these policies were theory-based but resulted instead from back-of-an-envelope calculations and collective intuitive judgments. A few habitual-offender statutes permitting lengthy or life sentences for third-time felons survived from earlier times. Between 1993 and 2006, 26 states enacted three-strikes-and-you're-out laws. Many of those states and others enacted 'career criminal' statutes that authorised or required longer sentences for defined categories of recidivist offenders (Shane-Dubow et al 1985; Chen 2008).

In England and Wales, matters have been more tortured (Downes and Morgan 2007; Newburn 2007). For much of the twentieth century, a habitual-offender statute allowed long-term incapacitative confinement of (mostly) recidivist property offenders (Morris 1951). Before 1991, judges had discretion to take previous convictions into account as they thought appropriate. The Criminal Justice Act 1991 for a time severely limited the weight previous convictions could be given, but the relevant provision was repealed in 1993. Three laws enacted in the Crime (Sentences) Act 1997 predicated mandatory minimum prison sentences on prior convictions. The Labour government continuously promoted a policy of incremental punishments for each prior conviction. The Halliday Report (Home Office 2001) proposed that laws be enacted prescribing additional punishments in respect of 'recent' and 'relevant' prior convictions and recommended indeterminate confinement for some 'dangerous' offenders. The Criminal Justice Act 2003 contained provisions embodying those recommendations. Andrew Ashworth and Estella Baker explore them and their uncertain meanings in this volume.

There matters stood when Julian Roberts began his efforts to focus renewed attention on the role of previous convictions. Policymaking on both sides of the Atlantic, save for the 1991–93 English hiatus, was based on seat-of-the-pants intuition and political calculation. Academics subscribed to a number of theoretical positions but none of them influenced policy very much. In the United States, and to a lesser extent in England, sentencing laws gave increasingly heavy weight to previous convictions. If a theory could be inferred from Anglo-American legislation, it was that previously convicted offenders deserve to be punished more severely—sometimes much more severely—than first-timers.[3] If a theory could be discerned in sentencing practice, it was a carryover from individualised, indeterminate sentencing: justice consists of judges imposing legally authorised sentences they to be believe appropriate under all the circumstances.

It is doubly curious that the subject has received so little theoretical attention. On so applied a subject as sentencing it is surprising that academics have not sought to engage more with policy and practice. More strikingly, most offenders being sentenced have previously been convicted. First offenders exist, of course, but they are a small minority of people charged with crimes. Roberts reports Home Office data on sentenced offenders in England and Wales in 2005: 88 per cent of those convicted of indictable offenses had prior convictions and 76 per cent of those convicted of summary offences (2008: table 5.2). Fully comparable US data are not available but patterns are unlikely to be very different.[4] Most writing about punishment theory implicitly addresses the sentencing of first offenders, which means it neglects most real-world cases.

There are reasons why normative theorists have little useful to say to policymakers and practitioners on this subject. Most modern theorists subscribe to post-Enlightenment ideas of liberalism, which imply limits on state power to interfere in the lives of individuals. Few subscribe primarily to utilitarian (or consequentialist) theories. Most therefore want to find principled arguments for the state's taking of increments of individual liberty. However, as Roberts and others have shown, many or most people share an intuition, or, stronger, a belief, that people who have been convicted of offences in the past should ordinarily be punished more severely than a first offender when they commit an additional offence. Reconciling theorists' normative presuppositions with non-theorists' beliefs has not proven easy to do, though Julian Roberts, Christopher Bennett and Youngjae Lee in this volume, and others, are trying to do so.

The 'recidivist premium' is difficult to justify in terms of any mainstream theory. Roberts, Bennett and Lee have not succeeded, and no one else—including most utilitarians—is likely to succeed. The only theoretical framework that comes close is Norval Morris's limiting retributivism, and that is so only because it is a hybrid retributive theory with utilitarian elements subject to liberty-respecting side constraints.

The rest of this chapter attempts to justify those observations. The first section more fully sets out the conflict between prevailing norma-

---

[3] Whether such laws were predicated on normative beliefs, political opportunism or expressive considerations no doubt varied across time and space.

[4] In 2002, the latest year for which national data have been published for the 75 most populated US counties, among *felony* defendants, 76 per cent had previously been arrested and 59 per cent had previously been convicted (Bureau of Justice Statistics 2006: tables 9 and 10).

tive frameworks and widely shared intuitions. Section B shows why none of the prevailing ways to justify the recidivist premium works. Section C explains why a limiting retributivist account offers the most plausible reconciliation.

A. THE PROBLEM: GUILT AND BLAME

Norval Morris (1992) posed the underlying problem in a short story, 'The Brothel Boy'. A mentally retarded boy, having lived his life in a Burmese brothel observing men pay women for sex, sometimes violent sex, attempts to have sexual relations with a young girl. In resisting, she falls, hits her head against a rock, and a few days later dies from the combined effect of the injury and inadequate medical care. The magistrate, Eric Blair, a fictionalised 1920s version of the writer better known as George Orwell, must decide whether the boy will be executed.

From the perspective of moral culpability, Blair is doubtful. The boy did not intend to kill, the fatal injury was inadvertent, adequate medical care would have saved the victim, and in the boy's weak mind he may have thought what he wanted to do was all right. 'I paid her', he repeats again and again during interviews. Blair has little doubt that in the eye of God, the boy is an innocent.

From other perspectives Blair feels pressured. The planter community, his primary constituency, thinks the boy should be executed ('just another over-sexed native'). So do the indigenous Burmese people. Blair has to worry about maintaining his personal authority and credibility in both communities, and about his institutional authority as a senior representative of the Raj, the British colonial administration.

In a commentary, Morris describes the story as a conflict between guilt and blame. 'Guilt' is moral culpability as a Kantian moral philosopher might see it: what did the boy intend, what did he know, how bad was he, did he have sufficient capacity for moral reasoning fairly to be held accountable? 'Blame' is the community construction: how upset and angry are people, what do they think should be done, what are the likely consequences of doing something else? The law must deal with both, Morris counsels, and sometimes blame takes precedence.

Julian Roberts in *Punishing Persistent Offenders* (2008) sets a similar stage. He first shows that most theorists allow no (Fletcher 1978; Singer 1979) or a closely constrained place (von Hirsch 1976, 1985) for previous convictions in the determination of deserved punishments. He then provides convincing evidence that offenders, judges, criminal justice officials generally and ordinary citizens agree that previous convictions justify additional punishment. A series of interviews in 2007 with convicted English offenders showed that many believed that a recidivist premium was appropriate; a sentencing exercise with hypothetical cases showed that they believed judges would impose one. Data on judges' sentencing patterns make it clear that judges do sentence recidivists more severely and surveys of practitioners and officials showed heavy support for doing so (ranging from 51 per cent of probation officers to 90 per cent or more of police and prosecutors). Finally, to gauge public views, subsets of a representative MORI survey of UK residents were asked to assess the seriousness of hypothetical cases; the offences were identical and the cases differed only in the extent of the offenders' prior criminal records. Respondents' assessments of the seriousness of the crime, of the offender's likelihood of reoffending and of the lengths of prison sentence they believed appropriate increased with the number of prior convictions.

Kevin Reitz in his ingenious essay in this volume makes the problem of the conflict between normative theory and widely shared intuition more bewildering. He demonstrates the dramatically different consequences to offenders sentenced under US sentencing guidelines between being sentenced for a group of offences at the same time or in sequential proceedings. A burglar arrested after a string of provable burglaries could be handled either way. If sentenced in the same proceeding, he is given a 'bulk discount', with the most serious offence providing a base sentence and the other offences leading to relatively small increments of additional punishment.[5] However, if the burglar is prosecuted in separate proceedings, he receives the prescribed sentence for the first offence in the first proceeding, that sentence plus a recidivist premium in the second, the aggregate second sentence plus another recidivist premium in the third, and so on. The lengths of imprisonment received by identical offenders whose cases were processed in the different ways might differ by a factor of four or five or more.

A prosecutor proceeding against two nearly identical offenders in the different ways would be seen by most people as having abused his discretion, and treated the multiple-proceeding offender unjustly. Two different prosecutors, however, might handle substantially similar cases in different ways, with staggeringly different consequences for the two offenders. It would be difficult for observers to complain that either had behaved inappropriately. The problem arises because two widely held intuitions are in conflict: the ideas that there ought to be a bulk discount for someone sentenced for multiple crimes in a single proceeding and that there ought to be recidivist premiums for people sentenced for separate offences in successive proceedings. If the offences occurred and were sentenced

---

[5] Many countries observe a 'totality principle' that works this way: no matter how many offences are involved, the total sentence cannot exceed the highest appropriate for the base offence (eg Lovegrove, 1988 (Australia); Jareborg 1993 (Sweden); Ashworth 2005 (England)). Petter Asp's chapter in this volume explains how and why Swedish law permits only a small recidivist premium.

at, say, two-year intervals, it probably would not occur to anyone to object in principle on the basis that the aggregate sentences exceed that which would have been imposed in one proceeding. But if the offences all occurred within one week, the differences that flow from handling all the offences in one proceeding or in separate proceedings feel, and are, morally arbitrary.

So there is the problem. Most theorists view punishment in terms of Norval Morris's guilt: the offender's culpability is the only, or primary, consideration. Most practitioners and the general public think in more holistic terms of blame.

B. UNSUCCESSFUL SOLUTIONS

Anyone who has talked or thought much about punishment theory has engaged in cocktail party-level analyses of the relevance of previous convictions. From most retributivist perspectives, they are irrelevant in a did-the-crime, did-the-time sense. If they are retributively relevant, some justification has to be provided. One possible one is that calculations of deserved punishment should relate both to the crime and to inferences about the offender's character that are derivable from the crime. A second is that reoffending demonstrates defiance of the court or the state. These arguments run into the immediate difficulty that in a liberal society the law prescribes specific behaviours, not bad character or bad attitudes; that neither is the law's business; and that 'characterological' assessments are highly vulnerable to contamination. Andrew von Hirsch (1981), for example, has argued that judges should not incorporate 'whole life' judgments into their consideration of sentences. That, he points out, opens the door to stereotyped, idiosyncratic and invidious judgments that are sure to redound to the detriment of the disadvantaged, the disreputable and the disheveled. No one should be punished for living an unconventional life or, in Mr Doolittle's terms, for defying middle-class morality.

The other conventional argument is that previous convictions are a proxy for elevated risks of reoffending. This might be acceptable to a utilitarian who is, after all, concerned to minimise crime and the human and other costs associated with it. To a retributivist, however, crime prevention is off-limits as a principal rationale for punishment. Below, I argue that a utilitarian who takes Bentham's injunctions against imposing unjustifiable pain seriously would also be sceptical about a systematic recidivist premium.

So we seem to be stymied. I think we are. To show why, I look backwards to imagine what the archetypal views of Kant, Hegel and Bentham might be, and then forward to various arguments posed in this volume.

1. Archetypal Arguments: Kant and Hegel

Kant and Hegel do not discuss the recidivist premium or the general question of how, if at all, to take account of previous convictions. Both discuss, in surprisingly modern terms, the question of how to apportion punishment to crime, and both try hard to make sure that the offender receives a punishment he or she deserves. The fairest inference to draw is that both would take the view that the punishment, once completed, ends the matter. Any additional punishment later on as a recidivist premium would result in the offender unjustly suffering more than is deserved as a consequence of the first offence.

Kant's views are well known albeit not free from ambiguity. Punishment is a 'categorical imperative'. Its imposition, irrespective of good or bad effects, is a moral requirement derivable from first principles. Three passages are especially well known and frequently quoted. The first is often interpreted to forbid taking consequential considerations into account:

> Judicial punishment can never be used merely as a means to promote some other good for the criminal himself or for civil society, but instead it must in all cases be imposed on him only on the ground that he has committed a crime; for a human being can never be manipulated merely as a means to the purposes of someone else. (Kant 1965 [1797]: 100)

The second is often understood to require that punishments be strictly apportioned to the seriousness of the crime:

> What kind and what degree of punishment does public legal justice adopt as its principle and standard? None other than the principle of equality. . . . Accordingly, any undeserved evil that you afflict on someone else among the people is one that you do to yourself. If you vilify him, you vilify yourself. If you steal from him, you steal from yourself. If you kill him, you kill yourself. Only the Law of Retribution (*ius talionis*) can determine exactly the kind and degree of punishment. (Kant 1965 [1797]: 101)

Out of context, Kant's allusion to the 'principle of equality' can be misinterpreted, and has been, as requiring that punishments perfectly correspond to crimes, as in a sense execution can to murder.[6] However, Kant gives examples of punishments that do not literally 'equal' the offence. For 'verbal injuries', for example, a fine might ordinarily suffice but not for a wealthy person: the 'humiliation' of a public apology and kissing the hand of a lower social status victim would be better. When a high-status person assaults a social inferior, he must apologise but might also be

---

[6] The *ius talionis* 'is obviously not capable of being extended. Crime and punishment are different things. Can they really be equated? What penalty equals the crime of forgery, perjury or kidnapping? For the state to exercise the same amount of fraud or brutality on the criminal that the criminal exercised on his victim would be demoralizing to any community' (Cohen 1940: 1010).

condemned to 'solitary and painful confinement, because by this means, in addition to the discomfort suffered, the pride of the offender will be painfully affected' (Kant 1965 [1791]: 101–02).

The third is often understood to make clear that the effects of punishment are immaterial and that the state's legal duty to enforce the categorical imperative of deserved punishment is unqualified:

> Even if a civil society were to dissolve itself by common agreement of all its members (for example, if the people inhabiting an island decided to separate and disperse themselves around the world), the last murderer remaining in prison must first be executed, so that everyone will duly receive what his actions were worth and so that the bloodguilt thereof will not be fixed on the people because they failed to insist on carrying out the punishment; for if they fail to do so, they may be regarded as accomplices in this public violation of legal justice. (Kant 1965 [1791]: 102)

Much in these passages is obscure.[7] Nonetheless, taken together, especially in the context of surrounding passages, they seem clearly to argue that punishment not only may, but must, be imposed on people who commit crimes (and who are duly convicted), and that the punishments imposed must be proportioned in a meaningful way to the seriousness of the crimes committed and nothing else (and in the extreme case, murderers must be executed).

Hegel's analysis of punishment is based on a more complex metaphysic, but shares two elements with Kant's: the idea that respect for the moral autonomy of the criminal, his capacity for making moral choices, requires that he be punished; and the idea that punishment must be apportioned to the moral gravity of the crime. Explaining why offenders should be punished, he wrote:

> [T]he *action* of the criminal involves not only the *concept* of crime . . . but also the formal rationality of the *individual's volition*. In so far as the punishment which this entails is seen as embodying *the criminal's own right*, the criminal is *honoured* as a rational being. He is denied this honour if the concept and criterion of his punishment are not derived from his own act; and he is also denied it if he is regarded simply as a harmful animal which must be rendered harmless, or punished with a view to deterring him or reforming him (Hegel 1991: 127, italics in original)

In explaining how decisions are to be made about punishments for spe-

---

[7] In the first passage, for example, the two uses of the word 'merely' might be argued to imply that a criminal may be used as a means to some good end if (but only if) he has 'committed a crime'. Similarly, the meaning of the proposition in the second passage that 'undeserved evil that you afflict on someone else . . . is one that you do to yourself' is not transparently obvious. Nor in the third passage is the allusion to bloodguilt.

cific crimes (except murder, for which he also argues that execution is inexorably appropriate[8]), Hegel offers a strikingly modern formulation:

> [T]he universal feeling of peoples and individuals towards crime is, and always has been, that it *deserves* to be punished, and that *what the criminal has done should be done to him.* . . . But the determination of *equality* has brought a major difficulty into the idea of retribution. . . . [I]t is very easy to portray the retributive aspect of punishment as an absurdity (theft as retribution for theft, robbery for robbery, an eye for an eye, and a tooth for a tooth, so that one can even imagine the miscreant as one-eyed or toothless); but the concept has nothing to do with this absurdity. . . . [E]quality remains merely the basic measure of the criminal's *essential* deserts, but not of the specific external shape which the retribution should take. . . . It is then, as already remarked, a matter for the understanding to seek an <u>approximate</u> equivalence. . . . [R]etribution cannot aim to achieve specific equality. (Hegel 1991: 128–29; italics in original; underscoring mine)[9]

Taken together, these passages from Kant and Hegel describe a theory of punishment not very different from those of many modern writers: people who have chosen to commit criminal offences deserve to be punished; punishments should be proportioned to the seriousness of crimes in such a way that relative punishments can meaningfully be said to be equivalent to the crimes for which they are imposed. Although Kant's and Hegel's explanations for why people deserve to be punished are different from those of most modern writers, the punishment calculus they describe is not very different from those generated by Andrew von Hirsch and Andrew Ashworth's theory of commensurate desert (2005) or Paul Robinson's stricter desert theory (1987). The 'equality' that Kant and Hegel insist on requires punishments that may change over time, and that may be attuned to the offender's sensibilities, but they must be apportioned to the nature of the offender's wrongdoing, and to nothing else. Whether a recidivist premium imposed following a second conviction is conceptualised as additional punishment for the first crime, or as additional punishment for the second, it violates the equality principle.

---

[8] 'For since life is the entire compass of existence, the punishment cannot consist in a value—since none is equivalent to life—but only in the taking of another life' (Hegel 1991: 129-30).

[9] Hegel makes his rejection of mechanistic or absolute punishment equivalence even clearer in another passage: 'Thought cannot specify how each crime should be punished; positive determinations are necessary for this purpose. With the progress of education, however, attitudes toward crime become more lenient, and punishments today are not nearly so harsh as they were a hundred years ago. It is not the crimes or punishments themselves which change, but the relation between the two' (Hegel 1991: 123).

2. Archetypal Arguments: Bentham

The inferences to be drawn from Bentham about the recidivist premium are less evident, particularly because most of his analysis is premissed on deterrence as the primary means of crime prevention. Nonetheless, it is reasonable to infer that he too would have opposed an across-the-board recidivist premium for several reasons: his overall system for calculating utility, in which the offender's suffering counts; his principle of parsimony which forbade infliction of punishment beyond what is necessary to achieve preventive goals; and his notion that punishments must be evaluated subjectively in each case to take account of their effects on particular offenders.

Bentham developed his analysis in excruciating detail in several works (Bentham 1970, 2008 [1830]). Penalties should be set so that the expected burden of punishment is greater than the benefits of crime. Punishments should be severer for more serious crimes than for less serious ones to provide incentives to commit the less serious. They should be adjusted to take account of each element of a crime so that the offender has incentive not to take each successive step.

The offender's situation, however, has to be considered in two ways. First, punishment should be parsimonious: 'The punishment should in no case be more than is necessary to bring it into conformity with the rules here given' (Bentham 1970: 169). Second, the offender's 'sensibilities' must be taken into account. That is, the punishment must take account of how it would affect that particular individual. People have different sensitivities and are affected in different ways by the same experience, including experiences of punishment. Accordingly, 'That the quantity actually inflicted on an individual offender may correspond to the quantity intended for similar offenders in general, the several circumstances influencing sensibility ought always to be taken into account' (Bentham 1970: 169).

The object of the criminal law for Bentham is to maximise happiness in order to 'augment the total happiness of the community' and 'to exclude as far as may be, everything that tends to subtract from that happiness: in other words, to exclude mischief' (Bentham 1970: 158). The goal is sometime expressed as achieving the 'greatest good for the greatest number'.

Critically, however, everyone's happiness—including that of offenders—counts: 'But all punishment is mischief: all punishment is evil. Upon the principle of utility, if it is at all to be admitted, it ought only to be admitted in as far as it promises to exclude some greater evil' (Bentham 1970: 158).

To make the point clearer, Bentham writes that 'It is plain' that 'punishment ought not to be inflicted' when 'it is unprofitable, or too expensive: where the mischief it would produce would be greater than what it pre-

vented' (Bentham 1970: 159). In describing cases where punishment is
unprofitable, he lists this first:

> Where, on the one hand, the nature of the offence, on the other hand, that of
> the punishment, are, *in the ordinary state of things*, such, that when compared
> together, the evil of the latter will turn out to be greater than that of the former.
> (Bentham 1970: 168, italics in original)

This proposition underpins what Richard Frase (2009, and in this volume)
refers to as one of two utilitarian proportionality doctrines: the ends–benefits test which requires that the value of the good sought be greater than
the cost incurred in seeking it.

It is also plain to Bentham that punishment ought not to be inflicted
when 'it is needless: where the mischief may be prevented, or cease of itself,
without it: that is, at a cheaper rate'. This is the basis of the second utilitarian proportionality doctrine: the alternative-means test which requires
that there be no less costly way to achieve a justifiably sought-after good
(Frase 2009, and in this volume).[10]

For Bentham, 'too expensive' means something different from retributive disproportionality. There it means that a punishment exceeds that
which is deserved on moral grounds. For Bentham, it means that a punishment is excessive in relation to either of the utilitarian proportionality
doctrines (Frase 2009). The alternative-means test requires that there be
no less costly way to achieve a justifiably sought-after good. No punishment or increment of punishment may be imposed that is greater than
is needed to achieve the good sought. If infliction of one unit of pain
on an offender is enough to achieve a desired preventive aim, infliction
of two units is unnecessary and the second unit is excessive and violates
parsimony constraints. The ends–benefits test requires that the pains to
be avoided by punishment be greater than the pains the offender would
suffer to achieve the sought-after end. The recidivist premium can pass
the parsimony test only if it can be shown to be effective as a deterrent,
to involve no greater infliction of pain than is minimally required, and
to be capable of achievement in no other less 'expensive' way.

The recidivist premium has a steep hill to climb to be justified in
Benthamite terms. If its end is primarily or substantially to prevent crime,
it is unlikely that currently available evidence on the deterrent and incapacitative effectiveness of sanctions is adequate (eg Nagin 1998; Tonry
2008). It cannot with a straight face be asserted that we know that the
additional suffering to an offender resulting from an additional increment

---

[10] In his chapter in this volume, Frase offers two other normative ideas that can be
invoked to limit amounts of punishment: retributive proportionality limits, and a normative
prescription against unnecessarily worsening social inequalities. The former is conventional
(but none the worse for that). The latter, however, is not a separate argument but part of
the ends–benefits analysis.

of punishment will be more than offset by additional suffering avoided through a diminution of crime attributable to the premium. If the end is primarily satisfaction of public preferences, increased public confidence or increased legitimacy of the criminal justice system in the public mind, it is hard to imagine that the evidence is available to satisfy the ends–benefits test, or that alternative means of pursuing those goals are not available that would trigger the alternative-means test.

In principle, Bentham's framework could justify a recidivist premium, *if* it were shown to be efficacious and not excessive. Satisfying those criteria requires empirical demonstration, and the burden or proof is borne by he or she who wants to impose pain. Three things must be shown. First, the positive effects of the recidivist premium must outweigh the additional suffering experienced by offenders over and above that inherent in suffering the punishment due a first offence. Second, there must be no alternative way to achieve those effects that involves less suffering. Third, the preceding calculations must take account of the incremental punishment's subjective effects on this individual offender.

Post-Benthamite utilitarianism makes some of those calculations easier. Individual subjective assessments of sensibilities were displaced by a decision to look at averages and not to make interpersonal comparisons of utility (eg Robbins 1938). Rule utilitarianism allowed analysts to calculate average utility and not have to show that utility is maximised in every case (eg Rawls 1955).[11] Nonetheless, the empirical burdens of proof to be made are heavy and it is unlikely that proponents of the recidivist premium can satisfy them.[12]

3. Implied Undertaking Claims

Two of the chapters in this volume develop arguments that something about the nature of a first criminal conviction imposes a special obligation on convicted offenders not to reoffend. Neither works, for the same three reasons. First, few offenders expressly undertake to behave in the future, or agree in advance to be punished more severely for a subse-

---

[11] Some contemporary mainstream utilitarians argue, however, that rule utilitarianism inexorably collapses into act utilitarianism; demonstration must be made in every case that it satisfies the characteristics of the set of cases to which the rule applies, and if it does not a separate utilitarian calculation must be made. Thus every case requires individualized calculations (Smart 1973).

[12] This is not a problem, however, for many modern economists. They simply make the a priori assumption that credible threats of increased punishment prevent crime. Nobel Prize winner Ronald Coase, a founder of the law and economics movement, observed, 'Punishment, for example, can be regarded as the price of crime. *An economist will not debate whether increased punishment will reduce crime;* he will merely try to answer the question, by how much?' (Coase 1978: 210, emphasis added). To like effect, Gary Becker (1968), another founder of the law and economics movement, and Isaac Ehrlich (1996: 43-44).

quent offence than they would otherwise deserve for a first offence. Such undertakings, if made, would be foolish, would lack consideration and would raise serious issues of involuntariness. It is unreasonable to imply undertakings when a reasonable person would not make them were they explicitly requested. Second, neither argument adequately explains why convicted offenders have different or greater obligations than other citizens to be law abiding. Third, the increment must measurably relate to something, but if it does not relate to an offence it is hard to see how it can be considered deserved or how its amount can be calibrated.

Possible bases for the incremental punishment are that the recidivist offender defied state authority, disappointed others' expectations, is incorrigible or is revealed by reoffending to be a person of worse-than-average character. All of these might arguably be germane in explaining private-sector relationships. None of them bears scrutiny in a liberal society as a basis for state deprivation of a citizen's liberty.

(a) Omissions Theory

Youngjae Lee argues elsewhere in this volume that something about state punishment creates an implied undertaking or obligation of first offenders to desist from offending in the future; reoffending constitutes a failure to honour the obligation, justifying additional, otherwise-undeserved punishment. Lee characterises the incremental punishment as predicated on the offender's omission or, less awkwardly stated, failure to satisfy his implied undertaking to be law abiding. There are a number of problems with this analysis. It does not explain where the obligation comes from. It implies an obligation that most offenders would refuse to accept, especially if they understood that acceptance would result in additional punishment if they failed to comply. It stretches omission liability much further than the criminal law would ordinarily allow.

The principal reason Lee's clever analysis fails is that it does not explain where the offender's obligation comes from. The offender in effect walks naked into a black judicial box carrying an indictment and exits carrying a punishment and an obligation not to reoffend, breach of which justifies an additional increment of punishment. Lee does not argue that defendants explicitly or implicitly agree not to reoffend. And were agreement explicitly requested, and a promise made, under ordinary contract law doctrine it would be unenforceable both because it would be without consideration and because it would be unconscionable as a contract by adhesion. No citizen is obligated not to offend. Every citizen is a free moral agent and may choose whether or not to offend. The citizen who chooses to offend is vulnerable to prosecution, conviction and punishment. That's it. People who have offended have the same choices and vulnerabilities as all citizens. Unless Lee can explain where the offender's special obligation comes from, and he does not, the argument fails.

An argument might conceivably be made that the recidivist premium is justifiable because punishment is a communicative process. A first conviction communicates the proposition that the crime committed was a wrongful act and was punishable, and, implicitly, that subsequent criminal acts will be punished. Every citizen, however, is presumed to know that and it is unclear why a first conviction and punishment puts an offender into a position different from that of any other citizen.

An argument might also be made that repeat offenders as an empirical matter often do receive harsher penalties than are imposed for first offences, should be presumed to know that, and can claim neither surprise or unjust punishment when that happens.

The no-surprise proposition is no doubt right. That claim that the recidivist premium is just because it is foreseeable effectively argues that what is, is, and, because it is, is just. That is a tautology. The normative case must be made; it cannot simply be declared.

Lee's analysis is expressed in terms of deserved punishments, and not in terms of instrumental effects of punishment. Deserved punishments, however, must ordinarily be justified in retributive terms as proportionate responses to criminal acts. Consequentialist theories justify punishments in other ways. We are in an era where retributive theories are predominant so I discuss only that perspective. A first offender who commits offence X should receive a punishment proportionate to X. A second offender who commits offence X deserves the same proportionate punishment. The additional increment of punishment must relate to something but it is difficult to say in desert terms what that something is. Lee explicitly rejects the claims that the premium is justifiable on the bases that the offender is defiant, disappointing, incorrigible or of questionable character. Those are states of being, not punishable acts.

Finally, Lee's analysis fails as an analogy. Criminal law usually requires an *actus reus*, an unlawful act, on which liability to punishment is predicated. Most crimes are acts of commission; an offender does something that the law forbids. In limited, carefully defined circumstances, however, criminal law liability in common law countries can rest on omissions. In those cases, a harm results under circumstances in which an offender was capable of preventing the harm without danger to himself and had a recognised or implied duty to do so. The most common situations involve failures to prevent harms to others when an actor has a clear duty of care, archetypically those of parents or recognised carers for children, or those of people who have undertaken contractually to care for another person. Less commonly, courts have recognised omissions liability in quasi-contractual circumstances in which a person has exclusive control over a vulnerable person and knows or has reason to know that the second person is in imminent peril. It is not easy to fit the citizen's general civic responsibilities to the state into that framework.

Lee's analysis involves no equivalent recognised or recognisable duty, nor any duty to a specific person. Basing the recidivist premium on a generalised obligation not to reoffend stretches omissions liability far beyond its traditional doctrinal reach. And it would stand omissions liability on its head. A typical omissions case involves a defendant who has failed to act to prevent harm. Lee's analysis involves actions, not failures to act. The analysis fails even common language tests. Literally, the claim is that the recidivist premium is just because of the offender's culpable omission to honour an obligation not to omit (or to fail) to honour a generalised obligation not to commit crimes. An omission to omit comes close to being a double negative, which conventionally is understood to mean a positive. To describe commission of a crime as an omission to abstain from crime is far from customary legal or plain-language usage.

(b) Apologies

Christopher Bennett argues elsewhere in this volume that punishment for a first offence should be understood as implying an apology by the offender. Commission of a second offence triggers a punishment deserved for the second offence and an additional increment of punishment that somehow relates to failure to behave in a law-abiding way implicitly required by the apology. The apology is thus understood to mean, 'I am sorry I committed the first offence and caused or threatened harm to the victim, I recognise that it was wrongful and unlawful, and I promise not to do it or commit any other offence again.' As an analogy or metaphor, Bennett describes a protracted set of interactions between a student and a professor in which a student repeatedly fails to appear at scheduled meetings, implying that he does not know or does not care that each failed meeting is an unwarranted imposition on the professor's time and incurs opportunity costs for the professor.

This argument encounters many of the same kinds of problems as Lee's. The student may well feel guilty each time he fails to appear, apologises and intends to appear on time for a next appointment. The professor may understandably feel aggrieved, and increasingly aggrieved each time the student fails to appear. Many observers might feel the professor was on sound ground in refusing to set another appointment or refusing to extend some other courtesy to the student or to meet some other special request.

For offenders, however, the apology is a fiction. Even if such an apology were required, it could not fairly be described as voluntary, and if it were sincerely made, the appropriate recipient, and the closer analogy to the professor, is the victim, not the state. In the private sphere the victim, like the professor, is entitled to be disappointed and to take private actions that signify that disappointment. The gravamen of the new offence, however, is its commission, not the failure to honour a promise, implied from a fictional apology, to be good. In any case, failure to honour an implied promise, or an overt one, is not a criminal offence, so it is hard to understand why a recidivist premium is justified even in respect of an explicit promise.

More importantly, it is hard to infer from an apology a promise not to do anything bad in the future, to anyone, and an agreement that such a future bad act will be met with an additional increment of punishment over and above whatever the second bad act deserves. Apologies in any case, as opposed to statements of guilt, regret or acceptance of responsibility, are made to victims, not to the state, and it is the state, not the victim of the first offence, which imposes punishment.

4. Public Attitudes Claims

Julian Roberts has demonstrated the existence of a widely shared view among judges, other practitioners and officials, citizens generally, and offenders that recidivists should be punished more severely than first offenders. This is said to justify the recidivist premium for some reason. One possible reason is that the people want recidivists to be punished more severely than first offenders and in a democracy the people's preferences should be respected. A second is that moral intuitions, possibly a product of natural selection, are part of what makes us human, and punishment as a human process should respect those intuitions. A third is that the legitimacy of the courts depends in part on their being seen to operate in ways that are consistent with widely held views of justice. A fourth is that punishment, though usually conceptualised as something done to an offender because of an offence, is actually something partly or fully done to an offender because of his or her bad character.

The overwhelming problem with the first argument is that it shifts the focus of punishment from the offender to the audience, from what the offender deserves to what observers want or expect. In Norval Morris's terms, second and subsequent offenders should be punished, and in an amount, on the basis not of their guilt but of the blame others attribute to them. Most prevailing conceptions of judicial process, however, call for judges to make decisions based on the facts of the cases before them and to ignore external pressures. US and British judges have of late sometimes departed from these conceptions and sometimes attempted to respond to the public will or mood, but in most legal systems judges consider this to be inappropriate. It is the defendant's liberty that is at stake, and the judicial task as ordinarily understood is to determine whether the defendant has committed the alleged offence and, if so, to determine the appropriate punishment. Most retributivist accounts would base the appropriate punishment on desert considerations. Consequentialist accounts would link it to prevention or to maximising happiness or something similar. Some economists' accounts would tie appropriate punishments to economic efficiency. None of them would tie it to providing satisfaction to the audience.

Ronald Dworkin's discussion of personal and external preferences in relation to integration of Texas law schools illustrates why the recidivist premium cannot be justified by reference to citizens' satisfaction (Dworkin 1986). The Supreme Court in *Sweatt v Painter*[13] addressed the question of whether Texas could refuse to admit blacks to the University of Texas Law School because a second state university law school existed to train them. Dworkin worked his way through a number of analyses. He distinguished between personal preferences, what one wants for oneself, and external preferences, what one wants for others, and between positive and negative versions of each. Then he asked, should the external negative preferences of some white Texans that blacks be denied admission to the Law School be taken into account? His answer was no: negative preferences based on invidious considerations should not count. Or, put more tendentiously, the happiness or satisfaction some people experience in the unhappiness or dissatisfaction of others should not count.

The stakes involved in the recidivist premium—loss of additional months or years of freedom beyond that deserved for committing the current offence—involves greater stakes than were involved in *Sweatt v Painter*. It also involves a class of people who are stigmatised and often from disadvantaged and minority backgrounds. It is not a class of people with whom the law-abiding majority is likely to identify or sympathise. It is hard to see why negative external preferences are any more appropriate in this context than in *Sweatt v Painter*, for many of the same reasons.

I do not have much to say about the second and third considerations—widespread intuitions about the recidivist premium and concerns for citizens' perceptions of the legitimacy of the criminal justice. Here I offer only two observations about public expectations based on intuition. First, ideas about justice based on referendums or plebiscites—the emperor allowing the audience to decide whether the defeated gladiator will live or die—make most people uncomfortable. I have difficulty distinguishing the appeal to public intuition. Second, although the intuition does appear to be widely shared, I see no good reason why its existence should be understood to justify the premium. In other contexts, and in other times and places, public intuitions would not be allowed to justify public policies. Examples include the common intuitions not so long ago that husbands should be able to discipline their wives, that homosexual-

[13] (1950) 339 US 629.

ity is the product of mental disorder and that the sky would fall if black people had equal access to public accommodation. Explanation is required for why intuition should be allowed to trump traditional normative analyses about deserved punishment and proportionality.

About legitimacy, I have little to say that is not said in my discussion of Bentham. Legitimacy is worth worrying about, but it is not obvious why offenders should bear the burden of seeking or achieving its enhancement. It is even less obvious when note is taken that most offenders convicted of common law crimes are socially and economically disadvantaged, and disproportionately many are members of groups that have traditionally been the objects of widespread invidious discrimination. There are many reasons why public perceptions of the legitimacy of the courts might be low—including the system's lack of transparency, mechanistic assembly-line processing of cases, lack of public knowledge, and widespread suspicions of class and race bias. It is not obvious that the presence or absence of a recidivist premium is a major causal factor.

Roberts's principal argument is about character:

> Repeat offenders are regarded as more culpable, more blameworthy, to the extent that their life choices embrace reoffending. (Roberts 2008: 220)

> [R]epeat offenders are more culpable as a consequence of their mental state at the time of the offence, in the same way that offenders who plan their crimes should be considered more blameworthy. . . . Thus previous convictions are relevant to the culpability branch of a proportional sentence. (Roberts 2008: 208–09)

> Having been convicted and sentenced, a person should desist from offending; committing further offences is evidence that the offender has elected an alternative moral course to that of a law-abiding citizen. (Roberts 2008: 88)

> [R]epeat offenders are more culpable by virtue of their mental state at the time of the crime, in much the same way that offenders who plan their offending may be seen as more blameworthy. (Roberts 2008: 66)

It is impossible to do justice to Robert's rich and nuanced book-length analyses, so I quote the preceding passages to represent his arguments why the recidivist principle can be justified in quasi-desert terms. There are two main claims. Recidivists are more culpable than first offenders in the same sense that people who commit crimes involving substantial planning and premeditation are more culpable than people who commit crimes impulsively. Recidivists are people of bad character who have not been catalysed by their first conviction into a law-abiding life and have in effect chosen to live outside the law; this makes them more culpable when they reoffend.

There is something to the first point, but not much. There is a small class of offenders—professional bank robbers, members of organised crime in senior management positions, perpetrators of complex white-collar and organisational crimes—who probably can meaningfully be said to be more culpable than garden variety offenders because of the studied professionalism of their villainies. The decisive characteristic, however, is not planning and premeditation per se but professionalism. Criminal law professors like to make the point by contrasting a man walking on a bridge who, seeing a small child leaning over the railing, whimsically pushes her to a certain death, with a chronically abused woman who plans for weeks or months to do away with her fearsome husband, and does so, and then asking students which is more blameworthy. Planning and premeditation may or may not signify enhanced culpability.

Most offenders, however, are not professional bank robbers or securities fraudsters. Roberts shows that 88 per cent of people convicted of indictable offences in England and Wales in 2005 had at least one prior conviction, 57 per cent had five or more, and 37 per cent had ten or more (Roberts 2008: table 5.2). Most of these are not Bernie Madoffs or Michael Milkens or Ivan Boeskys but people living marginalised, chronically disorganised lives like those described in an English White Paper:

> [M]uch crime is committed on impulse, given the opportunity presented by an open window or unlocked door, and it is committed by offenders who live from moment to moment; their crimes are as impulsive as the rest of their feckless, sad, or pathetic lives. (Home Office 1990: 6)

Recidivist offenders are much more likely to live 'feckless, sad, or pathetic lives' than to be Professor Moriartys, and to commit crimes impulsively rather than after lengthy deliberation and careful planning. Even assuming Roberts's point is valid for some offenders—greater culpability can be inferred from some kinds of premeditation and planning—such people constitute a small minority of repeat offenders.

The second part of Roberts's culpability argument—that past offending supports an inference of bad character that enhances the degree of culpability associated with the current offence—is less successful, for reasons I sketched above and others. It does not require legal training to recognise that the law is on a slippery slope when we start justifying punishments— or additional increments of punishment beyond that deserved in respect of an offence—on the basis of offender's bad character. A comparative advantage of retributive theories is they are premised on respect for the offender's moral autonomy and agency, and in principle limit punishments to those that can be explained by reference to the culpability expressed by particular offences. Consequentialist theories are open to a much wider range of considerations; their permeability to caprice, idiosyncrasy and bias was part of the widespread indictment of individualised and indeterminate sentencing and one of the reasons why retributive theories gained influence.

Allowing bad character a foothold by means of retrospective expansion of current culpability seems not a good idea. Roberts wants to limit bad character consideration to previous offending but it is not obvious once that door opens why such things as general fecklessness, a dissolute lifestyle, drug dependence and regularly keeping bad company should not also be allowed in.

There are other problems. If bad character evidenced by previous convictions justifies a recidivist premium for subsequent offences, why shouldn't bad character evidenced by other indicators support a first-offence dissolute-life premium? Or, if punishments can be deconstructed into a component relating to the current offence and another component relating to the previous conviction/bad character premium, why not separately criminalise and sanction bad character? These are far-fetched questions, but that is in the nature of slippery slope analyses. What is important is not whether such things are likely to be proposed or be adopted, but whether there are persuasive arguments showing that acceptance of the recidivist premium because repeated crimes reveal 'life choices embrac[ing] reoffending' can be distinguished from these other applications of bad character analysis.

C. A TENTATIVE SOLUTION

Neither Kant and Hegel nor Bentham is likely to countenance recidivist premiums, and the arguments about omissions, apologies, intuitions and bad character that have been made so far are unpersuasive.

Hybrid theories like Norval Morris's limiting retributivism could provide a mechanism to encompass the intuitions but constrain their influence, and might even solve the problem of competing and inconsistent conventional views about bulk discounts and recidivist premiums that troubles Kevin Reitz. Norval Morris (1974) provided a structure, and fleshed it out for the era in which he wrote. The basic argument and structure are simple. It is impossible to say in any absolute sense either generally or in a specific place and time what punishment a particular crime deserves (in retributive terms) or warrants (in consequentialist). Partly this is an epistemological problem—God knows but does not tell—and partly it is a relativist one—I may have a view, and you may, but how can we know which if either is right?

Morris's solution was to suggest that we cannot know what is in God's mind, and we will not reach easy agreement about what punishment is uniquely appropriate in a given case, but we can fairly easily reach agreements about punishments that are unjust because too severe or too trifling. Those agreements create limits above and below which punishments ought not go if they are to be 'not undeserved'. Hence the term 'limiting retributivism'. Retributive ideas about deserved punishments set limits outside which a punishment cannot reasonably be said to be deserved, and therefore to be regarded as just.

Within retributive limits, Morris argued that respect for ideas about equal treatment and Benthamite ideas about parsimony require that the default position be that punishments should fall at the bottom of the deserved ('not undeserved') range unless there is a good reason to do something more. In the 1970s, he believed that available evidence did not justify increasing punishments above the baseline for rehabilitative or incapacitative reasons. The evidence on the effectiveness of correctional treatment programs did not justify extending punishment for rehabilitative reasons. The evidence on prediction of dangerousness (at best, two false positives for every true one) was insufficient to justify extending punishment for incapacitative reasons. About deterrent (Morris 1974) and expressive (Morris 1992) punishments he was, oddly, less certain.[14]

The idea of ranges with a default starting point may provide a mechanism for addressing both Roberts's evidence about widely shared intuitions and Reitz's concerns about the anomalously and unjustly different ramifications in US guideline systems of sentencing for multiple offences in one or successive proceedings. Morris's aim was to establish a framework that respected ideas about deserved punishment and equal treatment but allowed some place for consequentialist considerations. He mostly wrote about the traditional troika of deterrence, incapacitation and rehabilitation. The structure, however, could easily accommodate previous convictions: subject to rules and presumptions, previous convictions could be invoked to justify imposition of punishments above the default minimum, but never above the upper limit of the range of deserved punishments for the particular offence.

Incorporating previous crimes into Morris's model would not be a radical augmentation, and is arguably implied by later writings on the appropriate role in sentencing of predictions of dangerousness (Morris and Miller 1985). There he set as a test for justifiable extensions of prison sentences for predictive reasons that

> the base expectancy rate of violence for the criminal predicted as dangerous must be shown by reliable evidence to be substantially higher than the base expectancy rate of another criminal with a closely similar criminal record and convicted of a closely similar crime but not predicted as unusually dangerous. (ibid: 37)

---

[14] The evidence about deterrent effects was then, and is now, even less informative for making decisions in individual cases than the evidence on rehabilitation and incapacitation. To my knowledge, there was then, and is now, no empirical evidence whatever on the effects of individual case decisions on public confidence in the justice system or on its perceived legitimacy.

Morris assumed that the influence of such predictions would occur within the limiting retributivist range.

Corralling previous convictions within desert limits would address several problems. If one believed (I do not) that evidence of widely shared intuitions about previous convictions requires or justifies a recidivist premium, this solution would permit it, but within bounds. Likewise, if one believed (I am ambivalent) that predictive or rehabilitative considerations relating to previous convictions justify a longer or more burdensome sentence, this solution would permit it, but within bounds. One implication of this analysis is that the pattern of steeply rising recidivist premiums in successive proceedings that troubles Reitz would be starkly revealed as unjust.

If with Kevin Reitz one is perplexed (I am) by paradoxical conventional views about the recidivist premium and the 'bulk discount', they could both be addressed within desert limits. For subsequent offences as for first offences, the upper limit for the current offence would set a bound. This would have the considerable advantage (in the United States) that it would effectively bring the totality principle to the United States and apply it to both simultaneous and sequential sentencing. The only arguments I can see for freeing sequential sentencing from the totality principle are that subsequent offences are predictive of future offending (which I have ruled out-of-bounds except within retributive limits), that they reveal the offender's persisting bad character (which I have ruled out-of-bounds for libertarian reasons), and that many people intuitively feel that repeat offenders deserve progressively harder treatment (with which I disagree, but in any case its influence must be held within limits).

Richard Frase's writings in this volume and elsewhere (eg Frase 2004) discuss Morris's views in greater detail and explore some of their imprecisions. For my purposes here, however, a description of the basic structure is sufficient with this important caveat. Andrew von Hirsch (eg von Hirsch 1985; von Hirsch and Ashworth 2005), and others, have observed that Morris was always insufficiently precise about the nature and limits of ranges of not-undeserved punishment. For my proposals here to work, some mechanism for identifying and constraining ranges is needed. If the ranges for most non-trivial offenses encompass many years, they will offer no more meaningful constraints on discretion than existed in the era of individualised, indeterminate sentencing. If a logic for identifying meaningfully constraining ranges can de developed, my proposals if adopted could solve some difficult and hitherto underappreciated problems.

REFERENCES

American Law Institute (1962) *Model Penal Code: Proposed Official Draft* (Philadelphia, American Law Institute).

Ashworth, A (2005) *Sentencing and Criminal Justice* (Cambridge, Cambridge University Press).

Ashworth, A and Baker, E, 'The Role of Previous Convictions in England and Wales' (this volume).

Asp, P, 'Previous Convictions and Proportionate Sentencing under Swedish law' (this volume).

Becker, G (1968) 'Crime and Punishment: An Economic Approach' 76 *Journal of Political Economy* 169.

Bennett, C, 'More to Apologise For: Can We Find a Basis for the Recidivist Premium in a Communicative Theory of Punishment?' (this volume).

Bentham, J (1970) 'The Utilitarian Theory of Punishment' in J H Burns and H L A Hart (eds), *An Introduction to Principles of Morals and Legislation* (London, Athlone,)

— — (2008 [1830]) *The Rationale of Punishment* (Amherst, Kessinger).

Bureau of Justice Statistics (2006) *Felony Defendants in Large Urban Counties, 2002* (Washington DC, Bureau of Justice Statistics).

Chen, EY (2008) 'Impacts of "Three Strikes and You're Out" on Crime Trends in California and Throughout the United States' 24 *Journal of Contemporary Criminal Justice* 345.

Coase, R (1978) 'Economics and Contiguous Disciplines' 7 *Journal of Legal Studies* 201.

Cohen, M (1940) 'Moral Aspects of the Criminal Law' 49 *Yale Law Journal* 987.

Downes, D and Morgan, R (2007) 'No Turning Back: The Politics of Law and Order into the Millennium' in M Maguire et al (eds), *The Oxford Handbook of Criminology*, 4th edn (Oxford, Oxford University Press).

Dworkin, R (1986) *Law's Empire* (Cambridge, MA, Harvard University Press)

Ehrlich, I (1996) 'Crime, Punishment, and the Market for Offenses' 10 *Journal of Economic Perspectives* 43.

Fletcher, G (1978), *Rethinking Criminal Law* (Boston, Little, Brown).

Frase, R (2004) 'Limiting Retributivism' in M Tonry (ed), *The Future of Imprisonment* (New York, Oxford University Press).

— — (2009) 'Limiting Excessive Prison Sentencing' 11 *University of Pennsylvania Journal of Constitutional Law* 39.

— — 'Prior-conviction Sentencing Enhancements: Rationales and Limits Based on Retributive and Utilitarian Proportionality Principles and Social Equality Goals' (this volume).

Hegel, GWF (1991) 'Wrong' ['Das Unrecht'] in AW Wood (ed), HB Nisbet (trans), *Elements of the Philosophy of Right* (Cambridge, Cambridge University Press).

Holmes, OW (1881) *The Common Law* (Boston, Little, Brown).

Home Office (1990) *Crime, Justice, and Protecting the Public* (London, Home Office).

— — (2001) *Making Punishments Work: Report of a Review of the Sentencing Framework for England and Wales* (London, Home Office Communication Directorate).

Jareborg, N (1995) 'The Swedish Sentencing System' in C Clarkson and R Morgan (eds), *The Politics of Sentencing Reform* (Oxford, Oxford University Press).

Kant, I (1965 [1787]) 'The Penal Law and the Law of Pardon' in J Ladd (trans), *The Metaphysical Elements of Justice* (Indianapolis, Liberal Arts Press/ Bobbs-Merrill).

Kleinig, J (1973) *Punishment and Desert* (New York, Springer Verlag).

Lee, Y, ' Recidivism, Retributivism, and the Lapse Theory of Previous Convictions' (this volume).

Lovegrove, A (1988) *Judicial Decision Making* (New York, Springer Verlag).

Michael, J and Wechsler, H (1937) 'A Rationale of the Law of Homicide' 37 *Columbia Law Review* 701 (Part I), 1261 (Part II).

Morris, H (1966) 'Persons and Punishment' 52 *The Monist* 475.

Morris, V (1951) *The Habitual Criminal* (London, Longmans Green).

— — (1974) *The Future of Imprisonment* (Chicago, University of Chicago Press).

— — (1982) *Madness and the Criminal Law* (Chicago, University of Chicago Press).

— — (1992) *The Brothel Boy and Other Parables of the Law* (New York, Oxford University Press).

Morris, N and Miller, M (1985) 'Predictions of Dangerousness' in M Tonry and N Morris (eds), *Crime and Justice: A Review of Research*, vol 6 (Chicago, University of Chicago Press).

Murphy, J (1973) 'Marxism and Retribution' 2 *Philosophy and Public Affairs* 217.

Nagin, D (1998) 'Deterrence and Incapacitation' in M Tonry (ed), *The Handbook of Crime and Punishment* (New York, Oxford University Press).

Newburn, T (2007) '"Tough on Crime": Penal Policy in England and Wales' in M Tonry (ed), *Crime, Punishment, and Politics in Comparative Perspective*, in M Tonry (ed) *Crime and Justice: A Review of Research*, vol 36 (Chicago, University of Chicago Press).

Rawls, J (1955) 'Two Concepts of Rules' 44 *Philosophical Review* 3.

Reitz, K, 'The Illusion of Proportionality: Desert and Repeat Offenders' (this volume).

Robbins, L (1938) 'Interpersonal Comparisons of Utility: A Consensus' XLVIII *The Economic Journal* 635.

Roberts, JV (1997) 'The Role of Criminal Record in the Sentencing Process' in M Tonry (ed), *Crime and Justice: A Review of Research*, vol 22 (Chicago, University of Chicago Press).

— — (2008) *Punishing Persistent Offenders: Exploring Community and Offender Perspectives* (Oxford, Oxford University Press).

— — 'First Offender Sentencing Discounts: Exploring the Justifications' (this volume).

Robinson, P (1987) 'Hybrid Principles for the Distribution of Criminal Sanctions' 82 *Northwestern Law Review* 19.

Shane-DuBow, S, et al (1985) *Sentencing Reform in the United States: History, Content, and Effect* (Washington DC, US Government Printing Office).

Singer, RG (1979) *Just Deserts: Sentencing Based on Equality and Desert* (Lexington, Ballinger).

Smart, JJC (1973) 'An Outline of a System of Utilitarian Ethics' in JJC Smart and B Williams (eds), *Utilitarianism: For and Against* (Cambridge, Cambridge University Press).

Tonry, M (2008) 'Learning from the Limitations of Deterrence Research' in M Tonry (ed), *Crime and Justice: A Review of Research*, vol 37 (Chicago, University of Chicago Press).

von Hirsch, A (1976) *Doing Justice* (New York, Hill & Wang).

—— (1981) 'Desert and Previous Convictions in Sentencing' 65 *Minnesota Law Review* 591.

—— (1985) *Past and Future Crimes: Deservedness and Dangerousness in Sentencing Criminals* (New Brunswick, Rutgers University Press).

von Hirsch, A and Ashworth, A (2005) *Proportionate Sentencing: Exploring the Principles* (Oxford, Oxford University Press).

7

Prior-conviction Sentencing Enhancements: Rationales and Limits Based on Retributive and Utilitarian Proportionality Principles and Social Equality Goals

RICHARD S FRASE

T HIS CHAPTER SEEKS to identify normative principles and practical rules both to justify and set real limits on the widespread
practice of enhancing sentence severity based on prior convictions.
The normative principles adopted for this purpose must be capable of
generating clear, workable formulas, telling judges and sentencing policymakers when and why prior-record enhancements are permitted, and
also when and why they are excessive. In order to achieve public, political and practitioner acceptance, such underlying principles must also be
informed by practice and public attitudes, and draw upon widely shared
values and intuitions.

Previous attempts to set normative limits on prior-record enhancements
have primarily looked to retributive principles. Moreover, writers working within a retributive framework have focused on the repeat offender's
supposed increased culpability (or the first offender's reduced culpability), and have not examined the possibility that a series of crimes might
cause greater social harm than the sum of the harms associated with
each offence. This chapter surveys various culpability theories that have
been proposed and also considers whether the justification for prior-record
enhancements could be based on increased aggregate social harm.

This chapter concludes, however, that these desert-based rationales are
each unconvincing and also unworkable—they are either too strict or too
lax, granting too small a role for prior record to gain practical accept-

ance, or, at the other extreme, failing to impose sufficient upper limits
on enhancement. This chapter therefore proposes an approach and several specific formulas under which prior-record enhancements are allowed
within a range of desert defined by the seriousness of the offender's
crime(s). This approach is based on the theory of limiting retributivism,
as implemented in Minnesota and several other US states with systems of
sentencing guidelines. Among the specific formulas proposed, a modified
(within-desert) version of the criminal history scores found in guideline
systems seems to provide the best way to define and limit prior-record
enhancements.

This chapter also proposes several other normative principles to further
limit prior-record enhancements. Two of these principles, grounded in utilitarian philosophy, have found widespread acceptance and application in
many areas of domestic and international law (Sullivan and Frase 2008).
In previous writings (Frase 2005; Sullivan and Frase 2008) I labelled
these two principles 'ends–benefits' and 'alternative-means' proportionality. Ends–benefits proportionality requires that the expected benefits of
a public measure not be outweighed by the private burdens and public
costs imposed by the measure. Alternative-means proportionality requires
that a measure not be more burdensome or costly than equally effective
alternative ways of achieving the same benefits.

A fourth normative theory to justify and limit prior-record enhancements draws on both utilitarian and deontological principles. This theory
posits that society has a particularly compelling moral duty, and a strong
practical need, to protect its most vulnerable citizens, especially those
who suffer from multiple disadvantages related to their poverty and race
or ethnicity. Although prior-record enhancements help to protect these
disadvantaged groups from the high crime rates that often afflict their
neighbourhoods, such enhancements also tend to have a disproportionate impact on racial and ethnic minority offenders, further increasing the
disadvantage they and their families and communities suffer, while also
increasing their risk of recidivism. Prior-record enhancements thus must
be kept within limits, to avoid worsening social inequalities.

The four limiting principles described above—retributive, ends–benefits,
alternative-means and social equality—operate independently: a violation
of any of them renders a sentence enhancement excessive. As shown in
later sections of this chapter, each of the four principles can be used to
derive practical formulas for identifying when a prior-record enhancement
is excessive. Each of the four principles also enjoys widespread public,
scholarly and judicial acceptance. The hybrid theory derived from these
principles thus provides a workable and effective system for controlling
prior-record enhancements.

Before I examine these normative theories in more detail, there is a preliminary, definitional matter—what do we mean by a 'prior conviction'?

Consider an offender who commits two burglaries, B(1) and B(2). In the paradigmatic situation there will be an intervening conviction and sentencing on B(1) before the offender commits B(2). But sometimes (especially when the offence dates of B(1) and B(2) are close together) the conviction and sentencing on B(1) does not occur until after the date on which B(2) was committed; at the subsequent sentencing of B(2), this offender has a 'prior' conviction, but not one that had already been entered when he committed B(2). In the United States some recidivist enhancements require an intervening conviction between the 'prior' and current offences; this approach is especially common in statutes that raise the maximum and/or minimum penalty for a second offence.[1] But other recidivist enhancements apply with or without an intervening conviction. For example, under the federal, Kansas, Minnesota and Washington guidelines, criminal history is calculated as of the date of sentencing, not the date on which the offence being sentenced (B(2), above) was committed,[2] and these rules appear to reflect less formal, pre-guideline sentencing practices.

The point being made here is that any justification for prior-record enhancement that depends on an intervening conviction and sentence (eg various 'notice' theories discussed below) cannot explain many of the formal and informal enhancements being applied in practice. A related point is that theorists should not assume a paradigm in which an offender (with or without an intervening conviction) commits the same crime again. Although 'similar' prior convictions often count more heavily, very dissimilar priors are also frequently used for enhancement (the only exception being that prior traffic offences are usually not counted in sentencing nontraffic crimes, and vice versa).

One further preliminary point needs to be addressed, since it relates to several theories of prior-record enhancement. A recurring question about these theories is why they give more emphasis to prior record than to other offender-based factors with the same relevance to desert—why does the theory privilege prior convictions over other evidence that could be used to enhance based on the same desert-based rationales?[3] Examples include evidence bearing on: how 'uncharacteristic' of the offender the current offence was; the wickedness of defendant's character; and how much 'notice' the offender had of the illegality or harmfulness of his conduct, and his need to take steps to control his criminal tendencies. The answer to such criticisms may be found in the practical need for workable enhancement criteria: accurate prior conviction information is more readily available than most other evidence supporting the underlying rationales, and lends itself to simpler decision rules.

---

[1] See eg Minn Stat § 152.01, subd 16a, defining 'subsequent' drug crimes.
[2] See eg Minn Sent Guidelines s II.B.
[3] See eg von Hirsch (1985: 79), applying this criticism to the notice theories discussed in section 4 below.

A. RETRIBUTIVE PRINCIPLES APPLIED
TO PRIOR CONVICTIONS

Desert theory is very underdeveloped when it comes to providing principles and practical decision rules that can both justify and limit prior-conviction enhancements (Roberts 1997, 2008, and this volume). Developing such principles and rules may be the most critical task for desert theorists at the present time. Up to now most such theorists have either ignored this topic or have provided a role for prior record which is either too strict or too lax. Strict theories, rejecting repeat-offender enhancements or positing reduced desert only for offenders with little or no criminal history, would invalidate so much of current sentencing practice that they are likely to be ignored by policymakers and courts. Other desert-based theories have the opposite problem: by positing enhanced culpability for repeat offending, above the culpability associated with the current offence(s), they suggest an open-ended escalation of sanction severity in proportion to prior record. Thus, whether desert theory is ignored by policymakers and courts or seen as justifying unlimited enhancement, the result is the same, particularly in the United States: sentences far in excess of what is deserved for the offender's current crime(s). Moreover, the obvious disconnect between desert theory and these punishment practices puts in doubt the validity and viability of retributive theory generally.

The remainder of this part of the chapter surveys various proposed or potential desert-based theories of prior-conviction enhancements and notes the theoretical and/or practical difficulties of each. It then proposes several specific formulas that would permit non-trivial prior-record enhancements while also maintaining clear, desert-based upper limits on these enhancements.

1. The 'Exclusionary' School

The 'exclusionary' school is the term given by Julian Roberts (2008) to the view of scholars who maintain that an offender's prior conviction record is unrelated to his desert and should have no bearing on the severity of his current sentence (see eg Fletcher 1978; Singer 1979; Bagaric 2000). Such a narrow view of desert may be correct in principle, given the problems with the desert-based enhancement theories discussed below. But when combined with a strict ('defining', not merely limiting) view of desert, this approach is unworkable in practice because it seems to rule out any consideration of prior record, and thus encourages sentencing policymakers and practitioners to ignore desert principles entirely.

2. Diminished Culpability of First Offenders (and Second Offenders? Third? Fourth?)

This theory argues that first offenders can plausibly claim their offence was out of character, and that society should be somewhat less willing to fully convert its condemnation of the offender's criminal act into condemnation of the actor (von Hirsch 1985; Wasik and von Hirsch 1994; Ashworth 2005; Roberts, this volume). This theory also asserts that we should give the first offender credit for his prior law-abiding life and, we hope, his ability to resume that life and learn his lesson. Under the narrowest version of this theory mitigation is limited to first offenders; a broader version, often referred to as progressive loss of mitigation, allows a lesser sentence reduction for second offenders, and some writers would continue to permit some mitigation for a third offence, or even a fourth, although the rationale for mitigation would seem to be quite strained at that point (Roberts, this volume).

Except for the last group, most variants of the reduced-desert theory reject the kind of steady escalation of penalties for each additional prior conviction which is found in the current sentencing laws and practices of many jurisdictions. These theories thus suffer (albeit to a lesser extent) from the weakness of the exclusionary approach—the theories (especially the narrower versions) would invalidate so much of current sentencing practice that policymakers and practitioners are likely to dismiss such theories, and perhaps all desert considerations. The broader versions of reduced-desert theory are more congruent with practice, but, as noted above, they are unconvincing when applied to an offender with several prior convictions. Another problem with all reduced-desert theories is that they may lack widespread support; it seems that many people's moral intuitions tell them that criminal record is a matter of enhanced culpability for repeat offenders, not reduced culpability for first or second offenders (Lee 2009).

On the other hand, reduced-desert theories do have one advantage over the desert-based rationales discussed below, all of which posit enhanced culpability for second and subsequent crimes—the reduced-desert approach has a clear upper limit, based on desert factors associated with the current offence(s), whereas the logic of enhanced-desert theories seems to permit an open-ended escalation of sanction severity. The idea that current offence(s) should set an upper limit on sanction severity finds support in sentencing guidelines systems, all of which recognise an offence-based 'cap' beyond which criminal history no longer raises the guidelines recommended sentence.

3. The Recidivist's 'Bad Character'

Character theories of enhanced punishment for repeat offenders seem to be based on the idea that such offenders have shown themselves, with each additional crime, to be more and more wicked and depraved, more anti-social and more indifferent to the rights of others. Julian Roberts (2008) has likened recidivism enhancements to the increased penalty and oppro-brium attached to killing with premeditation—in both cases, he argues, we are more likely to ascribe the current offence to the offender, rather than to his surroundings or environmental factors. But premeditation is a particular mental state that is directly associated with the offender's criminal act; punishing bad character comes much closer to violating the fundamental principle that people are punished for what they have done (and with what intent), not for who or what they are.[4]

There are also major practical problems in applying this approach—how much more blameworthy does the offender become with each additional crime, and is there any upper limit to penalty enhancements under this approach? Character theories have the opposite flaw from those discussed above—they eventually lead to the conclusion that the offender is such an outlaw that he has forfeited any right to have his punishment limited by retributive, human rights, or other deontological principles. Such an open-ended forfeiture concept may indeed be the core rationale of 'three-strikes' and other very severe habitual offender laws.

4. Heightened Notice and/or Defiance of Criminal Prohibitions

Another group of theories (summarized in Lee 2009) posits enhanced cul-pability for offenders who, after receiving formal condemnation of their prior criminal acts, ignore society's explicit warning and commit further crime in open defiance of these warnings. Both types of theory (especially notice theories) appear to assume an intervening conviction between the prior and current crime; but as noted previously, contemporary prior-record enhancement rules often sweep much more broadly than that. The notice theory may also assume some similarity between prior and cur-rent offences; again, actual criminal-record enhancement rules are much broader. Moreover notice theory does not explain further enhancements of punishment severity for a third, fourth or fifth offence.

As for defiance theories, some authors (eg von Hirsch 1985: 79–80) have questioned whether such a theory is acceptable in a liberal society where people are punished for their acts not their attitudes and thoughts. One possible answer to this criticism would be to invoke an expressive

---

[4] Eg an addict, see *Robinson v California*, 370 US 660 (1962).

theory under which offenders are punished to repudiate their false moral claim to act without regard to the rights of others or society (Hampton 1988); arguably, such false claims grow more offensive with each additional crime. But by how much and with what limits, if any?

5. Recidivism as Omission

This theory, recently proposed by Youngjae Lee (2009, and this volume), argues that the repeat offender's culpability is enhanced because he has failed to take appropriate action to control his criminal tendencies in light of his earlier crime, conviction, and punishment. Lee's theory seems to assume that, because of the prior conviction(s), the offender is or ought to be aware of his heightened risk of offending. From this actual or constructive awareness Lee derives a heightened duty on the part of the offender to rearrange his life in a way that ensures he will avoid further criminality. Elsewhere in this volume Christopher Bennett restates Lee's conception in terms of a communicative theory; on this view, punishment symbolises how sorry an offender *ought* to feel, and therefore, how strong an obligation he has to not offend again.

Compared to the desert theories previously discussed, this theory has the potential to better explain rules that steadily escalate sentence severity as the number of prior convictions increases—the duty of the offender to control his criminal tendencies becomes steadily more important and obvious. But Lee's theory suffers from some of the defects of the other theories: (i) it only seems to explain prior-record enhancements involving an intervening conviction; (ii) it also seems to apply mainly to offenders whose past and current crimes are similar, or at least caused by the same criminal impulses; (iii) the theory does not seem capable of generating a formula or useful guidelines for determining how much to enhance the repeat offender's sentence, and when to discontinue further enhancement for additional prior convictions; and (iv) this theory would seem to require courts to engage in difficult assessments of the extent to which the offender tried but was unable to control his criminal tendencies.

6. The Other Branch of Desert: Does Repeat Offending Create Broader 'Harms'?

Most desert theorists probably agree that a person's desert depends on the harms he has caused or risked as well as his intent and other offender-based culpability factors (von Hirsch 1993: 29–33). But thus far desert-based theories seem to have assumed that variations in harm do not explain or justify prior-record enhancements—the harm to the victim(s) of the current offence, say a burglary, is supposedly the same regardless of the offender's prior conviction record (Roberts, this volume).

It can be argued, however, that an offender's prior record of crime affects how we view his most recent criminal acts, and that the total harm of repeat offending is greater than the sum of the harms of each offence viewed in isolation. The repeat offender's current burglary is more disturbing, to both the victim and society, in light of—and in proportion to— his prior crimes. We are forced to conclude that this offender poses a heightened threat to all of us (and heightened to a degree roughly proportional to his prior record). This conclusion makes us fearful, and reduces our level of trust in others; it forces us to take extra precautions against people like this, precautions which may be expensive or inconvenient; it also forces officials to take additional, more expensive measures to deal with the heightened levels of risk posed by this and similar offenders. These are all real and substantial harms, foreseeably caused by the offender's past and current crimes. Just as we punish risky acts for reasons of blame as well as crime control, and punish them more severely the greater the risk that was taken, perhaps offenders deserve more punishment because their multiple, blameworthy criminal acts have made them appear (and be) more risky and therefore more disturbing to us and more expensive and difficult to deal with.

One problem with this theory is that it might be used to justify penalty enhancement based on our fear of what *other, similar* offenders may do; from a desert perspective, defendants are only accountable for the risks and harms which they or their criminal confederates have caused. Another problem with this theory is its potential to justify a limitless escalation of severity: our feelings of fear and distrust, and the extra precautions we and officials are forced to take, would if anything seem to accelerate with increases in the offender's prior record. Of course, such an accelerating effect could help explain severe habitual offender laws. But most desert theorists would probably agree that such laws cannot and should not be justified on desert grounds, and they would reject any desert theory that seemed to do this. Apart from the 'no-upper-limit' problem, the increased-aggregate-harms theory does not suggest any practical formula or guidelines for deciding how much to enhance for each additional offence.

7. The Need for Workable Desert-based Formulas to Limit Prior Record Enhancements

There are serious problems with each of the theories in sections 1–6 above, although each has some plausibility. Some theories give prior record so small a role that the theory will never be accepted in practice; other theories fail to provide any clear, desert-based scaling and upper limit to prior record enhancements.

There is a pressing practical need for workable formulas that tell judges, legislators and other sentencing policymakers which prior-record enhancements are justified on desert grounds, and which are not. The remainder of this section suggests several possible ways to do this. All three of the proposals below operate within the maximum deserved sentence for the defendant's offences; within that maximum each proposal gives judges discretion to consider prior record on non-retributive grounds (primarily recidivism risk). These proposals do not attempt to define desert-based enhancements proportionate to prior record. Such desert scaling is rejected because, as discussed above, the available desert rationales for prior-record enhancements are either unconvincing, too open-ended and/or impossible to translate into workable decision rules. Like Michael Tonry's solution described elsewhere in this volume, the proposals below presuppose a limiting retributive model in which desert defines a range of just sentences. Some version of that model is followed in virtually all modern sentencing systems (Frase 2004).

(a) The Statutory Maximum as a True Maximum

The first desert-based formula has a limited but critically important application: no matter how extensive the offender's prior record, this rule bans any sentence more severe than the statutory maximum for the current offence (cases of multiple current offences are discussed below). In other words, three-strikes, habitual-offender and other above-normal-maximum penalties would be banned.

The 'max means max' formula would change sentencing law and practice in many jurisdictions, but in most of these jurisdictions it would not actually affect the sentencing of very many offenders—with one exception: 'second-and-subsequent-offence' laws. These laws typically provide that the maximum penalty is X for a first offence and X+Y in all other cases (or the first offence is classified as a misdemeanour or petty offence, and a higher offence classification applies thereafter). Such laws are quite common and are probably frequently applied, so it may be unwise and perhaps inappropriate to propose a rule that would invalidate them all. The substantive rationale for permitting these enhancements would be that the enhanced penalty defines the desert maximum for this crime, with the first-offender penalty reflecting either a theory of diminished culpability (section 2 above) or utilitarian considerations (assumed lower risk and/ or greater amenability to treatment and supervision).

For the relatively narrow group of cases that remain, involving three-strikes and similar habitual-offender enhancements, desert theorists should stand firm; the statutory maximum should be seen as defining the most severe penalty anyone deserves for committing that crime. In most US jurisdictions such maxima (including second-and-subsequent maxima) are already quite high, providing more than ample sentencing power. An offender's prior convictions (along with other case-specific offence-gravity enhancements) may justify a sentence closer to the maximum, but the desert rationales for prior-record enhancement are sufficiently problematic (see previous discussion) that they cannot justify exceeding the maximum.

Three-strikes and habitual offender laws violate a fundamental principle accepted by all retributive theorists, whether they subscribe to limiting retributivism or a purer form of desert theory—no one should be punished in excess of their desert. Such laws also violate two other fundamental tenets of western legal traditions: the ban on double jeopardy, and the principle that no one may be punished solely for their status—for who or what they are. Double jeopardy is violated if an habitual offender is being resentenced and given extra punishment for his prior crimes. On the other hand, if we posit that the offender is being punished for some new crime—the crime of being an habitual offender—this is essentially punishment for a status, which the US Supreme Court has found to be unconstitutional.[5]

Multiple current offences pose additional problems (as more fully developed in Kevin Reitz's chapter in this volume). A strict interpretation of the 'max means max' rule would perhaps require multiple current offences to be sentenced concurrently, within the limits of the maximum penalty for the most serious offence. The rationale would be that with consecutive sentencing there is no defensible upper limit short of the sum of the maxima for the offences, resulting in an unacceptable risk of punishment exceeding desert. Some legal systems do in fact prohibit consecutive sentencing,[6] but this may be too strict a limit to gain support from practitioners and policymakers in most jurisdictions. Moreover, such a rule magnifies the disconnect between the treatment of multiple crimes sentenced sequentially versus simultaneously. In the former case offenders almost always receive what amounts to consecutive sentences (the only exception is when courts make a sentence for a new crime concurrent with an earlier sentence that has not been fully carried out at the time of sentencing on the second crime). Such sequential-consecutive sentences seem unproblematic, and categorically banning simultaneous-consecutives is hard to justify from a desert perspective; none of the repeat-offender rationales discussed above seems adequate to support the very different treatment of two offenders who have committed an identical set of crimes.

The conclusion seems inescapable: if fully consecutive sentences are not undeserved for sequentially sentenced offenders, the same is true for most

---

[5] See *Robinson v California*, ibid, invalidating the crime of 'being addicted to narcotics'.
[6] For discussion of the French rule prohibiting consecutive sentencing of multiple current offences, see Frase (1990: 618–19).

simultaneously sentenced offenders (subject perhaps to exceptions for multiple charges arising from a single incident, highly situational crime sprees and similar cases where consecutive sentencing exaggerates an offender's desert). It then follows that the frequent use of concurrent sentences in simultaneous sentencing must, in most cases, be justified by utilitarian considerations (perhaps applying a benefit-of-the-doubt presumption of lower risk—if the offender had been sentenced sequentially he might have desisted).

(b) Prior-record Enhancements Based on 'Reserved Desert' in Prior Sentencings

Since the 'max means max' proposals above will face strong opposition in many jurisdictions, alternative desert-based formulas need to be considered. One alternative would allow a limited degree of sentencing above the maximum for the most serious current offence based on the notion that, if the offender did not receive all of his deserved punishment in one or more prior sentencings, such 'reserved' severity is available to enhance his deserved punishment for the current crime. Norval Morris (1982: 185) and Julian Roberts (1997: 353–54) suggested a similar theory of reclaimed leniency from previous sentencings, as a possible desert-based rationale for prior record enhancements.

In practice, this approach would work as follows. First, the deserved punishment for the current offence(s) would be calculated based on the crime itself, without regard to prior record. Since statutory maxima reflect the worst case, in almost all cases the offender's deserved sentence should be well below the statutory maximum (and judges would be told that). The court would next make the same assessment for each prior crime, and compare the deserved prior sentence to the actual sentence served for that crime. The judge would then be authorised (but not required) to add some or all of any such 'reserved' punishment to the current sentence. As is common practice in many jurisdictions (again, reflecting the widespread practical support for a limiting retributive model), judges would also be encouraged not to execute fully the imposed current sentence, since a partially or fully suspended sentence can be used to encourage compliance with release conditions and criminal prohibitions. Such a stayed sentence on the current and/or prior crime(s) would, if never revoked, provide a substantial quantum of reserved desert that remains available to be reclaimed in future sentencings.

To avoid double-jeopardy objections, and to minimise the burden on courts in making reserved-desert assessments, such a system would have to operate prospectively. At each sentencing the court would calculate and impose (but normally not fully execute) a sentence equal to the court's assessment of the offender's maximum deserved penalty for the current offence(s), plus any additional reserved-desert penalty from prior sentencings. The offender would also be warned that if he is released from prison and supervision after serving less than that maximum deserved penalty, the remainder can be used to enhance his penalty if he is sentenced for another crime in the future (formally or effectively, the reserved deserved prison time is treated like suspended prison time that is later revoked). To make this system work, courts and correctional authorities would also need to improve and co-ordinate their record systems so that judges could easily determine how much of each prior deserved sentence was actually served.

(c) Enhancements within Redefined Statutory Ranges or Guideline Severity Levels

A third approach would allow prior record enhancements within a range of deserved penalties for the current offence(s).

In non-guideline jurisdictions the legislature would place all crimes in groups deemed roughly equal in their gravity and deserved penalties, similar to severity levels in sentencing guidelines systems. Criminal history and all other case-specific enhancements would operate within these ranges, thus placing a cap on the weight given to criminal history—beyond a certain number or severity of prior crimes, the sentence no longer increases. A similar approach is taken in US guideline systems, but in these systems the severity levels often overlap—the 'capped' top of one range is higher (sometimes, much higher) than the first-offender sentence for crimes of greater severity. A more desert-based approach would ensure that the highest penalties at one severity level are no greater than those at the bottom of the range of the (more serious) offence group above. This provides a greater degree of ordinal proportionality and further limits the magnitude of criminal history enhancements. Within each group, judges would be told that the low end is for offenders with no prior convictions and no other reasons to enhance the sentence, and the high end is for the worst-case offender. If the judge found any enhancement reasons to exist, he or she would estimate where within the range the offender falls. Alternatively, guidelines or other rules could provide formulas to assist judges in this exercise.

This approach would work much better in a guideline system such as Minnesota's, where the capped, high-criminal-history penalty for each group of offences (each offence severity level) is lower than the statutory maxima for almost all crimes in that group. In such a system, the severity-level ranges assume a 'typical' offence, without unusual offence-related factors which enhance the offender's deserved punishment. When such factors are found to exist, desert principles permit the upper end of the range to be exceeded, imposing a sentence greater than the recommended

guideline sentences for more serious offences (since those sentences are
also based on typical, unaggravated offence facts). But as with the proposed non-guideline version described above, and unlike existing guideline
systems, the proposed severity-level ranges do not overlap—the top of
each range cannot exceed the bottom of the (more serious) offence range
above. And unlike at least some existing guideline systems (see eg Frase
2005: 154–55, discussing Minnesota), within each range the guideline recommendations for offenders with low, medium or high criminal history
would not be viewed as desert-based, so judges could depart down or
up within that offence severity range based on non-desert (crime-control)
factors.

B. UTILITARIAN PROPORTIONALITY PRINCIPLES

Utilitarian goals (principally crime control) have often been used to justify prior-record sentence enhancements—offenders with prior convictions
are believed to be more likely to recidivate, and thus are in greater need
of incapacitation, specific deterrence and lengthy rehabilitative efforts in
a secure facility. In addition, repeat offenders may merit higher penalties
for reasons of general deterrence (of other offenders with similar conviction records).

However, utilitarian principles can also serve to limit sentencing
enhancements, even when such enhancements are not invalid under any
of the retributive theories discussed in section A above. There are actually two utilitarian limiting principles, and they operate independently; a
violation of either one renders a sentence invalid. In Germany and many
other legal systems, and in international law, both principles are viewed
as invoking concepts of non-retributive proportionality,[7] and this chapter
will also use that nomenclature. What utilitarian and retributive proportionality limitations have in common is the judgment that government
measures should not be excessive relative to their moral and practical
justifications.

1. Sentence Severity Limits Based on the Ends–Benefits Proportionality Principle

This principle stipulates that the costs and burdens of a measure (or the
added costs and burdens, compared to a less costly or less burdensome
measure) should not outweigh the likely benefits (or added benefits) of

---

[7] For further discussion of the application of proportionality principles in US, foreign and
international law, see Frase (2005) and Sullivan and Frase (2008).

that measure. This principle is well established in the writings of utilitarian philosophers, beginning with Cesare Beccaria and Jeremy Bentham (Frase 2005). When the issue involves a government measure, excessive cost is an important public policy concern, but such excess does not necessarily violate the rights of any individual. However, in a variety of contexts courts have found that the burdens which certain government measures impose on citizens are so excessive relative to the likely benefits that these measures violate constitutional rights or international human rights norms. When US courts make such a finding, they use a variety of legal standards, many of which only incorporate proportionality implicitly. For example, in deciding whether the police have violated the Fourth Amendment ban on 'unreasonable' searches and seizures, US courts ask whether the nature and degree of the intrusion on the citizen's liberty, privacy or property interests outweighs the government interests served by the intrusion (Frase 2002, 2005; Sullivan and Frase 2008).

As applied to sentencing, the ends–benefits [Ends] proportionality principle forbids penalties in excess of the likely crime-control or other benefits. For example, the principle is violated by a sentence of life without parole for a repeat property offender whose criminality is likely to decrease steadily with time, while the costs and burdens of imprisonment steadily rise, eventually exceeding the declining incapacitative benefits as well as the likely general deterrent and standard-setting benefits (the other common utilitarian sentencing goals, rehabilitation and special deterrence, are clearly inapplicable to such a sentence). Even a less severe prison term could violate ends–benefits proportionality if it extends beyond the likely criminal career of the offender, or prevents only minor repeat crimes; such was likely to have been true of both of the California three-strikes sentences (25 years to life, and 50 years to life) which the US Supreme Court nevertheless held not to be in violation of the Eighth Amendment Cruel and Unusual Punishment Clause.[8]

Another example of a sentence which violates ends–benefits proportionality is a lengthy prison term given to a drug seller whose criminal activity will quickly be taken over by new or existing drug dealers. The replacement effect results in minimal or zero incapacitative benefit, and also indicates that the offender's severe punishment has had very little general deterrent effect. This example appears to aptly describe many of the sentences imposed pursuant to the US 'war on drugs,' judging by the continued high volume of drug dealing (and the stable or falling street price of the drugs), notwithstanding massive incarceration of drug dealers. To the extent that the specific drug dealers who end up with lengthy prison terms are selected because they had a prior criminal record, the

[8] The California 'three-strikes' cases are more fully discussed and critiqued in Frase (2005).

ends–benefits proportionality principle invalidates those sentence enhancements.

2. Limiting Sentence Severity Based on the Alternative-Means Proportionality Principle

Utilitarian philosophy, beginning with Beccaria and Bentham, has always insisted that measures be efficient—they should not be more costly or burdensome than other available means of achieving the same objectives (Frase 2005; Sullivan and Frase 2008). Unnecessary measures are poor public policy because they waste limited public resources. And in some cases courts have found that unnecessarily burdensome measures violate constitutional or human rights. When US courts make such a finding they rarely use the language of proportionality, but the alternative-means proportionality principle is implicit in a wide variety of cases invalidating measures on grounds such as 'excessiveness' (eg bail), 'unreasonableness' (eg use of excessive force to arrest), use of unnecessarily intrusive measures (eg visible shackling in view of the jury), and lack of 'narrow-tailoring' or failure to use the 'least restrictive means' (eg under the 'strict scrutiny' standards applied in First Amendment and Equal Protection Clause cases) (Frase 2005; Sullivan and Frase 2008).

As applied to sentencing, the alternative-means proportionality principle is violated when a less severe penalty would have achieved the same crime-control or other practical benefits. A good example is a lengthy prison term imposed on a drug-dependent offender whose crimes are all motivated by the need to pay for his drugs, and who could have been safely and successfully treated and released after a much shorter period of custody (or perhaps without any time in custody).

Mandatory minimum prison terms provide another good example. These almost always violate alternative-means proportionality principles (as well as retributive and ends–benefits proportionality), since the targeted group subject to the penalty will inevitably include some offenders for whom a less severe penalty would have achieved all applicable utilitarian punishment purposes. This is true even for non-offender-related purposes such as general deterrence; since it is widely known that many targeted offenders do not receive these 'mandatory' penalties, universal application of the penalties is evidently not necessary to achieve whatever increased general deterrence the penalties provide.

In both of the examples above, to the extent that the offenders received a more severe penalty because they had a prior criminal record, the alternative-means proportionality principle invalidates those sentence enhancements.

C. LIMITING PRIOR RECORD
ENHANCEMENTS TO AVOID WORSENING
RACIAL AND ETHNIC INEQUALITIES

Constitutional equal justice norms and anti-discrimination statutes recognise that society has a compelling moral duty, and a strong practical
need, to protect citizens who suffer from personal and social disadvantages
related to their race, ethnicity or other inherent susceptibility to conscious
or unconscious bias (hereinafter, for simplicity, I refer solely to disadvantage due to race). Given the high correlations between race, social class
and crime in Western societies, racial minorities are at much higher risk
both of crime victimisation and of being drawn into crime and becoming
an offender. Offenders with more substantial prior-conviction records have
higher risks of committing further crime, and the victims of those crimes
are likely to be disproportionately racial minorities living in segregated,
economically and socially distressed communities. Thus, if giving repeat
offenders more severe penalties would reduce crime (by incapacitation,
deterrence, closer supervision and/or treatment), we owe it to potential
crime victims—especially those who suffer multiple disadvantages of race
and class—to impose those enhanced penalties.

But such penalties may hurt as well as help disadvantaged minorities.
Research has shown that prior-record enhancements have a strongly disproportionate impact—minority offenders are likely to have much more
substantial records of prior conviction (Frase forthcoming, citing Minnesota and national data). Research has also shown that, for a variety of
reasons, frequent and lengthy incarceration of minority offenders com-
pounds the disadvantages suffered by these offenders, their families and
their distressed communities (Western 2006; Clear 2008; Garland, Spohn
and Wodahl 2008). For these communities there comes a tipping point,
beyond which further increase in incarceration rates causes more harm
than it prevents, setting off a vicious cycle of disadvantage, crime, incarceration, release from prison to increased disadvantage, more crime, and
so forth.

Thus, in a broader, long-term perspective, it may be both unfair (to
vulnerable minorities) and unwise (more costly for society) to impose
prior-conviction enhancements which have a strongly disparate impact on
racial-minority offenders. Social equality norms, as well as strained government budgets, dictate that such enhancements should avoid worsening
existing inequalities.

The simplest way to apply this principle would be to eliminate any
prior-record enhancement which is shown to have a strongly disparate
impact on minority offenders. US sentencing guideline systems are particularly well equipped to assess such disparate impacts. Many of these
systems have long employed the greater predictability of guideline sen-

tencing to make prison population projections which help the system set priorities in the use of scarce prison space, and avoid prison overcrowding. Some of these systems are now using the same system-modelling technology to make demographic impact assessments which reveal whether a proposed change in sentencing rules will increase racial disproportionality in prison populations (Mauer 2009).

D. CONCLUSION

Criminal history enhancements pose practical and theoretical problems of immense importance. The majority of sentenced offenders have at least one prior conviction, and many offenders have numerous priors, so the enhancement issue arises frequently and has the potential greatly to increase sentence lengths and inmate populations.

Such enhancements present an especially serious theoretical problem under a retributive model. Some of the desert-based theories thus far proposed seem capable of justifying only a modest degree of enhancement. Since substantial prior-record enhancements are frequently employed in many jurisdictions it is doubtful that judges, prosecutors, legislators and other sentencing policymakers will accept a retributive theory that would invalidate much of current practice. Other retributive rationales go too far in the opposite direction, and could be cited to justify even the most extreme prior record enhancements. Thus, the challenge, for retributive theorists is to formulate a theory or theories giving prior record a more-than-modest role while at the same time drawing firm outer limits that prohibit very substantial enhancements. The further challenge is to translate these theories into fairly simple, workable formulas suitable for application in practice. Judges, especially those who sentence a high volume of repeat offenders, have limited time, and limited available data, to make highly nuanced, case-specific enhancement decisions.

This chapter reviews retributive theories of prior-record enhancement and concludes that none provides a suitable basis to justify but also place clear limits on more-than-modest, desert-based enhancements; a better approach would be to view these enhancements as operating within offence-based desert, under a limiting retributive model. The chapter then suggests three possible formulas to implement such enhancements:

1. Prohibit enhancement above the statutory maximum for the most serious current offence. Admittedly, this suggestion is likely to face strong opposition in many jurisdictions—even with an exception for 'second-and-subsequent' statutes, it makes a frontal assault on habitual-offender laws which are strongly supported by many policymakers (especially those subject to electoral politics), even though (or perhaps, because?) such laws

are not actually applied to many offenders. If faced with such opposition, the next formula might be proposed instead.

2. Allow enhancement above the maximum for the most serious current offence on a theory of 'reserved desert' from previous sentencings. This formula assumes, of course, that courts can determine what the maximum deserved penalty is for any given offender (based solely on his offence(s)), for both current and prior crimes. It further assumes that actual sentences are usually less than the maximum deserved, at least for offenders with little or no prior record. In addition, the proposal would require a prospective restructuring of sentencing procedures, to make it clear that the reserved desert is part of the prior-crime sentence, and that the offender is not later being resentenced for the prior crime in violation of double-jeopardy principles.

3. Allow enhancement within a range of deserved penalties for the crime(s) of conviction. This approach could be used in systems without sentencing guidelines, but would work much better with them. Unlike most existing guidelines systems, however, the top of each range would not exceed the bottom of the range for offences in the next-highest severity level. Within each guideline offence-severity range, the recommended 'typical-case' sentence would depend on the extent of the offender's prior record, but sentences could be adjusted up or down based on any relevant sentencing factors. Since each guideline severity range states the minimum and maximum desert for a typical offence, judges could sentence below the range or above it (up to the statutory maximum for that crime) upon a finding of atypically mitigated or aggravated desert. Consistent with the limiting retributive model, judges could grant further, conditional leniency by suspending the execution of the sentence subject to compliance with probation terms.

This chapter also argues that prior-record enhancements should be further limited by utilitarian proportionality principles. Two such principles were discussed: ends–benefits, and alternative-means proportionality. Each of these limiting principles operates independently of the other, and also independently of retributive proportionality limits—a sentence is deemed excessive and unjustified if it violates any of the three principles. One important value of utilitarian limits on prior-record enhancements is that they can compete directly with utilitarian arguments in favour of such enhancements. Utilitarian proportionality thus serves to limit excessive penalties even when policymakers reject or minimise desert limits or when there is disagreement about how to define or apply such limits.

Finally, the chapter argues that prior-record enhancements must be limited, for reasons both of fairness and social cost, when they are found to have a disparate impact on socially disadvantaged racial or ethnic minority offenders. To the extent that prior-record enhancements improve crime-control effectiveness, they benefit these disadvantaged groups, at least in the short run (since crime rates tend to be higher in the communities where these groups live). But accumulating research is showing that, in the long run, harsh criminal sentences only compound the disadvantage of these individuals, their families and their communities. And harsh sentences are especially likely to be imposed on minority offenders, in part because such offenders have more extensive prior-conviction records. It will be difficult, of course, to define the precise tipping point where prior-record sentencing enhancements shift from helping to worsening social inequalities. But the burden should be on those who would defend any enhancement which is shown to have a disparate impact on disadvantaged racial or ethnic minorities.

REFERENCES

Ashworth, A (2005) *Sentencing and Criminal Justice*, 4th edn (Cambridge, Cambridge University Press).

Bagaric, M (2000) 'Double Punishment and Punishing Character: The Unfairness of Prior Convictions' 19 *Criminal Justice Ethics* 10.

Bennett, C, 'More to Apologize For: Can We Find a Basis for the Recidivist Premium in the Communicative Theory of Punishment?' (this volume).

Clear, T (2008) 'The Effects of High Imprisonment Rates on Communities' 37 *Crime and Justice. A Review of Research* 97.

Fletcher, G (1978) *Rethinking Criminal Law* (Boston, Little, Brown).

Frase, RS (1990) 'Comparative Criminal Justice as a Guide to American Law Reform: How Do the French Do It, How Can We Find Out, and Why Should We Care?' 78 *California Law Review* 539.

—— (2002) 'What Were They Thinking? Fourth Amendment Unreasonableness in *Atwater v City of Lago Vista*' 71 *Fordham Law Review* 329.

—— (2004) 'Limiting Retributivism' in M Tonry (ed), *The Future of Imprisonment* (New York, Oxford University Press).

—— (2005) 'Excessive Prison Sentences, Punishment Goals, and the Eighth Amendment: "Proportionality" Relative to What?' 89 *Minnesota Law Review* 571.

—— (forthcoming) 'What Explains Persistent Racial Disproportionality in Minnesota's Prison and Jail Populations?' 38 *Crime & Justice: A Review of Research*.

Garland, BE, Spohn, C and Wodahl, EJ (2008) 'Racial Disproportionality in the American Prison Population: Using the Blumstein Method to Address the Critical Race and Justice Issue of the 21st Century' 5 *Justice Policy Journal* (http://www.cjcj.org/files/racial_disproportionality.pdf).

Hampton, J (1988) 'Punishment as Defeat' in JG Murphy and J Hampton (eds), *Forgiveness and Mercy* (New York, Cambridge University Press).

Lee, Y (2009) 'Recidivism as Omission: A Relational Account' 87 *Texas Law Review* 571.

—— 'Repeat Offenders and the Question of Desert' (this volume).

Mauer, M (2009) 'Racial Impact Statements: Changing Policies to Address Disparities', http://sentencingproject.org/Admin/Documents/publications/rd_abaarticle.pdf.

Morris, N (1982) '*Madness and the Criminal Law* (Chicago, University of Chicago Press).

Reitz, KR, 'Multiple Crimes and the Crisis of Theory' (this volume).

Roberts, JV (1997) 'The Role of Criminal Record in the Sentencing Process' 22 *Crime & Justice: A Review of Research* 303.

— — (2008) 'Punishing Persistence: Explaining the Enduring Appeal of the Recidivist Sentencing Premium' 48 *British Journal of Criminology* 468–81.

— — 'First Offender Sentencing Discounts: Exploring the Justifications' (this volume).

Singer, RG (1979) *Just Deserts: Sentencing Based on Equality and Desert* (Cambridge, MA, Ballinger).

Sullivan, ET, and Frase, RS (2008) *Proportionality Principles in American Law: Controlling Excessive Government Actions* (New York, Oxford University Press).

Tonry, M, 'The Questionable Relevance of Previous Convictions to Punishment for Later Crimes' (this volume).

von Hirsch, A (1985) *Past or Future Crimes: Deservedness and Dangerousness in the Sentencing of Criminals* (New Brunswick, NJ, Rutgers University Press).

— — (1993) *Censure and Sanctions* (Oxford, Clarendon Press).

Wasik, M, and von Hirsch, A (1994) 'Section 29 Revisited: Previous Convictions in Sentencing' *Criminal Law Review* 409.

Western, B (2006) *Punishment and Inequality in America.* (New York, Russell Sage Foundation).

8

The Illusion of Proportionality: Desert and Repeat Offenders[1]

KEVIN R REITZ

THEORIES OF JUST deserts—and other retributive conceptions of proportionality in criminal sentencing—have been built on the artificially pristine model of a first-time offender convicted of a single offence (Ashworth 2005: 207, 254; von Hirsch and Ashworth 2005: app 3). The theories fall into disarray when called upon to explain how the law does or should respond to offenders who are convicted of more than one crime (Bottoms 1998: 53).

Questions of plural or multiple offending are not obscure problems occurring at the margins of criminal law. They are bread-and-butter issues that must be confronted by any philosophy of criminal punishment. The majority of criminal cases across the United States involve multiple charges, and the majority also involve defendants with criminal histories (US Department of Justice, Bureau of Justice Statistics 2006: 3, 12). We find similar patterns in England and Wales, Australia, and New Zealand (Roberts 2008: 95; Lovegrove 2004). Plural offending is in fact the norm—the true paradigm case for criminal punishment. Theory failure in the realm of plural offending therefore has enormous practical implications.

The analytical framework for this chapter, and perhaps its main contribution to the debate, is to insist that any theoretical approach to the subject of plural offending in one context, to be defensible, must be consistent with the approach taken in a different context. Specifically, any construct for the law's actual or recommended response to offenders sentenced for multiple current counts of conviction must be built on

[1] I am grateful for comments from Richard Frase and Michael Tonry, and for many ideas generated at a workshop hosted by the University of Toronto's Centre of Criminology, a colloquium on 'The Role of Previous Convictions in Criminal Sentencing' hosted by Cambridge University, and a seminar on 'Repeat Offending' held at the University of Oxford.

premises compatible with those used to support the actual or recommended response to offenders with prior convictions. This test of theory validity has, to my knowledge, never before been employed. The related subjects of 'multiple' and 'repeat' offenders have each generated a small stand-alone literature, but are almost never considered together in the same mental space (see Jareborg 1998: 129; Roberts 2008: 180–81).

A. DESCRIPTIVE HEADACHES

The descriptive paradox is as follows: when plural offending comes to the courts in the form of prior criminal convictions, the quantum of punishment dispensed over successive prosecutions tends to explode in severity. When plural offending manifests as multiple counts of conviction, the quantum of punishment for successive crimes tends to collapse in severity.

Often, a single criminal transaction can generate numerous formal charges. To avoid distraction, this chapter concerns itself with multiple-count prosecutions in which individual counts represent distinct crimes, separable from other counts. I will assume there are large numbers of multi-count cases in which the individual charges are inarguably distinct from one another, much in the same way that prior convictions are ordinarily seen as distinct from the charges in a current prosecution. I may be too fastidious in limiting my analysis to unambiguously separable offences in multi-count cases. Austin Lovegrove found that there was little difference in judges' tendency to give a 'bulk discount' for multiple counts in same-transaction and separate-transaction cases (Lovegrove 2004). Andrew Ashworth has disparaged the distinction as irrelevant to desert analysis (Ashworth 2005).

B. WHAT SENTENCERS APPEAR TO BE DOING

One window into sentencing practices in US jurisdictions is provided by sentencing guidelines—in the 20 states where they exist (see American Law Institute 2007: 54–55). Because judges comply with the presumptions or recommendations of their state's sentencing guidelines most of the time, the guidelines are fair indicators of what actually happens in the majority of sentencing hearings (see Roberts 1997). The guidelines are also primary evidence of the intentions of the lawmakers who created them.

US guidelines usually include detailed provisions for the treatment of prior convictions as sentencing factors. On the question of multiple counts, US systems of guidelines tend to be less directive. In multi-count cases, some systems of guidelines place legal constraints on judges' discretion to impose consecutive sentences, or limits on the total severity of consecutive sentences, while some guidelines states allow judges unfettered choice in the matter (see eg *Oregon v Ice* 2009).

For purposes of illustration, I will focus on one jurisdiction that bears similarity to of a number of US states that use such guidelines.[2] Washington State's guidelines employ a familiar two-axis grid in which crime seriousness and prior convictions define the presumptive penalty for each case (see von Hirsch et al 1987). Study of the grid's application to plural offenders provides much provocative information. Washington is a state that has addressed punishment ranges in multi-count cases in a fairly specific way, so we can generate side-by-side comparisons of the treatment of criminal history and multiple current convictions as sentencing factors.[3]

Let us start with a simple case of two offenders who each have committed two armed robberies. For convenience we will treat the robberies as fungible. None of the offences, from a judge's perspective, would seem aggravated from the ordinary case, and none of the offenders exceptionally culpable.

Suppose Robber No 1 is to be sentenced following convictions for both crimes in a single prosecution. Robber No 2, in contrast, will be punished in two separate proceedings, each involving a single count.

Under the Washington Sentencing Guidelines, the 'presumptive' sentence following Robber No 1's single conviction is 48 months in prison.[4] For a single count alone, the presumptive penalty would have been 36

---

[2] I have made calculations, of the kind summarised in Tables 1–4 below, for other guidelines states such as Minnesota and Kansas. Total punishment disparities of the kind observed in Washington arise in the other states, although the magnitude of disparities in specific scenarios varies greatly. Kansas, for example, puts greater weight on criminal history than Washington or Minnesota. As a result, in Kansas compared to the other two states, total punishments in serial prosecutions diverge even more sharply from multi-count prosecutions for equivalent offences.

[3] Also, because Washington has a 'determinate' sentencing system, ie one that does not give a paroling authority the power to set actual prison durations, there is a predictable relationship in prison cases between the guideline sentence and the judicially imposed sentence, on the one hand, and the prison term actually served by the offender, on the other. In 'indeterminate' states, in contrast, knowledge of the sentence imposed generally provides little basis to predict the time that will in fact be served. That cannot be known until the parole board's discretionary release decision occurs, often years after the courtroom sentencing (see generally Reitz 2004).

[4] See Washington Sentencing Guidelines Commission, *Adult Sentencing Manual 2008* (2008: I-2, table 1, 'Sentencing Grid for Crimes Committed After July 24, 1999'; ibid: I-4, table 2, indicating that first-degree robbery is ranked at 'seriousness level' IX on the grid of guidelines). Washington's sentencing code provides that, in most instances, multiple counts of conviction are to be sentenced concurrently, although each count adds something to the presumptive penalty. The most serious count is treated as the primary offence, and additional counts are scored as criminal history under the guidelines. See Rev Code Wash § 9.94A.589 (2009). Although the presumptive sentence for an armed robber with one previous felony conviction is 40 months, the guideline grid indicates that a sentencing judge may impose any sentence from 36 to 48 months without 'departing' from the guidelines. Under Washington law, a departure from the guidelines requires a finding by the judge of an aggravating or mitigating circumstance that provides a 'substantial and compelling reason' for imposing a punishment above or below the presumptive range. See Rev Code Wash § 9.94A.535 (2009).

months.[5] The second robbery conviction adds 12 months. The fact that the second robbery is met with less punishment than the first is an illustration of what has been called a 'bulk discount' for multiple offenses (Ashworth 1995: 95).

For Robber No 2, the first of two convictions yields a presumptive sentence of 36 months in prison. Upon the second conviction, because the offender has one prior felony conviction, the presumptive sentence is boosted to 48 months. The first robbery, now counted as criminal history, adds 12 months.[6] This is an example of what has been called the 'recidivist premium'.

If we keep a balance sheet of penalties applied to Robber No 2, we can assign 48 months to the first robbery (36 months in the first proceeding and 12 in the second), and 36 months to the second robbery. Running totals of the punishments dispensed are displayed in Table 1. If we believe that Robber No 1's total punishment was 'proportionate' to his crimes, then it is awkward to maintain that Robber No 2 also received a proportionate total.

Table 1. Two robbers, two offences each, one versus two prosecutions

	Punishment for first crime	Punishment for second crime	Total punishment
Robber No 1 (1 case)	36 months	12 months	48 months
Robber No 2 (2 cases)	48 months	36 months	84 months

Moving to more complex cases under Washington law, the problems in need of explanation become even more striking. Suppose each robber committed three identical robberies, but Robber No 1 was sentenced for all three in a single case, while Robber No 2 was sentenced in three successive cases. Table 2 displays the balance sheet of presumptive sentences.

---

[5] A second conviction for a violent felony results in an 'offender score' of 2 under the Washington guidelines. See Rev Code Wash § 9.94A.525 (2009); *Washington Adult Sentencing Manual 2008*, at III-195 (Offense Reference Sheet for Robbery, First Degree).

[6] In some legal frameworks the courts have found it important to deny that the recidivist premium is in fact a punishment 'for' the prior offence, preferring to say that the premium is part of the penalty 'for' the current offence, which may be viewed as more serious in light of the defendant's past criminality. In the United States, for example, such a formulation is necessary to avoid the constitutional proscription of double punishments in the double-jeopardy clause, US Const Amend 5. See *United States v Witte*, 515 US 589 (1995). However one views attributions of this kind, there is no question that the existence of each prior conviction is the but-for cause of a specific increment of severity within the recidivist premium.

Table 2. Two robbers, three offences each, one versus three prosecutions

	Punishment for first crime	Punishment for second crime	Punishment for third crime	Total punishment
Robber No 1 (1 case)	36 months	12 months	12 months	60 months
Robber No 2 (3 cases)	60 months	48 months	36 months	144 months

One might say that Robber No 1 is met with *collapsing* desert for his successive crimes, while Robber No 2 experiences *exploding* desert with each new offence.

Other scenarios only add to the muddle. Offenders frequently come to sentencing with multiple counts of current convictions *and* criminal history. Table 3 assumes the following facts: Robber No 1 has committed three identical robberies sentenced over two proceedings. In the first case, he was prosecuted for only one of the crimes. In the second case, he was prosecuted for the second and third robberies together. Robber No 2 has likewise committed and been sentenced for three robberies over two cases, except that No 2's first case involved two counts, and his second case only one.

Table 3. Two Robbers, Three Offences Each, Two Prosecutions Each, Escalating versus Declining Patterns of Offending

	Punishment for first crime	Punishment for second crime	Punishment for third crime	Total punishment
Robber No 1 (Escalating)	48 months	36 months	12 months	96 months
Robber No 2 (Declining)	48 months	24 months	36 months	108 months

Oddly enough, the offender with increasing numbers of convictions in successive prosecutions receives the lighter total punishment. This is mathematically inevitable, however, given the twin effects of exploding desert for criminal history and collapsing desert for multiple convictions.

The mathematical distortion increases as criminal careers get longer and more complex. Table 4 compares total punishments for (1) an armed robber sentenced on one count, then two, then three in three successive proceedings, and (2) an armed robber with three, then two, then one.

Table 4. Two Robbers, Six Offences Each, Three Prosecutions Each, Escalating versus Declining Patterns of Offending

                              Total punishment

Robber No 1 (Escalating)   246 months (20 years, 6 months)

Robber No 2 (Declining)   462 months (38 years, 6 months)

The end results in total punishments are hugely disparate. They suggest a policy favouring heavy penalties for the robber who is de-escalating his criminal behaviour across cases, and/or a discount for the robber who is speeding up. A sensible rationale is not immediately obvious[7]

The available evidence suggests that Washington is no outlier in its approach to plural offending. It does not differ markedly from other US states or other English-speaking countries in the basic patterns of sentences imposed on plural offenders. Julian Roberts has found legal or statistical evidence of a recidivism premium (with different weightings) across US systems of guidelines and in such diverse countries as England and Wales, Canada, Australia (New South Wales), Finland, Sweden, the Netherlands, Italy, Korea, Israel, Turkey, India, Ghana and China (Roberts 2008: 102–03; Roberts 1997: 305–06, 309, 346). He reported that, 'After seriousness of the crime, criminal history of the offender is the most important determinant of sentence severity in common-law jurisdictions' (Roberts 1997: 12). One mission of the Canadian Sentencing Commission of the late 1980s was the (unsuccessful) attempt to mute the harsh impact of the recidivist premium (Canadian Sentencing Commission 1987;

---

[7] In fact, Table 4 does not come close to illustrating the full force of the recidivist premium in its most extreme expressions in US law. The California 'three-strikes' law—along with less potent three-strikes statutes and other habitual-offender provisions—probably marks the far end of this continuum. In one famous case, upon conviction for a current offence that would in most cases be sentenced as a misdemeanour, the defendant received a recidivist premium of a mandatory 25-year prison term without possibility of early release. *Ewing v California*, 538 US 11, 25–26 (2003) (plurality opinion) (holding that the sentence of 25 years to life imposed under state's three-strikes law, for the current offence of theft of golf clubs worth $1,200, is not grossly disproportionate under the Eighth Amendment when based on legislative 'judgment that protecting the public safety requires incapacitating criminals who have already been convicted of at least one serious or violent crime'). In another case, in which the unlucky misdemeanant was convicted of two shoplifting counts, *two* such premiums were assessed—their consecutive imposition is mandatory under the statute—so the total premium was 50 years without deductions for good time or parole. *Lockyer v Andrade*, 538 US 63 (2003) (finding no unreasonable application of clearly established Eighth Amendment proportionality law when the state imposed a mandatory prison term of 50 years to life for current offences of two counts of petty larceny arising from shoplifting of videotapes worth approximately $150). Woe betide the defendant subject to three strikes who has shoplifted on three separate occasions! That the sentences in *Ewing* and *Andrade* survived constitutional challenge illustrates the point made earlier in text, namely that theories of proportionality can be reverse-engineered to justify nearly any punishment.

see also Hogarth 2004). The bulk discount appears to be ubiquitous, as well. Nils Jareborg noted its operation in Germany, Sweden, and England and Wales (Jareborg 1998: 137). Austin Lovegrove, in the most comprehensive study of multiple-count sentencing in any jurisdiction, found the bulk discount to be *de rigueur* among sentencing judges in New South Wales (Lovegrove 2004). The precise computations of the recidivist premium and bulk discount are not by any means uniform from place to place, but their general outlines, their directionality and their comparative effects across and between cases appear to be roughly similar in many legal systems.

We may now ask whether leading desert-based theories of criminal punishment supply satisfactory explanations for the observed disparities in the treatment of plural offenders. It is not damning to a particular theory if it does not align in some respects with actual sentencing practices, of course. On the other hand, if a theory is wholly out of sync with applied law across many jurisdictions, doubts arise concerning the theory's practical value.

C. JUST DESERTS AS A DESCRIPTIVE TOOL

Just-deserts theory, perhaps the best-known deontological approach to criminal sentencing in the last 35 years, has been developed most famously by Andrew von Hirsch and Andrew Ashworth (von Hirsch 1993; von Hirsh 1985; Ashworth 2004; von Hirsch and Ashworth 2005). A central tenet of the theory is proportionality in punishment, which I will abbreviate as JDP (to denote the principle of 'just-deserts proportionality').

Von Hirsch and Ashworth have sought to use JDP to limit the sentencing impact of the recidivist premium, while allowing the premium some operation early in offenders' criminal careers. Other desert proponents such as George Fletcher, Richard Singer and Joshua Dressler would eliminate the premium entirely (Fletcher 1978: 460–66; Singer 1979: ch 5; Dressler 2001: 55).

In contrast, desert theory has generated little criticism of the bulk discount for multiple offences. There have been attempts to justify the phenomenon of collapsing desert, but no calls for change. Scholars including Ashworth and Nils Jareborg have recognised the difficulty in finding a satisfactory explanation for the bulk discount. Yet it has been treated as a problem at the margins of theory—a snag to be combed out. Anthony Bottoms captured the general attitude of the desert literature toward multi-count punishment when he wrote that it was one among other questions that 'perhaps require some revision or further development' (Bottoms 1998: 53).

No one writing from a desert perspective has sought to marry analyses of the recidivist premium and the bulk discount into a single, coherent account.

D. WORKING FROM JDP DETERMINANTS
OF CRIME SERIOUSNESS

Contemporary just-deserts theory has staked out a strong position on the appropriate retributive reference points for proportionate sanctions. As articulated by von Hirsch and Ashworth, punitive severity should vary with the seriousness of an offence, which in turn should be measured in light of (1) the harm done or risked by the offender and (2) the offender's culpability (von Hirsch 1993: 29–33; von Hirsch and Ashworth 2005; see also Roberts 2008: 78). Culpability goes primarily to the offender's state of mind when committing the offence—similar to, but more refined than, the *mens rea* doctrine in substantive criminal law (von Hirsch 1985: 71–74).[8] This is a tightly focused, snapshot view of culpability. It makes it hard to factor in, for example, whether a particular defendant grew up in such deprived circumstances that he should be spared the full measure of punishment we would give to a more advantaged defendant (von Hirsch 1993: 107–08; Ashworth 2004: 86).

Moreover, in the von Hirsch–Ashworth framework, the consideration of harm places a ceiling on penalty severity, which cannot be raised by anything having to do with culpability. Culpability comes in only to measure 'the extent to which' the offender should pay the full price in sentence severity—or only a fraction of the price—for the harm done or risked. The tight focus on the offense as the touchstone for JDP comes from benevolent impulses. Among other goals, JDP is meant to keep punishment severity in check and to ward off an alleged tendency of utilitarian, offender-based theories to result in heedless overpunishments.

E. EXPLANATIONS FOR THE RECIDIVIST PREMIUM

Let us see how well JDP holds up when looking at the case illustrations presented earlier. Starting with Table 1, can the JDP model explain the outsized punishment total for Robber No 2—175 percent of the punishment given Robber No 1?

Contemplating Robber No 2's total punishment as a stand-alone matter, the problem looks manageable. If we presume that 36 months in prison

---

[8] von Hirsch argues that culpability, for purposes of determining crime seriousness, includes refinements upon criminal law mental-state analysis, broadened consideration, beyond that in the substantive criminal law, of imperfect claims of duress, necessity, and insanity, and consideration of the actor's motives for committing the offence.

is the appropriately severe sanction for each of No 2's robberies, then simple addition yields an expected total punishment of 72 months for the two offences in two separate sentencings. There may be discomfort in explaining the additional 12 months imposed as a recidivist premium in the second case, but this is only 1/7th of the total punishment, so strict desert theory at least places us in the ballpark of observed policy and practice. Furthermore, if the JDP proponent is willing to relax the offence-centric view of culpability even slightly, she can account for the 1/7th discrepancy—or argue that it is justified but only as a smaller increment, say 1/14th, of the expected total punishment. Several notions of increasing culpability or decreasing entitlement to mitigation have been advanced to serve this limited purpose

Understandably, however, desert theorists are uncomfortable with any sizeable stretching of the culpability concept. For example, in Table 4, by Robber No 2's third sentencing, the recidivist premium under Washington law contributes a much larger share of punishment than the current conviction itself. The search for a culpability-based account for this result turns JDP on its head, suggests that open-ended culpability rather than harm has become the primary engine of severity, and opens up arguments in favour of individualisation in sentencing (based on an undisciplined view of culpability) that may yield sentencing patterns as disorderly and unconstrained as under any consequentialist approach. The best position from a JDP viewpoint, in cases of the Table 4 type, would seem to be a call for a drastic reduction in the recidivist premium for offenders with lengthy criminal histories.

In sum, current and evolving approaches to the recidivist premium in the just-deserts universe seem at first glance to be pursuing an achievable objective: one that can remain essentially faithful to JDP while tracking real-world behaviors tolerably well. As a reassuring bonus, JDP can summon prescriptions that are workable and slant in the direction of lenity.

F. THE BULK DISCOUNT

When one studies Table 1 with *both* Robber Nos 1 and 2 in view, however, serious difficulties ensue. Both offenders are accountable for identical harms, so their different total punishments are on the surface inconsistent. A bit of the gap can be closed by pulling back on the impact of the recidivist premium at No 2's second sentencing, as many have suggested. But this has limited effect. Even if we bring the premium down to, say, 4 months, the resulting differential of 48 months (Robber No 1) and 76 months (No 2) remains large. Indeed, eliminating the recidivist premium entirely cannot make the two total punishments comparable. The real source of the disparity is the bulk discount.

Holding harm per offence constant, there is no obvious harm-based rationale for the bulk discount. A strict harm-based account would require consecutive sentences for multiple counts—arithmetic rather than collapsing desert.[9] Looking back to the adaptations in JDP theory necessary to accommodate the recidivist premium, the quandary becomes worse. If we ascribe increasing culpability to repeated criminal acts, something more than additive punishments might be called for in multi-count cases. Perhaps JDP would hold the increment down, but the rationales used to address the recidivist premium are facing in the wrong direction when it comes time to address the bulk discount.

Attempts have been made to incorporate the bulk discount into the just-deserts canon, although none has held itself to a test of consistency with JDP premises in serial sentencings. Probably the best-known effort along these lines is the 'totality principle' offered by David Thomas (Thomas 1979: 56–58).[10] On this view, no matter how many offences are consolidated in a single case, punishment should not exceed the most severe sanction that could be imposed for the most serious offence. Alternatively, or supplementally, the punishment on all counts is not permitted to rise to the level of severity appropriate for a crime graded by the legislature as more serious than the most serious count of conviction. The totality rule posits a proportionality ceiling that is determined by *worst* crime or by crime *type*, not by the arithmetic logic that each quantum of offence seriousness is to be matched with a quantum of sanction severity. Ashworth describes this as a way of preserving 'a kind of overall proportionality'—a concept not defined in desert theory (Ashworth 2004: 54).

The totality principle is ingenious, but it does not withstand the test of common sense. It is implausible to say that one robbery plus ten burglaries cannot surpass the maximum seriousness threshold of one robbery, or that six sexual assaults upon different 14-year-old victims may never exceed the gravity of the most aggravated rape of a single 10-year-old. The doctrine is also indefensibly formalistic. Grading of distinctions between offences differs markedly across jurisdictions, and changes over time. Some grading separations are razor thin, while others are cavernous. In many

---

[9] People accustomed to thinking in severity/harm terms have greatest difficulty in cases of extraordinary numbers of counts, especially if each individualised harm is great. See P Bulluck, 'Defendant in Club Fire Draws a 4-Year Sentence' *New York Times* 11 May 2006 (the manager of a rock band was convicted of 100 counts of involuntary manslaughter following a nightclub fire started by a fireworks display on stage during the band's performance; the parent of one victim said, 'One year for every 25 people that died—it's crazy').

[10] Andrew Ashworth appears decidedly lukewarm to the totality principle. It is hard to know whether or not he endorses it, but if he does, it is for lack of a more satisfying rationale (Ashworth 2004: 250–54) (Ashworth calls the totality principle 'a pragmatic solution' that is 'extremely vague in its import').

codes, for many crimes, available penalties overlap significantly from one grade to the next.

Most tellingly, the totality principle fails the basic test of consistency laid down at the beginning of the chapter. When plural offending presents itself in successive prosecutions, no one pauses to think about a totality concept as integral to JDP analysis—and it is not clear how this could be done. When three or four burglaries are tried in series, for instance, the cumulative sanctions leap easily beyond the penalty for one armed robbery.

Anthony Bottoms, not convinced by the totality argument, has suggested an alternative understanding of the bulk discount as an exercise of 'mercy'. He argues that sentencing judges experience 'reluctance to exact the penalty which (on ordinary principles, treated cumulatively) is the commensurably appropriate one for [the offender convicted of many counts]'. It is not clear on Bottoms's account whether this reluctance can be theoretically justified. Nonetheless, Bottoms approves of the possibility that 'the court would exercise some mercy towards the defendant by reducing the total sentence to some degree' (Bottoms 1998: 66).

We should pause to notice the degree of understatement in Bottoms's formulation: the extension of '*some* mercy' and severity reductions in '*some* degree' adds up in many cases to vast departures from the penalties that would otherwise be derived 'on ordinary [JDP] principles'. We are not debating modest, fractional increments within overall deserved punishments, but violent implosions.

The intellectual crux of the mercy argument appears to be that judges naturally balk at the use of arithmetic desert in multi-count cases in favour of a feeling of overriding compassion for the multiple-conviction offender. JDP proponents are invited to endorse this common response. This injects an ungoverned emotional trump upon other considerations, however, and raises questions that challenge the viability of JDP: how are we to tell whether judges' emotional compunctions are reliable? How do we feed this new element into a reasonably precise scaling of proportionate penalties? How are we to limit the powerful impulses of mercy to multi-count cases, while keeping the harm-culpability model of JDP intact in other contexts? More specifically, and applying the criterion of theory consistency, why does JDP not call for mercy when judges are handing out cumulative and exploding punishments in serial prosecutions?

At base, the totality and mercy explanations fail for similar reasons. JDP cannot be applied smoothly across classes of plural offending cases without bending the theory so seriously out of shape that it is no longer JDP. In the thirty-odd years of the expanding just-deserts literature, no one has ever dwelled on this problem. Indeed, the subject of multiple current convictions—standing alone—has received extraordinarily sparing attention.

Proponents of just-deserts theory are motivated to understate or gloss over the multiple-offence problem in part because it is destabilising to the pillars of their programme. Maintaining a blind spot is preferable to everything else tumbling down. In addition, academic scholars of desert do not —in the main—toil in their chosen profession so they may argue for huge increases in criminal punishments. We would not expect the theory to be deployed to recommend significantly heavier sentences for multiple offenders than those already dispensed in the real world. If there is sharp dissonance between JDP and courtroom practice in this context, it can be overlooked as a benign discrepancy, or ranked as a matter of low priority, while to attack the bulk discount would run against deeply held policy preferences.

G. DISTINCTIONS IGNORED?

Perhaps the discussion of JDP as a descriptive tool has overlooked important distinctions between the repeat offender and the multiple offender. Some possible distinctions are discussed below under the headings of: (1) differences of timing, (2) JDP and intervening convictions and punishments, and (3) JDP as a chronologically isolated thought process.

1. Differences of Timing

Usually, but not necessarily, plural offences that come to the courts in multiple-count prosecutions will be more tightly bunched by dates of commission than plural offences distributed over a number of separate prosecutions. This is especially likely to be true with offences that are imprisonable from a first conviction—each prison stay should act as a temporal separator—and less probable for offences that would not result in confinement until the offender has built up an appreciable criminal history.

In two of the scenarios laid out in section A (see Tables 1 and 2), one would expect the offender sentenced serially to have committed his crimes over a period of many months to several years, while the defendant sentenced for all of his crimes in one proceeding may have had a much more concentrated period of criminal activity—a few months, weeks or even days. Is it possible, working within standard JDP analysis, that differences in timing can account for the large disparities in total punishment outcomes?

This does not seem likely. We are holding the harms of offences constant, so all of the theoretical work must be done through ascriptions of offender culpability. By many accounts, however, culpability should be understood to decline with longer intervals between criminal offences, while more crimes compressed within a shorter period should be seen as more blameworthy. Julian Roberts, for instance, observes that 'recency' is a widely accepted criminal history criterion in US systems and across Europe (Roberts, this volume). Likewise, crimes sufficiently in the distant past 'decay' and no longer count in the criminal history equation in most jurisdictions (Roberts 1997). Roberts also suggests that recognising a period of concentrated offending as more blameworthy than a more ponderous sequence would help the sentencing system focus on young offenders, still in an active period of their criminal careers, while not over-punishing older offenders whose careers may be winding down (Roberts, this volume). Lilia Kazemian, although not proceeding solely from JDP premises, agrees with Roberts's desert-based reasoning (Kazemian, this volume).[11]

We are not bound by these accounts, however. Andrew Ashworth proposes a 'contextual' approach to criminal history that would avoid automatic formulae such as recency and decay. In his view, the fact of repeat offending should not drive conclusions about an offender's culpability until we inquire into individualised reasons for the recidivism. Reoffending might stem from 'distress, addiction, or a person in the wrong crowd'.[12] Extrapolating, we might institute case-by-case consideration of culpability for all plural offenders in all settings. This approach could (perhaps) avoid the presumption of greater culpability for concentrated offending, but it would not supply a prima facie rule of greater culpability for widely spaced offending.

Using JDP tools to explain the paradox of exploding and collapsing punishment, it may be necessary greatly to reduce the emphasis placed on harms as retributive referents, and generously expand both the definition of and the weight given to culpability. For example, for a defendant convicted of many armed robberies in one prosecution, we might declare that we care little for aggregate harms, but choose to focus on an offender-based conclusion that the defendant has shown himself to be the type of person who commits armed robberies. If we think that an acted-upon propensity to rob is blameworthy—and we can restrict our thought process to *past* propensity if we are fearful of becoming consequentialists—this may be a promising argument.[13] Perhaps we do not care very much about

---

[11] Kazemian has also assembled data showing that, on predictive grounds, the expected length of an offender's residual criminal career declines as the time lag between the current and most recent offence grows.

[12] Andrew Ashworth, remarks at 'The Role of Previous Convictions in Criminal Sentencing: Normative and Legal Issues in International Perspective', Colloquium, Cambridge University, 9–10 May 2008.

[13] This is not altogether outlandish. John Monahan and Mary Ruggiero (1980: 150) reported experimental data showing that 106 college students equated propensity to commit crimes with increased culpability: 'Predictions of recidivism affected not only those sentences recommended on purely utilitarian grounds, as would be expected. They also had a significant and profound effect on sentences whose sole justification was to be moral culpability.'

the number of counts if we believe that most people with the defendant's propensity would tend to commit a series of offences, at least until apprehended. On this view, the number of counts in a given case is usually accidental, having more to do with luck or the efficiency of law enforcement than anything distinctive in the defendant's culpability.

This culpability-propensity approach would not require that single offenders and multiple offenders be given identical sentences. The multiple offender could be distinguished in two respects: We have hard evidence of propensity continuing over an extended time for the multi-count defendant, while we are only guessing about continuous propensity in a single-count case. Further, the multiple offender has inarguably caused the greater amount of harm—although we are now supposing harm to be a small part of the equation. On culpability-propensity reasoning, the defendant sentenced for multiple counts of armed robbery should receive a penalty that resembles, but is somewhat greater than, the robber sentenced on a single count. Judges' failure to impose consecutive punishments on most multiple offenders is explained, as are incremental increases in penalties moderated by the bulk discount.

How well does the culpability-propensity approach work in cases of serial prosecution? The one-count-at-a-time offender must continue forward, perhaps several years forward, before racking up the same number of counts of conviction as the multiple offender who gets it over with in one case. At each of the serial convictions, we must be able to say that the recidivist's culpability has increased very substantially since the last time around. Such an assessment could perhaps rest on the offender's acted-upon propensity to commit armed robberies *over a greatly extended period of time.* If the serial prosecutions have stretched over four or five years, we can reasonably conclude that the defendant has been the type of person disposed to commit armed robberies for a meaningful period of his life. As with the multi-count scenario, we choose not to care deeply about the total number of crimes—it is the longevity of the defendant's period as an outlaw that really counts. The multiple offender with tightly bunched crimes may have committed the same number of offences, and caused identical harms—maybe greater!—but during a relatively short 'bad patch' in his life course.

I do not endorse the culpability-propensity framework described here, and I doubt that JDP theorists would recommend it, either. The surrender of primary emphasis on harm, together with acceptance of an open-ended role for culpability, would obliterate much that is central to just-deserts theory, such as ordinal ranking by offence seriousness and the prospect of reasonably specific limitations on punishments in individual cases.

2. JDP and Intervening Convictions and Punishments

Reoffending post-conviction and post-sentencing is perhaps worse than reoffending without interruption by legal system actors. Arguments of this sort do appear in the literature. At one point von Hirsch embraced a 'defiance' theory that would add an increment of culpability to the offender who had been sent a moral message via conviction and sentence, yet defied authority and returned to crime. Von Hirsch later retracted this approach (this volume, ch 1), but it may be recoverable. Youngjai Lee (this volume, ch 4) suggests that the post-conviction, post-sentencing offender may have a moral obligation to make special effort to avoid future law-breaking, so that his reoffending carries greater culpability than someone else's reoffending without government interruption.

It is not necessary to pass on the merits of such arguments. Just as with the culpability-propensity theory, the culpability-extra-duty approach would be called upon to explain very large divergences in punishments between multiple and repeat offenders. Once again, in order to stretch so far, JDP would be forced to move culpability well forward of harm and the damage to JDP norms would be devastating.

In addition, the culpability-extra-duty construct cannot be turned to buttress the bulk discount. In this respect, it is a weaker tool than culpability-propensity. Who would maintain that repeat offending, in the absence of interruption by legal authorities, is attended by diminishing culpability with each new offence? Professor Bottoms once toyed with the idea of a comparative negligence theory that would ascribe some culpability to law enforcement for failing to stop a recidivist, but he rejected the idea as quickly as he raised it (Bottoms 1998). That seems correct.[14]

3. JDP as a Chronologically Isolated Inquiry

The chronological isolation viewpoint is the inverse of the longevity argument explored earlier. Instead of supposing that important residual effects on culpability survive an offender's experience of conviction and punishment, an understanding of JDP as chronologically isolated would posit that an offender's past crimes, and the legal consequences visited on him, largely or entirely cancel each other out.[15] We are thus called upon to ignore these past events when fixing a sentence today. We must think and act as if they had never occurred.

---

[14] Richard Frase informs me that French law includes exactly such a comparative negligence principle (see Frase 1990: 618–19).

[15] If we have accepted one of the many arguments in justification of the recidivist premium, then perhaps we would say that a small bit of forward-traveling culpability would not be cancelled out.

It is not intelligible on this account to keep running tallies of 'total punishments' as in Tables 1–4 above, and it is a non sequitur to critique JDP on these grounds. Never mind the overpowering importance of accumulating penalties to the offender, his family, and his community, proper determinations of JDP should always be assessed in the moment.

There may be more substance here than I perceive, but chronological isolation strikes me as a bad idea if it can be avoided. It privileges a short-sighted decisional process (like the consumer gone wild with credit card purchases) over any longer-term perspective. Nevertheless, such thinking may capture the way some desert theorists and sentencers perceive their subject. Strict desert proponents, who would prohibit the recidivist premium outright, argue openly in these terms (Fletcher 1978: 460–66; Dressler 2001: 55), although, to be fair, they were not at the time considering the application of their argument to multiple offenders.

If this is the moral universe of JDP, then fairness in punishment and distributive justice *over time* are defined away as concerns. Formal, technical fairness is maintained in the sense that every person is entitled to the same benefits and pains of a chronologically isolated sentencing theory. No attempt is made to explain the distortions in punishment experiences charted in section A. These occur outside the ambit of JDP—which has suddenly become a thin, sanitised theory unconcerned with the realities of punishment as experienced by human beings.

C. PRESCRIPTIVE SHORTFALLS

Averting our gaze from criminal courtrooms as they are, we may ask whether the harm-modified-by-culpability premises of JDP can move us toward an idealised or improved system of proportionate sentences for plural offenders. Failure in descriptive alignment may point to robustness of prescriptive power.

We will work forward from three alternative hypotheses: (1) that the sentencing of repeat offenders in separate prosecutions provides a good starting point for the derivation of an idealized JDP approach; (2) that the sentencing of repeat offenders in one consolidated proceeding provides the better starting point; or (3) that some wholly new starting point is needed. I will call these, respectively, the serial model, the consolidated model and the wild-card model.

1. Serial Model Applied to Consolidated Sentencings

JDP theory, with its focus on proportionate penalties for single offences, would seem committed to the serial model. If the seriousness of Crime X corresponds with severity of Punishment Y, then, under a pristine applica-tion of just deserts, the offender who is convicted of two identical Crime Xs in separate prosecutions may expect Punishment Y twice over. (Some deviation in punishment may be allowed, depending on one's attitude toward the recidivist premium.)

When the prescriptive thinking from serial prosecutions is mapped onto consolidated cases, however, unacceptable results follow:

For the desert purist who cannot countenance the recidivist premium, the same purity of thought suggests additive consecutive sentences in mul-tiple-count cases.

From many of the desert viewpoints that would allow a recidivist premium, the serial formula produces additive consecutive sentences in multi-count cases, plus an increment of punitive severity for increasing culpability or decreasing entitlement to mitigation.

For those who would require an intervening conviction in order to approve of the recidivist premium, the absence of such intervention in a multi-count case brings the deserved penalty back 'down' to additive consecutive sentences.

None of these results is tolerable as a matter of policy. No respectable proponent of just-deserts theory, to my knowledge, has recommended the routine use of consecutive sentences in multi-count cases.

2. Consolidated Model Applied to Serial Sentencings

Let us now suppose—without trying too hard to explain it in JDP terms—that the bulk discount afforded to multiple offenders should be our baseline for the derivation of proportionate sentences in serial pros-ecutions. This is plausible at least in the sense that proponents of JDP theory universally are comfortable with the bulk discount. They would surely want to include it in an idealised prescriptive scheme. But can any rationale for the consolidated model generate acceptable prescriptions for serial sentencings?

It challenges the imagination to picture a system in which a first-time robber is sentenced to a prison term of 18 months and, upon a second conviction, receives a sentence of 6 months. What would happen upon a third, fourth, and fifth conviction? As the number of serial sentencings grows, the penalty imposed would dwindle to zero.

Perhaps the consolidated model could be honoured in serial cases by starting off with very low penalties, allowing for the possibility that the offender will be back to court many times. In effect, the bulk discount would be awarded from earliest to latest offence. Thus, the first-time robber might receive probation and, in successive cases, 2 months, then 4 months, then 6 months, and so on. It would take quite a few prosecutions before the penalty meted out would actually reflect a crime's placement on the ordinal and cardinal desert scale.

Delivering the bulk discount backwards may sound appealing, particularly to those whose preferences lean in the direction of lighter sentences. It should be noted, however, that the appearance of lenity in the backwards-discount system might is unreliable. All depends on how the cardinal scale for severity in punishments is formulated. The backwards-discount approach is algebraically no different than a rule mandating consecutive sentences in multi-count cases.

3. Wild-Card Model?

Because so many cases involve multiple counts of conviction, usually with criminal history thrown into the mix, in permutations much more varied and complex than the basic scenarios rehearsed in this chapter (see Wasik, this volume), one begins to despair that JDP can supply useful guidance to the lawmaker or sentencer who earnestly wants to locate, or not to exceed, proportionate sentences in every case.[16]

The operative model may itself be one forged of unmanageable complexity, in concession to the confusing, irregular, kaleidoscopic packaging of plural offences that one sees routinely in the criminal courts. No sentencing judge can be expected to wrap her mind around the compound problems of desert in cases, for example, with seven current counts of conviction and eleven prior convictions, for a host of different crimes, with many stops, starts, and prior sanctions applied. Just getting the facts straight is too hard, let alone finding moral meaning in the mix.

Maybe the practical limits of what can be thought about in real-world adjudication demand a reductionist model of punishment. Jamming plural-offender scenarios into the single-case model is one way of doing this: no matter how many offences we encounter in a multi-count case, for pragmatic reasons we must root JDP analysis in the single most serious offense. Other counts can be placed under the catch-all heading of 'aggravation'. (A useful storage room for overcomplicated considerations.) In serial sentencings, we will likewise concentrate on one crime, and a JDP-appropriate punishment for that single incident. Criminal history, if admissible, may again be placed the ever-malleable aggravation category.

We appear to have accounted for everything, and sentencing judges are now given a task they can perform without becoming mental magicians. The pragmatics may be there, but such a model lacks compelling moral force. If the original motivation for the exercise was to establish *persua-*

---

[16] For different routes to a similar conclusion, see Ristroph (2006) and Zimring and Hawkins (1995: 73–75).

sive deontological constraints on punishments, the goal was leached out along the way.

D. ALTERNATIVE ROUTES TO DESCRIPTION

So far, we have not examined the many utilitarian theories that might explain the opposing phenomena of exploding and collapsing punishments in plural-offending settings. Anthony Bottoms has written that, if one is a consequentialist, it is 'not too much of a problem' to justify the bulk discount, and perhaps he would take the same view of the consequentialist asked to justify the recidivist premium (Bottoms 1998: 64). I am not at all certain this is an easy task if we require the consequentialist, as we did of the JDP theorist, to maintain consistency of analysis across consolidated and serial sentencings. At first glance, many consequentialist approaches do not look up to the task.

A serious journey through utilitarian theories—or other possible explanations of the paradoxes of plural offending—will not be undertaken here. That is a subject for a later work. Indulging in preliminary speculation, however, it appears unlikely that incapacitation theory will align very well with the bulk discount and the recidivist premium considered as a piece. While the recidivist premium may reflect the belief that offenders with lengthening criminal histories are more dangerous than those without, it is difficult to account for the failure to perceive a similar (or greater) risk of future offending in the multiple offender who has committed an equally impressive number of crimes, probably in a shorter period of time. On similar reasoning, the premium and the discount, applied across cases, are probably not sorting those offenders who most need sustained rehabilitative interventions from those who do not. The defendant who comes to court with the longest criminal history, for example, may be nearest the point of desistance on the age–crime curve.

General deterrence does not look to be a promising explanation, either. Why would society want to deter previously convicted offenders from committing a second offence with the threat of very heavy penalties, while offenders who have committed a number of crimes, but who have not been apprehended or convicted, should face receding disincentives with each offense?

At the moment, it seems to me that one must be a particular kind of consequentialist to rest comfortably with both the recidivist premium and the bulk discount. One must be devoted entirely to the goal of specific deterrence, and insensitive to meaningful limitations of retributive proportionality. Other utilitarian programmes are ruled out—along with mixed

philosophies like limiting retributivism.[17] A large descriptive gap remains
even here, however, because sentencers whose behaviour is explicable on
the specific deterrence account would probably disagree with it. In other
words, they do not experience themselves as regularly handing down undeserved punishments. We need a further explanation of the moral comfort
level of such judges and policymakers.

It may be that a description conforming to both conduct and belief
can be found in biology. Perhaps human beings are hard-wired to punish
transgressors on a specific-deterrence programme, consciously or uncon-
sciously. The same hard wiring could also be responsible for a reinforcing
sense of moral propriety. The literature of evolutionary biology posits an
instinct for 'retributive aggression' (Wilson 1988). There is some evidence
in the experimental setting that humans are wont to overpunish 'cheaters'
in role-playing games, if overpunishment is defined as assuming a cost to
oneself that is greater than any expected benefit. Because it is a net loss,
such overpunishment has been characterised as a form of altruism—in
this case explicable on group-selection theory. The punisher assumes a disproportionate personal cost in order to increase the long-term chances of
the group's survival (Hoffman and Goldsmith 2004; Henrich et al 2006;
Hauert et al 2007). One can imagine that a feeling of being on the moral
high ground would be included as part of the evolutionary programming.
(It is intriguing to think how this hypothesised hard-wiring would mani-
fest itself in the behaviour of sentencing judges, who do not personally
assume the costs of punishments they impose.)

Even if this route to description is promising, however, it is unlikely
to tell us how the law of criminal punishment *should be* arranged.[18]

E. ALTERNATIVE SOURCES OF LIMITATIONS
ON PUNISHMENT SEVERITY

This chapter does not end with prescriptions of its own. My tentative
conclusion is that theories of proportionality built on JDP-like premises
are disappointingly weak instruments. Yet I would not be prepared to
cast retributive proportionality constraints aside. They may do important
work in single-offence and single-transaction cases, and in constructing an
ordinal ranking of single-offence seriousness. They may supply guideposts
for ceilings on punishments within a schema of limiting retributivism.
(This would have to be a version of LR that does not pay much atten-

---

[17] I should note a possible exception here for limiting retributive theories that are so loose
that they have almost no bite, such as in the original Model Penal Code, which understood
statutory maximum penalties to provide adequate retributive ceilings for individual cases.
See American Law Institute 1985: 1–30).

[18] For an argument that biologically based intuitions about punishment are sound bases
for legal policy, see Robinson, Kurzban and Jones (2007).

tion to lower limits on severity, because it would permit or encourage the generous underpunishment of multiple offenders.) Generally speaking, a preference for restraint in the use of criminal punishment suggests that moral inhibitions should be consulted when possible, even if they are not reliable across the board.

If retributive theory is patchy, we need other forms of proportionality analysis, or proportionality-like limitations on penalties, all the more. Richard Frase's vision of utilitarian proportionality tests (as supplements to the deontological ones) could be a step in the right direction. In his latest writing, he further suggests that societal concerns about racial and ethnic disparities in aggregate correctional populations should translate into counsels of restraint at the policymaking level. Downstream, this would affect many case-specific outcomes (Frase, this volume).

Other systemic considerations might prove proportionality-like in their flow-down effects. It is quite familiar for students of US sentencing systems to think in terms of resource constraints as limiting, ultimately, what can be done in individual cases. Resource allocations depend on many big-picture considerations, such as the total of government revenues, popular resistance to tax increases, the feasibility of deficit spending, perceptions of costs and benefits within correctional spending, and opportunity costs outside the justice system.

The size of the total pool of correctional resources, and decisions about sub-allocations, are likewise subject to deontological critique. Many Americans are instinctively ashamed of their nation's status as world leader in incarceration rates. Although the underlying moral premises are rarely stated,[19] the US incarceration rate is widely cited (in comparison with rates in other countries) as complete proof of moral indefensibility. If these are valid moral intuitions, there may be an associated deontological cap on what a society may spend on prisons. And within the category of prison spending, there are surely humanitarian requirements of the minimal conditions of life that must be maintained for inmates. Cuts in spending intended to increase the pain of imprisonment can only go so far. Indeed, governments may have a moral obligation to spend on expensive rehabilitative treatment for prisoners, even in the face of doubts about programme efficacy (Rubin 2001). Whenever money flows toward one priority, budgetary support for the system's capacity to deliver severe punishments is diminished elsewhere.

* * *

[19] This is trenchantly observed in Zimring and Hawkins (1991: 206): 'Because [assumptions about the scale of imprisonment] are implicit rather than explicit in contemporary dialogue, there is little to suggest how decisions about appropriate penal scale might be derived. The dominant tone of the debate is the expression of strong feelings rather than the statement of particular value premises.'

In an assessment of my work as Reporter for the Model Penal Code, Robert Weisberg has written that the Code takes the intellectual approach of 'tragic skepticism' in its pursuit of forward-looking goals in the face of deep uncertainty that they can be achieved with regularity, or to the degree anyone would want (Weisberg, 2009). On this view, if it is indeed my own, most of the effort poured into sentencing and corrections is futile, but societies nonetheless have the obligation to look for ways to reduce the quotient of futility where they can.

This chapter may be heading to a similarly sceptical view of programmes that purport to deliver proportionate sentences. We may celebrate those occasions in which deontological limits can be persuasively articulated, or can be seen at work, but the larger picture remains (mostly) tragic, and in need of a more eclectic toolbox of remediations than desert theory alone can provide.

REFERENCES

American Law Institute (1985) *Model Penal Code and Commentaries, Part I: General Provisions, §§ 6.01 to 7.09* (Philadelphia, American Law Institute).

—— (2007) *Model Penal Code: Sentencing, Tentative Draft No 1* (Philadelphia, American Law Institute).

Ashworth, A (2005) *Sentencing and Criminal Justice*, 4th edn (Cambridge, Cambridge University Press).

—— (1995) *Sentencing and Criminal Justice*, 2nd edn (London, Butterworths).

Bottoms, A (1998) 'Five Puzzles in von Hirsch's Theory of Punishment' in A Ashworth and M Wasik (eds), *Fundamentals of Sentencing Theory: Essays in Honor of Andrew von Hirsch* (Oxford, Oxford University Press).

Bureau of Justice Statistics (2006) *Felony Defendants in Large Urban Counties, 2002* (Washington DC, US Department of Justice).

Canadian Sentencing Commission (1987) *Sentencing Reform: A Canadian Approach: Report of the Canadian Sentencing Commission* (Ottawa, Canadian Government Publishing Centre).

Dressler, J (2001) *Understanding Criminal Law*, 3rd edn (New York: Lexis Publishing).

Fletcher, G (1978) *Rethinking Criminal Law* (Boston, Little, Brown).

Frase, RS (1990) 'Comparative Criminal Justice as a Guide to American Law Reform: How Do the French Do It, How Can We Find Out, and Why Should We Care?' 78 *California Law Review* 539.

Hauert, C et al (2007) 'Via Freedom to Coercion: The Emergence of Costly Punishment' 316 *Science* 1905.

Henrich, J et al (2006) 'Costly Punishment Across Human Societies' 312 *Science* 1767.

Hoffman, MB and Goldsmith, TH (2004) 'The Biological Roots of Punishment' 1 *Ohio State Journal of Criminal Law* 627.

Hogarth, J (2004) *Sentencing as a Human Process* (Toronto, University of Toronto Press).

Jareborg, N (1998) 'Why Bulk Discounts in Multiple Offence Sentencing?' in AA Ashworth and M Wasik (eds), *Fundamentals of Sentencing Theory: Essays in Honor of Andrew von Hirsch* (Oxford, Oxford University Press).

Lovegrove, A (2004) *Sentencing the Multiple Offender: Judicial Practice and Legal Principle* (Canberra, Australian Institute of Criminology).

Monahan, J and Ruggiero, M (1980) 'Psychological and Psychiatric Aspects of Determinate Criminal Sentencing' 3 *International Journal of Law and Psychiatry* 143.

Oregon v Ice (2009) 129 S Ct 711 (US Supreme Court).

Reitz, KR (2004) 'Questioning the Conventional Wisdom of Parole Release Authority' in M Tonry (ed), *The Future of Imprisonment* (Oxford: Oxford University Press).

Ristroph, A (2006) 'Desert, Democracy, and Sentencing Reform' 96 *Journal of Criminal Law and Criminology* 1293.

Roberts, JV (1997) 'The Role of Criminal Record in the Sentencing Process' in M Tonry (ed), *Crime and Justice: A Review of Research*, vol 22 (Chicago, University of Chicago Press).

— — (2008) *Punishing Persistent Offenders: Exploring Community and Offender Perspectives* (Oxford, Oxford University Press).

Robinson, PH, Kurzban, R and Jones, OD (2007) 'The Origins of Shared Intuitions of Justice' 60 *Vanderbilt Law Review* 1633 (2007).

Rubin, EL (2001) 'The Inevitability of Rehabilitation' 19 *Law & Inequality* 343.

Singer, RG (1979) *Just Deserts: Sentencing Based on Equality & Principle* (Cambridge, MA, Ballinger).

Thomas, DA (1979) *Principles of Sentencing*, 2nd edn (London, Heinemann).

von Hirsch, A (1976) *Doing Justice: The Choice of Punishments* (New York: Hill & Wang).

— — (1985) *Past and Future Crimes: Deservedness and Dangerousness in the Sentencing of Criminals* (New Brunswick, NJ, Rutgers University Press).

— — (1993) *Censure and Sanctions* (Oxford, Clarendon Press).

von Hirsch, A and Ashworth, A (2005) *Proportionate Sentencing* (Oxford, Oxford University Press).

von Hirsch, A, Knapp, KA and Tonry, M (1987) *The Sentencing Commission and Its Guidelines* (Boston, Northeastern University Press,).

Weisberg, R (2009) 'Tragedy, Skepticism, Empirics, and the Model Penal Code', 61 *Florida Law Review* 797.

Wilson, EO (1988) *On Human Nature* (Cambridge, MA, Harvard University Press).

Zimring, FE and Hawkins, G (1995) *Incapacitation: Penal Confinement and the Restraint of Crime* (New York, Oxford University Press).

Zimring, FE and Hawkins, G (1991) *The Scale of Imprisonment* (Chicago, University of Chicago Press).

9

Dimensions of Criminal History: Reflections on Theory and Practice

MARTIN WASIK

A CENTRAL QUESTION addressed in this book is whether sentencing policy for persistent offenders should be based upon progressive loss of mitigation or on a recidivist premium. While the former approach has been identified as reflecting English sentencing practice at least from the 1970s onwards (Thomas 1979: 197), changes in the Criminal Justice Act 2003 are meant to move towards the second position (Home Office 2001; von Hirsch 2002). Each model can be presented schematically by way of a line on a graph to reflect the criminal record of a persistent offender. For such an offender the former theory would generate a sloping line which runs upwards for the first two or three such convictions and then flattens off, while the latter theory would produce a line which continues to slope upwards with each further such offence.

I have no doubt of the importance of this debate, but the purpose of my chapter is not to refine further either or both of these theories. It is, rather, to test the insights they provide by setting them in the context of practical issues that arise in the course of sentencing. The device employed to achieve this end is a fictional criminal record, drawn up by me, and set out below. While this fictional record is intended to be typical of many defendants who appear before the courts in England and Wales, it has been compiled in a particular way to illustrate the various points that I wish to make. In what follows I have drawn upon my own impressions from sitting as a judge in a part-time capacity in the Crown Court. The focus is therefore upon issues which arise in the Crown Court, but many of the points are relevant to the magistrates' courts and, perhaps, to other jurisdictions.

In this chapter I am mainly concerned with the defendant's previous convictions as they affect the sentencing stage of a criminal trial, but it is important to note from the outset that the record is also important at other decision-making stages of the criminal process. The defendant's record will have influenced decisions over arrest and charge, prosecution or diversion from prosecution, and whether the defendant is bailed or remanded in custody (eg Blumstein, Cohen, Roth and Visher 1986: ch 6). The criminal record may also have been relevant if the defendant entered a not guilty plea at trial, and the prosecution sought leave to lead evidence of one or more of the defendant's previous convictions under the 'bad character' provisions of the 2003 Act.[1] The document which contains the list of previous convictions is deployed at different stages of the criminal justice system, by different actors, for different purposes. For the police, a criminal record check may help to identify a suspect, for the prosecutor it may form the basis of a decision to caution rather than to prosecute, and for magistrates it will be crucial in deciding if the defendant can be released on bail or must be remanded in custody. Given that the focus of this chapter is on sentencing, I shall not expand on this general issue any further at this point (see Jackson and Wasik 2000), but I will return briefly to the question of bail a little later.

A. SOME BACKGROUND ON CRIMINAL RECORDS

Criminal records in England and Wales are compiled from data supplied by the courts, and by the police from the Police National Computer (see Thomas 2007: ch 3). They are part of the file of papers made available to the court. The list of previous convictions forms the main part of a larger set of materials known as the 'antecedents', which contains other material, such as the defendant's non-conviction disposals. These include formal cautions for adults, and reprimands and warnings for juveniles. Although these forms of diversionary disposal do not count as 'convictions' (since a 'conviction' can only be returned by a court), they are listed in a separate sheet in the antecedents, so that if the defendant later falls to be sentenced for an offence the court will know about them. As far as the use of antecedents more generally in sentencing is concerned, there is a Practice Direction[2] designed to ensure consistency in operation but, apart from that, this area is essentially a matter of convention derived from day-to-day court practice

When it comes to the sentencing stage the judge will consider the previous convictions alongside all other material relevant to the sentencing process. Typically in the Crown Court this will include, first and foremost, the full facts of the offence(s) for which the defendant is to be sentenced. When the prosecutor opens the facts at the sentencing hearing it is usual

[1] Criminal Justice Act 2003, s 101ff.
[2] *Consolidated Criminal Practice Direction*, part III.27.

to take the judge through the antecedents, drawing the judge's attention to any conviction(s) which the prosecutor regards as particularly significant. If there are many previous convictions, the prosecutor will concentrate on offences similar to the present one, to recent disposals, and to previous custodial sentences.

Second, there will usually be a pre-sentence report, prepared by a probation officer. This, in addition to setting out the defendant's background and personal circumstances, will if appropriate contain a risk assessment of the defendant and make a suggestion as to suitable sentencing outcome. The risk assessment will be based, in part, on information derived from the antecedents.

Third, there will always be a plea in mitigation, from defence counsel. If the defendant has no previous convictions, the defence will stress that point, as a key matter in mitigation. If there is a record, the defence will often offer a commentary on the previous convictions, noting any matters which might serve as mitigation, such as a slow-down in the rate, or seriousness, of offending, the existence of a recent conviction-free gap in the record, and so on.

B. BASIC PRINCIPLES

The defendant's record (or, of course, its absence) is a matter relevant to every sentencing decision made in the courts. But its role and importance has to be kept in context and in proportion. The previous convictions of the defendant are one aspect, albeit an important one, of the sentence decision-making process in England. While US sentencing guidelines use the 'criminal history score' as one of the two defining parameters of sentencing, this is not the case in England and Wales. There is no graduated scale in existence in England by reference to which a defendant's provisional sentence is adjusted upwards or downwards to take the record into account. Recently it has been proposed that the impact of previous convictions on sentencing in each case should be made more explicit and clearly structured.[3] That suggestion is resisted by the judiciary and has been shelved for the moment, but the issue might well return when the new body responsible for issuing sentencing guidelines is set up and starts its work.[4]

For the moment, then, there is little by way of substantive law or sentencing guidelines on previous convictions in sentencing, and it is necessary to glean the existing principles from commentators and from occasional

[3] Sentencing Commission Working Group (2008) paras 3.12–3.18 and Annex I.
[4] Provisions for the setting up of a Sentencing Council (to replace the existing Sentencing Guidelines Council and Sentencing Advisory Panel) are set out in the Coroners and Justice Act 2009.

judicial comments in appellate cases. Long-standing Court of Appeal cases say that while a criminal record deprives the offender of personal mitigation which he would have had if he had been a first offender, the sentence for the new offence should not be excessive, and should be kept in proportion to the seriousness of the latest offence.[5] Even if a more severe sentence is required for a persistent offender, the rate of escalation should be gradual, and proportion should be retained. Old offences on the record, and offences falling into a different category from the latest offence, may be of little or no relevance, especially if they were committed years ago. The number of past convictions is obviously important, as is their similarity to, or difference from, the new offence. The persistence of the offender, as measured by the shortness of gaps between his recorded offences, and the nature of the defendant's response to previous sentences, are also relevant. All these points are well known by practitioners, and routinely form the basis of representations made by counsel to the sentencing judge.

The law, as it has developed since the first statutory provision on the relevance of previous convictions was enacted in 1991, has been considered in other chapters of this book. Suffice it to say here that, despite academic interest,[6] none of the versions of statutory guidance on previous convictions have generated any significant appellate case-law.[7] The current provision is to be found in section 143(2) of the Criminal Justice Act 2003:

> In considering the seriousness of an offence ('the current offence') committed by an offender who has one or more previous convictions, the court must treat each previous conviction as an aggravating factor if (in the case of that conviction) the court considers that it can reasonably be so treated having regard, in particular, to—
>
> (a) the nature of the offence to which the conviction relates and its relevance to the current offence; and
>
> (b) the time that has elapsed since the conviction.

The subsection has not been the subject of appellate consideration, and the Sentencing Guidelines Council has issued no guidelines with regard to it, although the Sentencing Advisory Panel has consulted on the issue.[8] From my own experience in practice I can report that I have never been addressed by prosecution or defence counsel on the terms of that section. It has never once been mentioned. The impression from everyday practice

---

[5] See eg *Queen* (1981) 3 Cr App R (S) 245, where it was said that nobody should be punished again for offences which had already been dealt with, and *Carlton* (1994) 15 Cr App R (S) 335, where it was said that previous convictions were relevant because the offender could no longer pray in aid his good character.

[6] Apart from the current volume, see Roberts (2008) and Roberts and von Hirsch (2009).

[7] For discussion of earlier versions, see Wasik and Taylor (1993: 33–38) and Wasik and von Hirsch (1994).

[8] Sentencing Advisory Panel (2008) paras 42–60.

is that the section has had little, if any, impact, or at least that it has not taken matters in a different direction from earlier practice.

I turn now to consider the antecedents of John Villan (JV), whose latest offence is before us for sentence today at Anytown Crown Court. Since dates are important, for these purposes 'today' is Monday, 3 August 2009. The case falls to be sentenced at the end of a typical Crown Court list. Before turning to this case, the judge has dealt with two bail applications, three plea and case management hearings, and five sentences.

As explained above, the list of previous convictions (Table 1) will have formed part of the judge's papers in the case of JV. In order to keep matters simple I have included no non-conviction disposals. Such disposals are generally removed from the criminal record after five years, and

Table 1

JOHN VILLAN
This printout is produced for the use of the court, defence and probation service only and must not be disclosed to any other party. Your attention is drawn to the provisions of the Rehabilitation of Offenders Act 1974.

SURNAME: Villan
FORENAME: John
DATE OF BIRTH: 1.4.1982
ADDRESS: 1 Oddball Street
                Anytown
                Anyshire

CONVICTION(S)

(1) 2.5.1995 *Anytown Youth Court*

1. Possession of offensive weapon in a public place	Supervision order 12 months Forfeiture of kitchen knife. Bound over 12 months (parent) in sum of £100
2. Handling stolen goods (undertaking to, or assisting in retention etc)	Fine £50 (parent)

(2) 1.6.2000 *Anytown Magistrates Court*

1. Handling stolen goods	Fine £150 Costs £75
2. Interference with vehicle	no separate penalty

(3) 5.9.2000 *Anytown Magistrates Court*

1. Burglary and theft—Dwelling	Conditional Discharge 1 year Compensation order £300

continued

Table 1—*continued*

(4) 15.6.2001 *Anytown Crown Court*

1. Obtaining property by deception 2 months DYOI
(+ 15 tic)

2. Theft (from motor vehicle)   1 month DYOI (consecutive)

3. Breach of conditional discharge   1 month DYOI (consecutive)

4. Failure to surrender to bail   no separate penalty

(5) 13.1.2002 *Anytown Crown Court*

1. Racially aggravated assault   9 months DYOI
occasioning actual bodily harm

2. Use disorderly behaviour or   1 month DYOI (concurrent)
threatening/abusive/insulting words

(6) 10.3 2003 *Anytown Magistrates Court*

1. Threat to damage or destroy   Community Punishment Order, 150 hours
property

2. Theft from motor vehicle   Fine £200, Restitution order

3. Failure to surrender to bail   Fine £100

(7) 1.5.2007 *Anytown Crown Court*

1. Burglary and theft (dwelling)   12 months imprisonment, suspended for
(+ 1 tic)   2 years, supervision requirement, alcohol
                                      treatment requirement, 100 hours
                                      unpaid work requirement

2. Attempted burglary (dwelling)   4 months imprisonment, suspended for
                                      2 years, concurrent

since JV is now 27 years old they would almost certainly now be of little relevance. Near the beginning of the document there is mention of the Rehabilitation of Offenders Act. At one time, if there were convictions on a criminal record which were 'spent' under the terms of the Act, they were stamped over with the word 'SPENT'. This practice seems now to have ceased, and it is left to counsel or the judge to identify spent convictions, if there are any. The convictions acquired by JV in 1995 are spent, but little is likely to be made of this point in practice. I have assumed that the record itself is not factually in dispute. As with any form of record, there can be errors and omissions (see further Thomas 2001, 2007: ch 3). A defendant may assert that a particular conviction appearing in the list does not belong to him and, if that entry is important to the sentencing exercise, the matter will have to be adjourned for this to be resolved.[9] The prosecution will have to prove the relevant conviction.[10] Recently I had to adjourn a sentencing hearing because a brother claimed that a conviction attributed to him actually belonged to his sibling. Problems can be compounded by defendants with similar names or (a common problem) defendants who have several aliases. I have also assumed that there are no outstanding matters against the defendant, such as a prosecution pending in the magistrates' court. Given all these assumptions, the sentencing exercise should be relatively straightforward.

C. WHAT COUNTS IN A CRIMINAL RECORD? WHO IS A FIRST OFFENDER?

Consider the form and shape of JV's record. It is, of course, an invented criminal record, but it is designed to reflect what experience indicates is typical. The record is quite long. Statistics show that one-quarter of offenders appearing for sentence have 15 or more previous convictions (Ministry of Justice 2009). The list of previous convictions is an official list of recorded offending and, of course, may be very different from the actual rate of offending by the offender. Criminological research shows that self-reported offending is at a consistently higher rate than that suggested by official records. It also shows that the onset of offending as revealed by self-report data is generally earlier than criminal records would suggest. Of course while self-report records, arrest records and non-conviction data are important for criminological purposes, when it comes to sentencing, reliance can properly only be placed on convictions, since only they are the outcome of a criminal process operating to proper standards of evidence and proof (Weis 1986). There is an exception in the dangerousness provisions, and I will return to that point later.

Focusing on the official record, then, there are some obvious questions about its length and composition. The theory of progressive loss of mitigation is built around the idea of a reduction in sentence severity for first offenders, and some lesser discount for the first few convictions, with a flattening off thereafter. This assumes that it is clear who counts as a first-time offender, a second-time offender and so on. An obvious question is: what counts? Is it the number of previous convictions recorded against the defendant, or the number of previous court appearances? In JV's criminal record there are 7 previous court appearances, but 16 offence convictions, or 31 offence convictions if the offences taken into consideration are also

[9] The relevant *Practice Direction* states that any points of accuracy arising from the antecedents should be resolved at least seven days before the hearing date, at which point the police will check the record again and add any recent convictions.

[10] Police and Criminal Evidence Act 1984, s 73

included. A similar computation issue besets the recidivist premium, since by that approach there is a world of difference for sentence today depending on whether JV has 7, 16 or 31 previous convictions.

So, what counts as a previous conviction, and who can be regarded as a first offender? There are different approaches. From the sentencer's point of view, the most important guide is that of the Sentencing Guidelines Council (SGC), which bases all of its sentencing guidelines on the starting point of a 'first-time offender' convicted after a trial. The SGC defines a 'first-time offender' as someone who does not have a conviction which, by virtue of section 143(2) of the CJA 2003, must be treated as an aggravating factor. This formula seems to disregard all non-conviction disposals and to take the view that some previous convictions (where not 'relevant' or 'recent', to paraphrase section 143(2)) should be disregarded, too. On the other hand, the official Sentencing Statistics, published by the Ministry of Justice, are ambivalent on this point, sometimes providing figures based purely on previous convictions, but most of the tables in the relevant chapter on criminal history include cautions, reprimands and warnings as well (Ministry of Justice 2009). As far as the competing theories of progressive loss of mitigation and recidivist premium are concerned, all this is rather important, because we need to know what to count, and at what stage we should start counting.

In Andrew von Hirsch's writings on this topic he proposes that a degree of tolerance should be extended to the first offender, who has 'lapsed':[11]

> A transgression (even a fairly serious one) should be judged less stringently when it occurs against the background of prior compliance. The idea is that the inhibitions of even an ordinarily well-behaved person can fail in a moment of weakness or wilfulness. Such a temporary breakdown of self-control is a kind of human frailty for which some understanding should be shown.
>
> (von Hirsch, Ashworth and Roberts 2009: 158)

This notion of a 'lapse' suggests a genuine first offence[12] committed against a blameless past. When such cases arise in practice they stand out from the rest. Defence counsel will make much of the fact that her client has never been in trouble before, and this is one of the strongest arguments available for personal mitigation. Other cases are not so clear. Many defendants have non-conviction disposals, such as a caution. A prerequisite of a caution is that the defendant admits that he committed the offence. It might therefore be argued that such a defendant on their first court appearance is not blameless, nor is it a true 'lapse'. Perhaps we can agree that the first court appearance for any defendant is a matter of special significance, even if he has previously been cautioned, and we

---

[11] von Hirsch, Ashworth and Roberts (eds) (2009) 158.

[12] Of course if the genuine first offence is nonetheless extremely serious, such as a murder, it cannot helpfully be characterised as a lapse. I do not discuss this point further here.

could stretch a point and still treat the first offence in court as a 'lapse'. This is in line with the SGC formulation. We are counting 'convictions', and that excludes non-court disposals.

There is a further complication. Often when a defendant appears for sentence it is for more than one offence, as is the case on JV's record. The criminal record, as it is presented in court, has a front 'summary' sheet on which separate figures are provided for the number of previous court appearances and the total number of offences sentenced (but not taken into consideration) on those occasions. These numbers can be very different. On one recent occasion I had to sentence a defendant on a single occasion for more than 30 different offences, spread over five indictments, committed when he was at large during an 18-month period. So, should we be counting the number of offences for which the defendant has previously been convicted, or the number of court appearances on which he has been sentenced? The official statistics rely upon court appearances. If the offender has been convicted of several offences on one occasion, it is nonetheless regarded as one previous conviction, with the most severe sentence imposed on that occasion being the one which is recorded. This is consistent with a number of specific sentencing provisions in English law. A section in the 2003 Act deals with the case of a 'persistent offender' who has previously been fined.[13] This provision deems a persistent offender to be someone who has 'on three or more previous occasions . . . had passed on him a sentence consisting only of a fine'. Here, it is the number of occasions which counts. Similarly, the 'three-strikes' rule in domestic burglary (on which more, below) requires that the offender must have been convicted of domestic burglary and sentenced for domestic burglary sequentially, on three different court appearances. For the purposes of this rule a defendant dealt with for several domestic burglaries on the same occasion incurs just a single 'strike'.[14] So, again, what matters is the number of court appearances, and not the number of past offences. But if an offender is sentenced on his first court appearance for several offences, can this be described convincingly as a 'lapse'? This is of some practical importance, since it can often be a matter of chance whether different offences lead to sequential court appearances or to a single one. If different offences come to light at or around the same time, the usual practice is for these to be gathered together for sentence on a single occasion, allowing the sentencer to form an overall view. If, say, three offences are dealt with on the defendant's first court appearance, again the theory must assume that these together count as the 'lapse',

---

[13] Criminal Justice Act 2003, s 151; Criminal Justice and Immigration Act 2008, ss 6 and 11.

[14] It is possible for one offender to infringe the 'three-strikes' rule after committing just three burglaries, but for another offender not to infringe the rule after committing many more such offences.

whether or not they were all part of the same piece of criminal behaviour. The theory of progressive loss of mitigation says that tolerance is likely to be exhausted after (say) three convictions. This surely cannot include three offences dealt with on the same occasion. The idea of a 'lapse' therefore seems better associated with the number of court appearances, but the competing tensions are obvious.

The interplay between the number and timing of offences, the number of court appearances and the relevance of non-court disposals is illustrated by a group of Court of Appeal decisions in relation to sentencing juveniles. The relevant provision states that a detention and training order cannot be imposed on a young offender aged under 15 at the time of conviction, unless he is a 'persistent offender'.[15] The term 'persistent offender' is not defined. In *S(A)*,[16] the young offender pleaded guilty to three counts of robbery, two counts of possession of an offensive weapon (a kitchen knife) and one count of false imprisonment. The offences were committed over two days. Despite the fact that the defendant had never appeared in court before the Court of Appeal upheld the judge's finding that he was a 'persistent offender', and that a custodial sentence of two years was appropriate. In *C*[17] a 14-year-old boy had committed one burglary and one offence of allowing himself to be carried in a vehicle which had been taken without consent. He had been granted bail in respect of those matters and, while on bail, had committed two further burglaries and an offence of aggravated vehicle taking. Again, despite the absence of any previous court appearances, the Court of Appeal upheld the decision of the judge to impose a detention and training order for 12 months on C, as a persistent offender. It is perhaps not surprising, in light of these decisions, that in the same context the Court of Appeal held[18] that non-conviction disposals appearing on a juvenile's record are relevant to the question of whether he qualifies as a 'persistent offender'.

D. A MIXED OFFENDING PATTERN

JV's record is mixed, in the sense that he is not a specialist in offending. Both the sentencing statistics, based on official records, and longitudinal research on criminal careers, show that this is the norm. It is common in practice to see a record which contains a mix of property offences, motoring offences, public disorder and lesser violent offences. Versatility is usual throughout offending careers (Piquero, Farrington and Blumstein 2007). If we seek specialism, the offences most commonly committed

---

[15] Powers of Criminal Courts (Sentencing) Act 2000, s 100(2)(a).
[16] [2001] 1 Cr App R (S) 62.
[17] [2001] 1 Cr App R (S) 415.
[18] In *AD* [2001] 1 Cr App R (S) 202.

by offenders who have three or more previous convictions for the same
offence include burglary (38 per cent), drunkenness (30 per cent), failing
to surrender to bail (29 per cent), driving while disqualified (29 per cent)
and, especially, theft from a shop (60 per cent) (Ministry of Justice 2009:
130–31). While offenders who confine their offending to a particular type
of offence do sometimes come before the courts, they are likely to prompt
further inquiry by virtue of being out of the ordinary. Sometimes specialisation indicates a 'professional' dedication to crime as a way of life,[19]
and sometimes it may suggest a form of personality or mental disorder.[20]

As explained above, a central question in this book is whether sentencing policy for persistent offenders should be based upon progressive
loss of mitigation or a recidivism premium. Each model can be presented
schematically, the former theory producing a line which moves upwards
for the first two or three such convictions and then flattens off, the latter
theory producing a line which continues to slope upwards with each
further such offence. Both these lines are based on the (unarticulated)
assumption that we are dealing with a persistent specialist offender. Such
offenders are rarely encountered in practice, and so it is hard to discern
either of these theories being reflected in practice.

One point is clear, however. Neither theory allows for what may seem
counterintuitive but which commonly happens in practice—the imposition of *lower* sentences on persistent offenders. Criminological research
shows that criminal careers tend to increase in seriousness over time,
before tailing off in most cases, but there is rarely a clear and obvious
pattern or progression. Offending fluctuates in volume and seriousness.
In a record where seriousness does vary, a reduction in seriousness of the
latest offence will tend to produce a lower sentence, despite the record.
A persistent burglar who is now before the court for a minor motoring
infraction will be sentenced as a motoring offender and not as a burglar.
JV's offending has gone up and down in seriousness, and so has the
nature of the sentences which he has received over the years. But there
is more to this point. A persistent offender who has received a range of
financial, community and custodial sentences in the past is by no means
certain to receive a sentence at the same level as last time (as suggested
by the theory of progressive loss of mitigation) or a more severe sentence
(as suggested by the recidivism premium). An offender with 15 or more
previous convictions is very likely to have served a custodial sentence
already, but in 2007, although 40 per cent of offenders with 15 or more
previous convictions received a custodial sentence for the latest offence,
60 per cent did not—14 per cent received a discharge, 16 per cent a fine
and 19 per cent a community penalty.

---

[19] An extreme case is *Brewster* (1980) 2 Cr App R (S) 191 and [1998] 1 Cr App R (S) 181.
[20] An example is *Bowler* (1994) 15 Cr App R (S) 78.

A reduction in sentence severity for a repeat offender might be for a whole range of reasons. The first is a reduction in seriousness of the latest offence, attracting a proportionately less severe sentence. Or there may be some other aspect of the case, such as a time gap between this offence and the one before, or evidence in the pre-sentence report that the defendant is finally settling down, maturing and starting to desist from offending, or material to show that the defendant has been making real efforts to overcome the underlying factors behind the offending (such as drug dependency).[21] This approach to sentencing persistent offenders is clearly illustrated in sentence guidance from the Court of Appeal on the appropriate use of drug treatment and testing orders.[22] The Court stated that judges should be alert to passing sentences which had a realistic prospect of reducing drug addiction wherever it was possible sensibly to do so. Such an order, it was said, was likely to have a better prospect of success earlier rather than later in a criminal career, but there would be exceptional cases, and it could be appropriate even where a substantial number of offences had been committed. In such cases many judges are prepared to try a community sentence on a persistent offender.

This tendency was identified many years ago by Thomas as 'last chance probation' and it is still common today. As we have seen, progressive loss of mitigation encompasses the notion of 'lapse'. A lapse typically occurs for a first offender, but perhaps something similar can occur for a persistent offender. Cessation of offending rarely happens overnight, but is a stuttering change associated with a range of obstacles to reform and a number of false starts (Farrall and Calverley 2006: 7). The literature suggests that desistance occurs when a number of relevant factors, such as gaining employment, forming a significant personal relationship and becoming tired of a cycle of punishment and reoffending, happen at around the same time,[23] and that this process can be cemented by the use of an imaginative, constructive (on some views, lenient) sentence appropriately timed. This everyday sentencing practice runs counter to the ever-rising line associated with the recidivist premium, and is also more radical and inventive than the flat line associated with progressive loss of mitigation.

JV's case falls to be sentenced today, Monday, 3 August 2009. JV was

[21] According to the Court of Appeal in *Bowles* [1996] 2 Cr App R (S) 248, there are occasions when, in the case of persistent offenders, it is appropriate to impose a community order rather than a custodial sentence provided there is sufficient reason to think that a cycle of reoffending can be broken.

[22] *Attorney-General's Reference (No 64 of 2003)* [2004] 2 Cr App R (S) 106. The drug treatment and testing order has been replaced by the community order with a drug rehabilitation requirement, but the principles set out in this decision appear to be equally applicable to both.

[23] For a striking recent example, see *Attorney-General's Reference (No 45 of 2009) (Barratt)* [2009] EWCA Crim 1759.

remanded in custody by the magistrates on April 7, and an appeal against the decision not to grant bail was refused by a Crown Court judge on April 17. The decision over whether to grant bail is essentially a judgment about the reliability of the defendant to abide with the conditions of that bail. In this case bail was refused on two grounds: that there were substantial reasons to believe that JV would fail to attend court; and that there were substantial reasons to believe that he would commit further offences if granted bail. In refusing the appeal the judge would have borne in mind several matters relating to JV's criminal record, especially the two previous failures to surrender to bail, together with breach of an earlier court order (breach of the conditional discharge) and the alleged breach of an operational suspended sentence. By today's date for sentence JV has served, on the information provided by the prison authorities, 119 days on remand, a period which should normally be deducted by the judge from any custodial sentence imposed for the offence.

I now turn to consider the way in which the information in the hypothetical criminal record would be treated by a judge in the process of sentencing for a new offence. One of the points I wish to draw out is that the record will be accorded different significance and weight depending upon the nature of the new offence. I shall try to show this by considering the relevance of the record in two different sentencing scenarios, involving sentencing JV for two different hypothetical new offences. It is argued that, depending on the nature and seriousness of the new offence, the record will take on a different significance. This is partly to do with long-standing principles relating to the relevance of record (number, similarity, and frequency of convictions and so on, mentioned above) but also that the presence of a given offence on the record can be a bar to imposing a particular sentence today,[24] or provide a 'trigger' for a presumptive disposal (see further Wasik 2001).

SENTENCING SCENARIO 1:
NEW OFFENCE DOMESTIC BURGLARY

The offender pleads guilty today to entering a house as a trespasser in the early afternoon of 4 April 2009 while the female owner-occupier was out shopping. A rear window had been forced. The offender ransacked two downstairs rooms and one of the bedrooms before being disturbed by the woman returning home from shopping. The offender ran down the stairs, pushed past the householder and left through the front door. He was detained the following day. No property was taken.

---

[24] For example, a conditional discharge cannot be imposed within two years of a warning.

Factual details of relevant convictions and disposals

Domestic Burglary sentenced in 2000—this offence committed was committed on 1 December 1999. No information is available from the records about the facts of this offence

Domestic Burglary in 2007 the offender, on 20 October 2006, entered a terraced property at 25 High Street, Anytown by an unsecured back door and stole £100 in cash and a portable radio from the kitchen table. The attempted burglary was committed at the neighbouring property, 27 High Street, on the same afternoon. The offender tried to force a rear window, but was seen and detained at the scene by a neighbour.

In the first scenario the offence for which the defendant is to be sentenced today is a domestic burglary which took place on 5 April 2009. The appearance on the criminal record of earlier convictions for domestic burglary should alert counsel and the judge in the Crown Court that this may be a 'three-strikes' burglary case.[25] Section 111 of the Powers of Criminal Courts (Sentencing) Act 2000 provides that

  (a)   where a person is convicted of a domestic burglary committed after 30 November 1999;
  (b)   at the time when the burglary was committed he was aged 18 or over and had been convicted in England and Wales of two other domestic burglaries; and
  (c)   one of those other burglaries was committed after he had been convicted of the other, and both of them were committed after 30 November 1999,
the Crown Court shall impose a custodial term of at least three years except where the court is of the opinion that there are particular circumstances which relate to any of the offences or the offender which would make it unjust to do so in all the circumstances.

This provision contains a number of technicalities. It will be necessary for counsel and the judge to consider JV's criminal record in some detail to ensure that the relevant criteria are made out. It would need to be shown that the defendant is now aged 18 or over (he is), that the domestic burglary sentenced in 2000 was committed after 30 November, 1999 (it was, just) and that the domestic burglary sentenced in 2007 was committed after the defendant was convicted for the earlier offence (it was). Although the defendant was dealt with for two domestic burglaries (one of which was taken into consideration) on one sentencing occasion in 2007, this counts as one burglary for the purposes of section 111. It should also be noted that the attempted burglary dealt with in 2007 does not count for the purposes of section 111, since only completed offences are within the

---

[25] There is an earlier point in that it is the responsibility of the magistrates' court to consider whether the provision applies. If so, the case is triable only on indictment, and should be committed forthwith to the Crown Court.

terms of the section.[26] So, with the burglary which falls to be sentenced today, the defendant does appear to fall within the section.

The defence may raise a further objection to the applicability of the section. The burglary sentenced in 2000 was sentenced by way of a conditional discharge. The conditional discharge is a disposal which counts as a previous conviction only for certain purposes (see Wasik 1997), and it is clear in law that this disposal would not count for the purposes of section 111, save for the fact that the defendant subsequently breached the discharge by committing further offences (see the sentences imposed in 2001). This breach means that the domestic burglary conviction does count for the purposes of section 111 and the defence argument can safely be rejected.

Having worked through this exercise it becomes apparent that the court today must impose a prison sentence of at least three years on JV unless there are 'particular circumstances' which would make that outcome 'unjust'. There is very little appellate guidance on the criteria which might permit a court to exercise its discretion and avoid the minimum sentence. It is clear that such reasons may relate to the seriousness of the burglary offences themselves, or to aspects of JV's criminal record. In *McInerney*,[27] Lord Woolf CJ observed that:

> The sentence could be unjust if two of the offences were committed many years earlier than the third offence, or if the offender has made real efforts to reform or conquer his drug addiction, but some personal tragedy triggers the third offence, or if the first two offences were committed when the offender was not yet 16.

There is no other appellate guidance on this important provision. In our case it is likely that the defence submission for avoidance of the minimum sentence would be based on the fact that, despite the fleeting encounter between the offender and the householder, the most recent burglary was not of the most serious kind, the fact that the first burglary was committed nine years ago (when the defendant was 18) and that since the convictions in 2007 the defendant has complied (or substantially complied, depending on the date on which the current burglary was committed) with the suspended sentence of imprisonment. I will return to that point in a moment. How binding in section 111? The sentencing statistics show that 581 offenders fell within the criteria of section 111 in 2007, the latest year for which the statistics are available. Of these, surprisingly enough, only 236 (48 per cent) received at least the minimum sentence.[28] Ninety offend-

---

[26] *Maguire* [2003] 2 Cr App R (S) 40.

[27] [2003] 1 All ER 1089 (at [16]). This case has been superseded as the guideline case by *Saw* [2009] EWCA Crim 1, but the remarks of Lord Woolf CJ still appear to be valid.

[28] Offenders pleading guilty to the third qualifying burglary can receive no more than a 20 per cent reduction in the minimum sentence, which works out at 28.8 months. The 236 includes offenders so sentenced as well as those actually sentenced to three years or more.

ers (15 per cent) did not receive a custodial sentence at all for the third qualifying burglary. This shows that, despite the apparently clear terms of section 111, Crown Court judges resist its application in over half of sentencing cases in which it applies, by finding 'particular circumstances' in the offences or the record which make the three-year sentence unjust. In turn, this indicates that judges are not held in sway to the criminal record, despite the section's emphasis on that aspect of the sentencing decision, and that they look at all the circumstances before deciding on the appropriate sentence for the new offence. In the statistics for 2007, 42 offenders received a community sentence for the third qualifying burglary, and there were two conditional discharges and one absolute discharge.

If we are to apply section 111 properly, we need to know about the facts of the previous convictions for burglary. The factual details supplied about the earlier offences have been provided by the prosecution in accordance with the relevant Practice Direction, which requires the police to 'provide brief details of the circumstances and/or of the convictions likely to be of interest to the court, the latter being judged on a case by case basis'.[29] In practice, a four- or five-line summary is produced for each such offence, and is printed separately and attached to the antecedents. It turns out in JV's case that no information is available from the records about the facts of the burglary dealt with in 2000. In my experience it is not uncommon for there to be no information, especially where the matter was dealt with in the magistrates' court and is not a recent conviction. The defence will probably invite the judge to infer from the conditional discharge imposed for it that this was not a very serious offence[30] and, since the prosecution will not be in a position to dispute the matter, the defence point will have to be accepted. There is a deeper issue here. Burglary is a widely defined offence, and its seriousness 'can vary almost infinitely from case to case'.[31] The stark entry in JV's criminal record is uninformative. One can only speculate why this offence was sentenced in the way it was. It may be that this really was an example of an offence at the lowest end of the scale (such as reaching through a kitchen window to steal a bottle of milk[32]), or it may be that the offence was a more typical burglary but the defendant played a minor role, such as by acting as lookout. Criminal records do not distinguish between principal offenders and secondary parties. In the absence of details provided by the police from the original record, one cannot discern from an entry in a person's criminal record whether they were acting alone, or

---

[29] *Consolidated Practice Direction*, para III.27.1.

[30] In fact, several hundred offenders each year are discharged following convictions for burglary in a dwelling.

[31] *Brewster* [1998] 1 Cr App R (S) 181.

[32] It might more appropriately have been charged as theft, in which case it would not have been a qualifying conviction.

with an accomplice, or whether they played a leading or peripheral role in the offence. Finally, it could just have been a lenient sentence. There is simply no way of knowing.

As well as deciding whether section 111 applies in this case, there is the further issue of the outstanding suspended sentence imposed on 1 May 2007. The criminal record should always provide information about the status of the defendant when he committed the latest offence—such as whether he was on bail (a statutory aggravating factor when passing sentence) or was under a conditional sentence, or within an unexpired licence period following release from a custodial sentence. If these circumstances apply, the sentencer must know about them and deal with them, such as by imposing an additional sentence for breach of the earlier order, or revoking such an order, or requiring the offender to serve some or all of the unexpired licence period.

In this case a sentence of 12 months' imprisonment was imposed on 1 May 2007, but suspended for 2 years. Today is 3 August 2009, which is more than 2 years later but, of course, what matters is not the date of sentence but the date of the offence. To constitute a breach of the suspended sentence the new offence must have been committed within the operational period of the order. The record shows that the burglary to be sentenced today was committed on 4 April 2009, which tells us that the offender therefore had less than one month of the operational period of the suspended sentence left when he breached it. Commission of a new offence towards the end of the operational period may be a ground for activating only part of the suspended term. The defendant's compliance or otherwise with the requirements of the suspended sentence will also be an important consideration.

SENTENCING SCENARIO (2):
NEW OFFENCE RACIALLY AGGRAVATED
WOUNDING OR INFLICTING GBH (OFFENCES
AGAINST THE PERSON ACT 1861, SECTION 20)

The offender was drinking in a pub with a friend when he saw a Pakistani man, previously unknown to him, whom he thought was 'looking at him oddly'. The offender was verbally abusive, using racist language. When the injured party remonstrated with him, the offender struck him in the face with his beer glass in the area of the left eye, causing a cut needing 20 stitches, a serious injury which would disfigure and leave a permanent scar. The prosecution accepted a plea of guilty to the section 20 offence on an indictment originally charging a section 18 offence.

Factual details of relevant convictions and disposals

2002 Assault occasioning actual bodily harm—late in the evening of 5 September 2001, when the offender was much affected by drink, he approached a taxi driver in the street to ask for a ride home. The Sikh taxi driver refused to take him because of his intoxicated state. The offender became abusive and aggressive, using racial epithets, before striking the taxi driver twice in the face and running off.

2003 threat to destroy or damage property—the offender had been involved with other neighbours in a long-running dispute with a Pakistani family living in the same street. The offender, in company with two co-defendants, on the evening of 15 July 2002, confronted members of the Pakistani family and threatened to throw the contents of a can of white paint (which the offender was holding) at the front door and over the steps of the injured party's house.

In the second scenario the defendant falls to be sentenced for an offence of racially aggravated section 20. As we have seen, JV's record reveals a previous conviction for racially aggravated section 47. These offences are two of a number of such offences created by statute in 1998. They provide higher maximum penalties when the standard offence is aggravated either by racist motivation or racist abuse at the time of the offence.[33] The maximum penalty for the aggravated form of section 20 is 7 years, while for the basic offence it is 5 years. These same two maxima also apply to section 47.[34] Because Parliament chose in 1998 to create these additional offences, rather than simply entrusting the sentencer to take racial motivation into account as an aggravating factor, the racially aggravated offences appear as such on the face of the criminal record. So 'racially aggravated assault occasioning actual bodily harm' in 1992 appears clearly on the record.

This can be contrasted with the offence of threatening to damage or destroy property, with which the defendant was convicted in 2003. There is no racially aggravated version of this offence, and so any racial element on the facts will not be apparent from the criminal record. In JV's case details of that offence, and the racial context in which it took place, have been provided by the police, and so the latest offence can now be seen in the context of two earlier and relatively recent incidents involving racist offences. The court relies on the police to look into the background of JV's previous offending, and to recognise the significance of this particular previous conviction. While this conviction for threatening to damage or

---

[33] Crime and Disorder Act 1998, s 28. These provisions have been added to by the Crime and Security Act 2001.

[34] Which is bizarre, given that s 20 is regarded as the more serious offence, since it requires that the victim incur 'grievous bodily harm', whilst s 47 requires 'actual bodily harm'.

destroy property was of little or no importance when we were considering the sentence for a third domestic burglary, in this context in becomes all-important. Now that the facts are revealed, the court may be inclined to consider that this now provides important evidence of a pattern of racist behaviour, and to consider a more severe custodial sentence in light of the record than might otherwise have been imposed. Such a pattern, as identified in the antecedents, has always been recognised as making the most recent offence more serious and justifying an increased sentence. Even at the time of the Criminal Justice Act 1991, when the significance of previous convictions was played down, this was specifically catered for.[35]

There is another record-based issue in this case, which is whether by virtue of the latest offence, as seen in the context of his criminal record, JV qualifies as a 'dangerous offender'. The relevant provisions are set out in the 2003 Act as amended. The complexities of these provisions are notorious, and I gloss over most of them here. The first point is that the new offence was committed on or after 4 April 2005 and we are to sentence JV after 14 July 2008, so the dangerous offender scheme as amended by the Criminal Justice and Immigration Act 2008 applies.[36] The second point is whether the new offence is a 'specified offence', listed in schedule 15 to the 2003 Act (it is[37]).

The third point is whether it is a 'serious' specified offence (since the new offence is not punishable by a maximum sentence of 10 years' imprisonment or more, the answer is no). This means that the sentence of imprisonment for public protection is not available. If the court considers that JV is dangerous, the available sentence is an extended sentence (which comprises the appropriate custodial term plus an extended licence period of not more than 5 years), but only if there is an offence on JV's record which is an offence listed in schedule 15A to the 2003 Act (there is not) or, if the court were to impose an extended sentence, the term of that sentence would be at least 4 years. The judge would be assisted by counsel in these matters and would have to explain in open court before announcing sentence how these various decisions had been reached.

The legislative test for the assessment of dangerousness is whether the court is of the opinion 'that there is a significant risk to members of the public of serious harm occasioned by the commission of further specified offences'.[38] This is a forward-looking predictive exercise and, in assessing the degree of dangerousness posed by the offender, the judge is required to

---

[35] Criminal Justice Act 1991, s 29(2).

[36] The amended scheme is a more flexible and much improved version of the original: see *Attorney-General's Reference (No 55 of 2008)* [2008] EWCA Crim 2790.

[37] As an offence under the Crime and Disorder Act 1998, s 29, rather than the Offences Against the Person Act 1861, s 20.

[38] Criminal Justice Act 2003, s 225(1)(b).

consider, by virtue of section 229(2) of the Act, 'all such information as is available' to the court. According to the decision in *Lang*[39] the court will rely principally upon two sources of information: the pre-sentence report prepared in accordance with the relevant National Standards which will generate an assessment of risk, and details of JV's previous convictions.[40] The criminal record is being used here not for the purpose of gauging the seriousness of the latest offence but as a key basis for the judicial prediction of JV's law-breaking trajectory and degree of future risk that he poses to others in the future. The case of *Lang* tells us that wherever possible the prosecution should be in a position to describe the facts of any previous offences on the record which may seem to be relevant to this exercise. In fact we already have the facts of the two most relevant offences. The section 47 assault is a specified offence, while the threat to commit criminal damage is not, but both would be taken into account. If there is still doubt about the facts of either of these offences, then it may be necessary to adjourn for further inquiries to be made.[41]

The 2003 Act says that the court may 'take into account all such information as is available to it about the nature and circumstances of any other offences of which the offender has been convicted', and 'about any pattern of behaviour of which the offence forms part'.[42] Rose LJ in *Lang* stressed that an assessment of dangerousness might be indicated by an escalating pattern of seriousness in the previous convictions, a consideration which might well be applicable in JV's case. In JV's case the prosecution also has information that in January 2007 the defendant was barred by the landlord of a public house in Anytown after JV made racially abusive comments to another man at the bar. The police were called and logged the incident, but the injured party did not want matters to be taken any further, and so no prosecution was brought. The Court of Appeal authorities clearly indicate that the sentencing court can have regard to such 'information', since that phrase in section 229 is not limited to convictions or to other evidence which has been tested in court.[43]

E. CONCLUSIONS

The purpose of the discussion over the last few pages has been to set the models of progressive loss of mitigation and the recidivist premium in the context of everyday sentencing practice in the Crown Court. I have

[39] [2006] 1 WLR 2509.
[40] In fact a first offender can qualify under these provisions but in the great majority of cases the offending history forms a crucial part of the assessment of dangerousness.
[41] *Samuels* (1995) 16 Cr App R (S) 856 (decided in relation to earlier dangerous offender laws).
[42] Criminal Justice Act 2003, s 229(2).
[43] *Hillman* [2006] 2 Cr App R (S) 565; *Considine* [2008] 1 WLR 414.

drawn upon my own experience, which is necessarily subjective. I have suggested that neither of the two models can be seen operating in practice with any degree of clarity. Neither of the models is articulated by lawyers in practice, and the relevant statutory provisions on the relevance of previous convictions are not referred to in court. My impression is that while mitigation will be accorded to a 'genuine' first offender wherever the gravity of the offence permits, that flexibility will evaporate quickly with further court appearances. Those with a criminal history are likely to receive more severe sentences. But there is no sharp or inevitable increase in sentencing severity.

The sentencing statistics show that, across the courts in 2007, 28 per cent of first-time offenders received a custodial sentence, while 40 per cent of offenders with 15 or more previous convictions received a custodial sentence (Ministry of Justice 2009: table 6.6). This modest 12 percentage point gap between first offenders and the most persistent offenders receiving imprisonment certainly suggests that, taken in the round, sentencing is driven mainly by offence seriousness. I have also suggested that neither model captures an important reality of sentencing practice, which is the imposition of lower sentences on repeat offenders. There needs to be some better connection made between the principles of sentencing and the literature on desistance from crime. In this context, theory needs to engage more fully with practice.

As we have seen, there are limitations in the system of criminal records, and the entries in the record often fail to capture important details of what happened, and the context in which it took place, but the record nonetheless provides a background against which the latest infringement is to be judged. The courts are engaging here in a process which is comparable to that undertaken in many other life contexts, when we form a judgment about a person and make decisions for the future based on their past record. The football manager will prefer to sign a striker who has a record for scoring goals. The editors of this volume would probably not invite a chapter from a writer with a history of defaulting on deadlines. But inferences drawn from past behaviour are negotiable. The football manager might think, despite the record, that the striker is maturing, is about to 'come good', and will start scoring goals in a different team. The editors might think that, despite a patchy record on delivery, it might be worth giving the contributor another chance.

Records can be interpreted in different ways. The main dimensions of a record are fairly clear—the number of previous failures, their similarity to the latest failure, the frequency of failure, the existence of a failure-free gap, the defendant's response to previous failures, and so on. I have suggested that, in sentencing, the criminal record is treated partly as a document of fact, and partly as a document requiring interpretation. Both prosecution and defence lawyers try to present the defendant's record to the judge in a particular way. Like other historical documents the criminal record contains a number of basic facts which are indisputable, but in and around which there is much scope for interpretation.

Lawyers tell stories around the history—in particular defence lawyers in mitigation. A poor record can be explained away or at least qualified in terms of youthful indiscretion, past association with an undesirable peer group, or a history of dependency on alcohol or drugs. A conviction-free gap can be shown to coincide with a time when the defendant was employed, or living in a different area, away from his former associates, or was in a settled relationship. There are almost always, despite the past, positive signs to be found, such as a new-found maturity, a new relationship, a child on the way, an offer of employment, real efforts being made to seek help for an addiction, or to engage in a positive way with support services. Finally, the significance of the record varies according to the nature of the latest offence, because of particular rules applicable to dangerous offenders, or the 'three-strikes' provisions which stress particular offences on the record and which can be all-important in the cases to which they apply.

REFERENCES

Blumstein, A, Cohen, J, Roth, J and Visher, C (eds) (1986) *Criminal Careers and 'Career Criminals'*, vol II (Washington DC, National Academy Press).

Farrall, S and Calverley, A (2006) *Understanding Desistance from Crime* (Maidenhead, Open University Press).

Hayton, D, (ed) (2000) *Law's Future(s)* (Oxford, Hart Publishing).

Home Office (2001) *Making Punishments Work: Report of a Review of the Sentencing Framework for England and Wales* (London, Home Office).

Jackson, J and Wasik, M (2000) 'Character Evidence and Criminal Procedure' in D Hayton (ed), *Law's Future(s)* (Oxford, Hart Publishing).

Ministry of Justice (2009), *Sentencing Statistics 2007*, ch 6 (London, Ministry of Justice).

Piquero, A, Farrington, D and Blumstein, A (2007) *Key Issues in Criminal Career Research* (Cambridge, Cambridge University Press).

Rex, S, and Tonry, M (2002) *Reform and Punishment: The Future of Sentencing* (Cullompton, Willan,).

Roberts, J (2008) *Punishing Persistent Offenders* (Oxford, Oxford University Press).

Roberts, J and von Hirsch, A (2009) 'The Recidivist Premium: For and Against' in A von Hirsch, A Ashworth and J Roberts, *Principled Sentencing: Readings on Theory and Policy*, 3rd edn (Oxford, Hart Publishing, 2009) ch 4.6.

Sentencing Advisory Panel (2008) *Consultation Paper on Overarching Principles of Sentencing* (London, Sentencing Advisory Panel).

Sentencing Commission Working Group (2008) *A Structured Sentencing Framework and Sentencing Commission: A Consultation Paper* (London, Sentencing Commission Working Group,).

Thomas, D (1979) *Principles of Sentencing*, 2nd edn (London, Heinemann).

Thomas, T (2007) *Criminal Records* (London, Palgrave Macmillan).

—— (2001) 'The National Collection of Criminal Records: A Question of Data Quality' *Criminal Law Review* 886–96.

von Hirsch, A (2002) 'Record-enhanced Sentencing in England and Wales: Reflections on the Halliday Report's Proposed Treatment of Prior Convictions' in S Rex and M Tonry (eds), *Reform and Punishment: The Future of Sentencing* (Cullompton, Willan,).

von Hirsch, A, Ashworth, A and Roberts, J (2009) *Principled Sentencing: Readings on Theory and Policy*, 3rd edn (Oxford, Hart Publishing).

Wasik, M (1997) 'Discharge Provisions and the Restricted Meaning of "Conviction"' 113 *Law Quarterly Review* 637–66.

—— (2001) 'The Vital Importance of Certain Previous Convictions' *Criminal Law Review* 363–73.

Wasik, M and Taylor, R (1993) *Blackstone's Guide to the Criminal Justice Act 1991*, 2nd edn (London, Blackstone).

Wasik, M and von Hirsch, A (1994) 'Section 29 Revised: Previous Convictions in Sentencing' *Criminal Law Review* 409–18.

Weis, J (1986) 'Issues in the Measurement of Criminal Careers', in A Blumstein, J Cohen, J Roth and C Visher (eds), *Criminal Careers and 'Career Criminals'*, vol II (Washington DC, National Academy Press).

IO

The Role of Previous Convictions in England and Wales

ESTELLA BAKER AND ANDREW ASHWORTH

T HE AIM OF this chapter is to assess the role that previous convictions play in the sentencing of offenders in England and Wales. It traces the development of the current law; analyses the policy that underpins it (or purports to do so); sets the law in the context of a number of broader trends; and provides a critique of current provision from a variety of perspectives. Historically, it has been difficult cleanly to distinguish measures to deal with 'ordinary' recidivists from those to deal with dangerous offenders. Therefore, it is arguable that a complete account ought to consider how the law stands now in relation to both of these categories. Over time, however, it has become increasingly well accepted that different penological considerations should govern the sentencing of the two groups. For that reason, and because the case for drawing a distinction between the applicable penal responses has found favour in the current sentencing legislation, the discussion here will not deal with the treatment of dangerous offenders[1] but is restricted to those who indulge in other forms of persistence. Nor will it deal comprehensively with a further category of measure: that of the 'three-strikes' type.

In the mid-1990s, the UK government became frustrated that, in its view, sentencers were not making adequate use of their sentencing powers to deal with certain repeat offenders (see Home Office 1996). That caused it to enact three measures that were intended to cajole courts into exercising their discretion to impose more severe punishments. Two of them, the presumptive minimum seven-year term for a third or subsequent conviction of drug trafficking and the presumptive minimum three-year term for a third or subsequent conviction of domestic burglary, remain on the stat-

---

[1] For a discussion of the current 'dangerous offender regime', see Ashworth (2010: ch 6.8).

ute book.[2] The third, the automatic life sentence for a second conviction of a serious violent or sexual offence, has now been repealed.[3] None of these sentences has had much practical impact in terms of affecting significant numbers of offenders.[4] Therefore, despite their symbolic importance in signalling to the public that sentencing policy was toughening up (see Baker and Roberts 2005), and to the courts that the political time was ripe for greater legislative intervention in sentencing policy, they will only be discussed incidentally here. Finally, although it makes some attempt to set current law and policy in a longer historical context, the chapter is concerned primarily with evolutions in law and policy since 1990 as the last two decades have been marked by a notably lively phase in sentencing development.

The chapter contains four parts. Section A provides a sketch of the current statutory provisions that govern the use of previous convictions in sentencing decisions and outlines the way in which the legislative approach has changed during the last twenty years. Section B then links the pattern of change to the parallel changes that have occurred to strengthen the constitutional regulation of sentencing discretion and examines the extent to which the policy steer that has been provided by legislation does, or does not, appear to have had any impact on the actual sentencing practices of the courts. Section C uses that enquiry as the basis for a deeper analysis of some of the problems and uncertainties that surround the current legislative provision. The final part extends that discussion to investigate the policy that the legislation purports to implement. The conclusion then sets the issues in the broader context of fluctuations in the prevailing political trends and of technological development that help to explain the direction in which law and policy has evolved. This will pave the way for a brief prospective look at where they may go next.

A. CURRENT LEGISLATION AND ITS DEVELOPMENT

The key statutory provision that governs the use of previous convictions in sentencing is section 143(2) of the Criminal Justice Act 2003. It provides:

> In considering the seriousness of an offence ('the current offence') committed by an offender who has one or more previous convictions, the court must treat each previous conviction as an aggravating factor if (in the case of that

---

[2] Powers of Criminal Courts (Sentencing) Act 2000, ss 110 and 111; originally enacted by the Crime (Sentences) Act 1997, ss 3 and 4.

[3] Originally enacted by the Crime (Sentences) Act 1997, s 2; the need for which is now extinguished by the comprehensive dangerous offender regime under the Criminal Justice Act 2003.

[4] For discussion, see Ashworth (2010: ch 6.7).

conviction) the court considers that it can reasonably be so treated having regard, in particular, to—

(a) the nature of the offence to which the conviction relates and its relevance to the current offence, and
(b) the time that has elapsed since the conviction.

The drafting of this provision creates an obvious tension. On the one hand, it indicates that a court is bound to ('must') treat each previous conviction as a factor that aggravates the current offence, and should do so each time the offender is sentenced.[5] This appears to require a cumulative approach, so that, for example, on sentencing a fifth-time offender, the court must treat each of the four previous offences as rendering this one more serious. On the other hand, the force of the mandatory words, 'must treat . . . as an aggravating factor', appears to be softened by the later clause, 'if the court considers that it can reasonably be so treated'.[6] Rather than providing a 'get-out clause' for sentencers who reject the cumulative model, reasonableness seems to be connected in turn with the offender's previous conduct. Thus the court should have regard to each previous conviction's relevance and recency, as set out in paragraphs (a) and (b), and perhaps to any other factor arising from those previous convictions.

Precisely how the relationship between these various factors combines to produce a judgment that the offence is more serious than it might otherwise be (or not) is important because, like the legislation that it replaced (and leaving aside the separate statutory provision for dangerous offenders), the Act purports to establish a desert-based sentencing scheme.[7] Consequently, the primary determinant of decision-making is stated to be offence seriousness. Therefore, how section 143(2) is interpreted has a tangible bearing on how a court assesses whereabouts on the penalty scale the current conviction sits, as well as the appropriate quantum of punishment that the offender should receive. As later sections of this chapter will explain, however, the wording of section 143(2) provokes important questions, to which most of the answers remain unsettled.

One of the reasons for this uncertainty is that its orientation and wording are significantly different from the statutory provision that it replaced. The divergence points to an uncertainty that affects the sentencing measures of the 2003 Act as a whole. Were they intended to sweep away the body of sentencing law that the legislation replaced; or were they instead meant to build upon that accumulated body of sentencing wisdom, albeit

---

[5] Convictions from other jurisdictions may also be taken into account (sub-ss (4) and (5)), but it is unclear whether a conviction followed by a discharge counts as a previous conviction in this context.

[6] Notably, the Explanatory Notes to the Act stated baldly that recent and relevant convictions 'should be regarded as an aggravating factor which should increase the severity of the sentence', leaving no room for judicial discretion or for other factors.

[7] Of a sort: see Baker and Clarkson (2002).

modifying it in certain identifiable respects? Taken on its face at least,[8] the enactment of section 143(2) provides one of the strongest signals that Parliament intended the 2003 Act to make real changes to sentencing policy.

The previous provision, section 29(1) of the Criminal Justice Act 1991, certainly did not require the courts to take a cumulative view. According to its noticeably milder language:

> In considering the seriousness of any offence, the court may take into account any previous convictions of the offender or any failure of his to respond to previous sentences.

If this wording licensed courts to aggravate sentences on account of previous convictions, then it was as a matter of discretion, not obligation. Its correct interpretation was not uncontentious (Wasik and von Hirsch 1994), because the Criminal Justice Act 1993 had inserted this version of section 29(1) into the 1991 Act in substitution for the original provision.

Contrasting even more markedly with what is now stated in section 143(2), in its initial guise, section 29(1) read:

> An offence shall not be regarded as more serious for the purposes of any provision of this Part by reason of any previous convictions of the offender or any failure of his to respond to previous sentences.

The White Paper that had preceded the 1991 Act (Home Office 1990: para 2.18) left no doubt that the intention behind this provision was to prevent offenders from being sentenced 'on the record'. Instead, it asserted that the seriousness of the current offence was to be the primary factor in sentencing. It endorsed the decision in *R v Queen* (1981),[9] where the Court of Appeal had reiterated the principle of progressive loss of mitigation, ie the proposition that a first-time offender should receive a mitigated sentence on account of good character, but that the amount of mitigation should reduce with the second and subsequent convictions. Thus there seemed to be a consensus between the executive and the judiciary as to the preferable approach for the law to adopt. Although it is arguable that the way in which the intention to transfer the policy onto a statutory footing was effected by the original wording of section 29(1) was inept,[10] there is no doubting what the policy was meant to be. Nor can it be disputed that, during the interval between 1990 and 2003, Parliament appeared completely to revise its view as to the bearing that previous convictions should have on sentencing decisions.

---

[8] But see section B below.

[9] (1981) 3 Cr App R (S) 245.

[10] For interpretation of s 29, see the Court of Appeal's ruling in *R v Bexley* (1993) 14 Cr App R (S) 462.

B. SENTENCING DISCRETION AND THE REGULATION OF SENTENCING

Coinciding with the transformation in approach towards repeat offenders has been a separate transformation in the constitutional structures through which sentencing policy is determined and implemented. At the time of the 1990 White Paper the bulk of this work was done by the courts, there being relatively little applicable legislation. Since then, however, the situation has changed markedly as a succession of reforms has attempted to impose ever greater constraints on judges' exercise of sentencing discretion.

On the one hand, a statutory sentencing framework has long since been put in place that applies to all offenders, across both tiers of trial court. Now contained primarily in the Criminal Justice Act 2003, the concept first found its way onto the statute book courtesy of the Criminal Justice Act 1991. On the other, what is becoming a series of extra-judicial bodies has been created, initially to offer advice on sentencing levels, and more recently to draw up actual guidelines. The trend was begun by the Crime and Disorder Act 1998 which established the Sentencing Advisory Panel; was continued by the Criminal Justice Act 2003, which added the Sentencing Guidelines Council; and has now been taken a stage further by the Coroners and Justice Act 2009, which (in effect) merges both the previous bodies into a new Sentencing Council.

Deciphering the relevance of these changes to the current discussion is more involved than might at first appear. Superficially, they suggest that Parliament has made a concerted effort to assert its authority over that of the courts to determine sentencing policy. However, the actual state of affairs is more subtle because the reforms have left the judiciary in a commanding position to influence policy development, albeit within the evolving statutory context. Thus, reproducing the model of the Sentencing Guidelines Council,[11] the new Sentencing Council will have a majority judicial membership;[12] and, before the former body was established, the Sentencing Advisory Panel advised the Court of Appeal directly.[13] These arrangements mean that, to gain an informed understanding of how English sentencing law treats previous convictions, it is not enough to look at the applicable statutory provisions. That enquiry must be complemented by an examination of applicable sentencing guidelines and what is known about the actual sentencing practices of the courts. So what additional information can be gleaned from these sources?

Whereas many of the US guideline systems treat the criminal history score as one of the two main determinants of sentence, and ascribe a

---

[11] Criminal Justice Act 2003, s 167.
[12] Coroners and Justice Act 2009, sch 15.
[13] Crime and Disorder Act 1998, s 81.

cumulative effect to it, that approach is rejected by the more flexible approach to guidelines in England and Wales. After a relatively slow start, the Sentencing Guidelines Council has been moving towards greater specificity on the significance of previous convictions in the sentencing process. Its current guidance on 'sentence ranges and starting points' states that a sentencing range is 'the bracket into which the provisional sentence will normally fall after having regard to factors which aggravate or mitigate the offence': the possible sentence ranges will be indicated by the guidelines established for the particular type of offence. Then:

> Where the offender has previous convictions which aggravate the seriousness of the current offence, that may take the provisional sentence beyond the range given, particularly where there are significant other aggravating factors present.[14]

This gives courts the liberty to go outside the indicated sentence range where previous convictions are treated as aggravating, but it gives no guidance on the extent to which previous convictions may aggravate sentence.

Guidelines on specific offences adopt a similar line. For example, that on theft from a shop indicates a range of 'fine to community order (medium)' for a moderate theft evincing some planning, but the Council's 'factors to take into consideration' state that 'where an offender demonstrates a level of "persistent" or "seriously persistent" offending, the community and custody thresholds may be crossed even though the other characteristics of the offence would otherwise warrant a lesser sentence'.[15] One notable consequence of this approach, to be discussed below, is that the guidelines provide no clear warning about disproportionality of sentence, an omission that is shared by the wording of section 143(2). The Court of Appeal may be expected to supply overall supervision of the length of sentences; but previously, the Court has neither exhibited an enthusiasm for engaging with the statutory sentencing framework nor demonstrated a reliable sense of perspective in these matters.

After the law on previous convictions was altered by the Criminal Justice Act 1993, there was no judicial consideration of the legislative provision in the following decade: only one substantive discussion of the legislation took place,[16] despite the fact that courts were sentencing thousands of offenders with previous convictions each year. Since the implementation of the Criminal Justice Act 2003, section 143(2) is among the pivotal provisions of the current framework that have yet to receive any authoritative consideration. It seems that sentencing appeals

---

[14] This wording is found in most definitive guidelines. See eg Sentencing Guidelines Council, *Theft and Burglary in a Building other than a Dwelling* (London, Sentencing Guidelines Council, 2008) 8.

[15] Ibid, 16.

[16] *R v Spencer and Carby* (1995) 16 Cr App R (S) 482, at 485–86.

are simply not based on these important provisions. One explanation is that this is because they are being applied perfectly by the courts, but its credibility is stretched by the fact that the legislation is amenable to different interpretations.

Turning to the Court of Appeal's own previous history of dealing with these issues, there has been a demonstrable inconsistency between its language and its actions. An example of this is provided by the case of *Woods* (1998).[17] A vicar returned to his vicarage to find the offender dozing on the floor, having broken in and put various items from the house in a bag ready to take with him. The offender had 121 previous convictions for offences of burglary and theft, not of great seriousness, and had been released from prison only 21 days before the burglary. The trial judge sentenced him to six years' imprisonment, saying that there was no hope of his rehabilitation or deterrence and that therefore an incapacitative sentence was needed in order to protect the public.[18] The Court of Appeal acceded to the proposition that the offender was not a professional but an incompetent yet frequent opportunist, usually looking for small amounts of food or money. The Court reduced the sentence from six to four years—still a substantial custodial sentence, and difficult to justify in law.

Moving beyond specific decisions such as *Woods*, there are good reasons to suspect a long-standing ambiguity in the Court's attitude to the treatment of previous convictions. Contrary to what the White Paper of 1990 had implied, the Court's judgments did not establish an unequivocal commitment to the progressive-loss-of-mitigation approach. Although advocated in *Queen* and in some of its other judgments,[19] there were also instances in which it took a different view.[20] Therefore, the position that had been portrayed in the White Paper was not borne out by the facts. Perhaps linked to that inconsistency, it was never clear that the doctrine of progressive loss of mitigation commanded authority in the lower courts. And perhaps the most cogent evidence of a divergence of judicial opinion on the matter emerged once the Criminal Justice Act 1991 entered into force. Section 29(1) (as originally drafted) became one of three focal points of judicial opposition to the statutory scheme that the Act put in place because of the way in which it was asserted to fetter judicial discretion. In a notorious 'sound-bite', Lord Taylor, the then Lord Chief Justice,

---

[17] [1998] 2 Cr App R (S) 237.

[18] Under the 1991 Act it was not lawful to impose a disproportionate sentence for reasons of public protection unless the special provisions of s 2(2)(b) of the Act applied, and they were limited to sexual and violent offences. The question arises whether the position is different under the 2003 Act because s 142 appears to allow courts to pass sentence for 'the protection of the public'.

[19] Apparently, over a reasonable time span: see *R v Griffiths* (1966), cited in Thomas (1970: 43).

[20] Eg *Bailey* (1988) 10 Cr App R (S) 231.

speaking extra-judicially, described the Act as forcing sentencers 'into an ill-fitting straightjacket' (Lord Taylor 1993: 129).

As has been well documented, this is just one, particularly prominent, example of a body of statements and actions by magistrates and the professional judiciary which helped to fuel a vociferous media campaign against the supposedly ridiculous consequences of the legislation. Combined with a variety of extraneous factors that had served to make the then government vulnerable for other reasons, the product was a political decision to replace section 29(1) by the new section that was introduced in the Criminal Justice Act 1993. It was evident from the reception of this new section that there was a substantial reservoir of opinion among the magistrates and judiciary that sentencing 'on the record' could be an acceptable and appropriate response to repeat offending. Looking back further into the history of the law's development, it is possible to identify at least one factor that might help to explain why such an idea could have taken root. At three earlier points in the twentieth century, Parliament enacted measures that were intended to deal with persistent offenders: 'preventive detention' under the Prevention of Crime Act 1908; a different sentence of 'preventive detention' under the Criminal Justice Act 1948; and 'extended sentences' under the Criminal Justice Act 1967. In each case the scope of the measure was such as to catch offenders who repeatedly broke the law, but whose level of offending was not serious. The legacy may have been to lend lasting credence to the proposition that persistence should attract a harsher punishment than would be justified on the basis of the seriousness of the offence alone, and to establish it as part of the courts' sentencing culture.[21]

Whether that explanation for the phenomenon holds or not, this body of evidence challenges a provisional conclusion that was reached earlier. It was suggested that the effect of the statutory reforms that have occurred since 1991 has been to forge a growing divergence between the natural inclination of the courts to adopt a progressive-loss-of-mitigation approach and that of Parliament, which has become increasingly persuaded by the cumulative model. In fact, instead of regarding the 1990 White Paper as marking the point of consensus, there is some basis for saying that it has only occurred in recent years as the policy set by legislation has moved into closer alignment with the underlying sympathies of the courts. That revised conclusion throws fresh light in turn upon the question of the extent to which the sentencing framework established by the Criminal Justice Act 2003 represents continuity or change. Contrary to the expectation that is set up by the progressive revisions in statutory wording from the two versions of section 29 to the current provision in

---

[21] See the discussion in Thomas (1970: 41).

section 143(2), it might be inferred that the policy of the courts, and so sentencing practice itself, has remained remarkably stable.

C. ANALYSIS OF THE LEGISLATION

It was seen above that section 143(2) of the Criminal Justice Act 2003 requires sentencing courts to treat previous convictions as aggravating factors, when they consider it reasonable to do so in the light of the relevance and recency of those convictions. Analysed in terms of the extent to which the legislation confirmed established sentencing principles or brought about change, the selection of these two factors was in line with doctrine that had previously been developed by the courts.

Attribution of significant weight to convictions of a qualitatively distinct kind or to ones that have grown stale runs counter to accepted sentencing culture. An unusually well-focused indicator was provided by early appeals against the imposition of automatic life sentences.[22] The legislation permitted courts to avoid imposing the measure if there were 'exceptional circumstances' that would justify not doing so. Both the existence of a pronounced dissimilarity between the qualifying and trigger offences (ie the lack of relevance of the first to the second), and/or a long interval between the two convictions, were circumstances that were argued to be 'exceptional' in a number of cases.[23] Returning to section 143(2), it is plain that much hinges on how the concepts of 'relevance' and 'recency' are interpreted; and then how that interpretation proceeds to influence a court's judgment of the reasonableness of taking earlier convictions into account in its assessment of the current offence.

What should be the criterion of whether prior convictions are *relevant* to the current offence? Much of the sentencing framework that was put in place by the 2003 Act is founded in the recommendations of a major review of the previous framework: the Halliday Report (Home Office 2001). This Report noted that most persistent offenders have a mixed criminal record, and therefore argued that 'less weight should be given to whether previous and current offences are in the same category', so that 'the key point is whether the previous offences justify a more severe view' (ibid: para 2.17).[24] Insofar as this suggests that the *seriousness* of

---

[22] These appeals were heard before the Court of Appeal held in *R v Offen (No 2)* [2001] 2 Cr App R (S) 44 that this provision was only compatible with the European Convention on Human Rights if courts were to satisfy themselves, before imposing such a sentence, that the offender posed a significant risk to the public.

[23] On dissimilarity, see eg *R v Kelly* [1999] 2 Cr App R (S) 176 (robbery using a firearm and GBH with intent); *R v Stephens* [2000] 2 Cr App R (S) 320 (unlawful sexual intercourse with a girl under 13 and GBH with intent); and on time lapse, see eg *R v Kelly* (18-year gap); *R v Turner* [2000] 2 Cr App R (S) 472 (a gap of over 30 years).

[24] Later in the same paragraph, however, the report states that 'completely disparate . . . previous convictions should be given less weight'.

the previous offences is the crucial issue that is quite different from section 143(2) as drafted. 'Relevance' is surely to be taken as indicating a similarity of subject matter. In the past, the practice in sentencing for offences of violence has been for courts to pay more attention to previous convictions for offences of violence than to others; and the same might be said of sexual cases (see Wasik 1987: 108–09), and offenders interviewed by Julian Roberts thought that 'specialists' should be treated more severely (Roberts 2008: 153–54). Where there is a record of offences of dishonesty or burglary, courts may decide to treat the person as a 'professional'. Attractive as such views may initially appear though, later discussion will suggest that they may not be robust when reviewed in the light of what is known about actual offending patterns.

Would desert theorists' notion of lapse[25] have any application here? Human weakness in losing one's temper momentarily and punching another may be regarded as different from human frailty in succumbing to the temptation of economic crime. There is therefore some ground for arguing that a first sexual offence by someone with previous property convictions should be treated as 'out of character', and should be mitigated to some extent.[26] But this argument cannot be pressed too far. It would be absurd to imply that everyone is entitled to one 'discounted' crime of violence, one 'discounted' fraud, one 'discounted' sexual offence and so on. This may have been why Halliday suggested that the *seriousness* of the prior offences should be the primary determinant, in terms of 'whether there is a continuing course of criminal conduct' (Home Office 2001: para 2.17). But, again, this is not what section 143(2)(a) says: it rests on the notion of relevance, presumably interpreted in terms of types or categories of offending.

What about recency? By requiring courts to have regard to the time that has elapsed since each previous conviction, section 143(2)(b) seems to restate the common law principle that a gap in offending should be taken to diminish their effect upon the current punishment. An old example is *Fox* (1980),[27] where the Court of Appeal reduced the sentence on a man aged 35 convicted of grievous bodily harm who had two previous convictions many years earlier: 'In our judgment, his previous record of violence when he was in his late teens and mid-twenties should have been left out of account in deciding what action to take.' Various justifications may be offered for this concession—for example the offender deserves credit for going straight, or the present offence is to some extent

---

[25] See eg the discussions by von Hirsch, Roberts and Ryberg in this volume.

[26] See *R v Davies* [2006] 1 Cr App R (S) 213: D with 36 previous court appearances for 'more than 100 offences covering a wide variety of criminal activities' convicted of first sexual offence. The Court of Appeal evidently did not regard previous convictions as aggravating, but did not mention the 2003 Act.

[27] (1980) 2 Cr App R (S) 188; see also *R v Bleasdale* (1984) 6 Cr App R (S) 177 (four years without trouble for a man of 22 'is an important feature in his favour').

'out of character' in terms of his recent behaviour, or the conviction-free gap makes it less likely that he will reoffend—but the most straightforward approach is to affirm the underlying principle of the Rehabilitation of Offenders Act 1974. Generally speaking, it is unnecessarily harsh if a person has to bear the burden of previous convictions indefinitely: after a number of years a person should be able to regain full rights as a citizen, and such a principle may even provide an incentive not to reoffend. Many US guideline systems provide for the 'decay' of previous convictions after 10 years, and this has been adopted, for example, in the proposed South African sentencing code.[28] Although it appears that there is little public sympathy for this principle (Roberts, Hough, Jacobson and Moon 2009), it forms part of English law and, applying the principle of decay, rightly so.

Turning to the matter of how the factors of relevance and recency might be weighed up, it is interesting to speculate what the effect of section 143(2) might be on sentence in a case such as *Woods*.[29] Under the 2003 Act a court would be bound to find that his previous convictions were both recent and relevant, and the sentencing guidelines (underpinned by the presumptive minimum sentence for the third domestic burglary)[30] would indicate a starting point of at least three years. If a court were really to regard each of his 121 convictions as aggravating the current offence, then it might well impose a sentence even longer than the four years that was upheld by the Court of Appeal. That observation raises perhaps the most fundamental issue in relation to section 143(2), namely that it lacks any reference to an overall proportionality constraint.

The absence of such a constraint, it has already been seen, is not redressed by an appropriate warning about disproportionality of sentence in the sentencing guidelines. Halliday insisted that 'the effects of previous convictions would always be subject to outer limits resulting from the seriousness of the current offences' (Home Office 2001: para 2.20). At the time, ministers stated that section 143(2) merely 'modifies the proportionality principle so that previous, relevant convictions can act as an aggravating factor', and that it was not intended to lead to 'wildly disproportionate sentences'.[31] But the wording of section 143(2) discloses no such constraint, leaving English sentencing law at odds with the recommendations of the Council of Europe (1993) and out of step with that

---

[28] South African Law Reform Commission (2000), s 42: 'where a period of 10 years has passed from the date of completion of the last sentence and the date of commission of any subsequent offence . . . the last conviction and all convictions prior to that must be disregarded for the purposes of sentencing'.

[29] See n 17 above.

[30] Under the Powers of Criminal Courts (Sentencing) Act 2000, s 111 this is set at three years' imprisonment.

[31] Baroness Scotland, HL Deb 24 Feb, 2003.

in other jurisdictions where the recommendations have been adopted, eg Sweden (von Hirsch and Jareborg 2009: 258).[32]

In terms of forecasting the likely consequences, it may prove salutary that this defect in the 2003 Act reproduces one found in the earlier English measures to deal with persistent offenders.[33] Its effect then was that repetition of offending behaviour of a relatively minor nature led many to be caught within their net. That created a tendency for them to have an unwarranted impact on relatively trivial offenders that led to their falling into disrepute and, ultimately, to their being excised from the statute book. In gauging the relevance of this experience to the prognosis for section 143(2), it should be borne in mind that the earlier provisions created special sentences that were targeted at particular groups of offenders, whereas section 143(2) purports to establish a general rule. Nevertheless, the precedent supplies additional reason to be concerned about the impact of the 2003 provision.

Finally, attention should return to the mandatory wording of section 143(2). Does the injunction to courts to 'treat each previous conviction as an aggravating factor' mean that Parliament intended to rule out the use of community sentences for repeat offenders? Judge Peter Jones put the case of offenders who commit frequent thefts of items such as toiletries, with a view to selling them in order to raise money to buy drugs (Jones 2002). Such an offender may come before the court with 30, 40 or more previous convictions. If the court wishes to tackle what it regards as the underlying cause of offending (drug-taking) by making a community order, would it be lawful to do so? Halliday himself wanted to see community sentences used more widely in such cases, but that was always in conflict with his proposed policy on persistent offending (ibid: 185–86, citing Home Office 2001: para. 6.6), and the mandatory wording of section 143(2) heightens the conflict. On one view a court would be acting unlawfully if it dealt with an offender, whose record disclosed many recent and relevant convictions, by means of a community sentence: each previous conviction ought to be treated as an aggravating factor, and 30 or 40 previous convictions would therefore take the offence well beyond the custody threshold.

---

[32] See c 29.4, 'the court shall . . . to a reasonable extent take the offender's previous criminality into account'. See also chapter by Asp in this volume.

[33] 'Preventive detention' under the Prevention of Crime Act 1908; the different sentence of 'preventive detention' under the Criminal Justice Act 1948; and the 'extended sentence' under the Criminal Justice Act 1967.

D. ANALYSIS OF POLICY

The policy issues that arise in connection with section 143(2) centre upon two core themes. One concerns the question of what the target of punishment is meant to be, and whether the statutory scheme is apt to translate intention into practice. The other is the extent to which the policy that is implemented by the legislation is and/or ought to be consistent with the accumulating body of empirical knowledge of the phenomena of recidivism and desistance.

The first of these matters has to some extent been dealt with. To reiterate what has been said so far, neither section 143(2) nor the policy documents upon which it was based has established an unequivocal position as to whether it is repetition per se that should earn additional punishment, or repetition coupled (somehow) with the further factors of relevance and recency. Like earlier measures to deal with persistent offenders, the Act indicates that the latter considerations should influence the sentencing decision but nonetheless leaves the fundamental issue unresolved. This failure to be clear and specific has a number of contributory causes. Among them is the lack of a consistent adherence to an underlying set of moral and philosophical principles that might guide the policy choice. That is not to allege that such a philosophical foundation is entirely absent; after all, with justification, the statutory sentencing scheme can be described as desert-based. But this is a version of desert that has been tempered, if not compromised, by extrinsic political considerations.[34] As such, section 143(2) cuts a contrast with the Criminal Justice Act 1991: although section 29 of the latter Act may have suffered from other defects,[35] its desert-based aim was not similarly watered down.

A further reason for the ambiguity of section 143(2) stems from a related failure adequately to articulate why the dimensions of relevance and recency might be regarded as germane in determining the appropriate penal response to reoffending. That is not to say that the implied rationale is hard to discern. On the face of it, somebody who develops a track record of similar sorts of criminality thereby gains credentials as a specialist, and signals that previous sentences have not had a meaningful deterrent impact. Meanwhile, somebody who has engaged in a spate of criminal activity within the recent past, and is now convicted again, is readily cast as having a present disposition towards offending and so as an obvious candidate for incapacitation. In both instances, the argument for a 'more intrusive and intensive sentence' (Home Office 2001: para 2.11) seems as transparent as it is compelling. The trouble is, however,

---

[34] A matter that is discussed further below.
[35] See *R v Bexley & others* (1993) 14 Cr App R (S) 462.

that the logic that drives that deduction appears less irrefutable in the light of available information about actual offending behaviour.

To take the specialisation issue first, both Appendix 3 of the Halliday report and David Farrington's review of criminal career research lead to the conclusion that the typical pattern is a small degree of specialisation 'superimposed on a great deal of generality or versatility in offending', and that the majority of previous offences of violent offenders are non-violent (Farrington 1997: 380). On the other hand, research commissioned by the Sentencing Advisory Panel into persons convicted of theft from shops did uncover a degree of specialisation. It found that:

> Of the 1,443 offences where information on previous convictions and sentence was known, only 5% had no previous convictions. On average, an offender had been sentenced on 19 previous occasions for a total of 42 offences, of which 21 were for theft and kindred offences and 12 for theft from a shop.
> (Sentencing Advisory Panel, 2008: para 9)

What is most striking is the staggering magnitude of these figures; multiple previous convictions amongst shoplifters are clearly not a rarity. Moreover, data drawn from the 2007 sentencing statistics suggests that they share that characteristic with other offender groups. For example, of those sentenced in that year, it was only a minority who had no previous convictions or cautions at all (9 per cent in the magistrates' courts and 20 per cent in the Crown Court). Rather, the trend during this decade has been for offenders to come before the courts with more and more previous convictions: the proportion of sentences for indictable offences given to persons with 15 or more previous convictions or cautions rose from 17 per cent in 2000 to 25 per cent in 2007. Nevertheless, previous criminal history varies considerably according to the type of offence: only 5 per cent of those convicted of burglary were first offenders, compared with 36 per cent of sex offenders and 40 per cent of those convicted of fraud or forgery (Ministry of Justice 2009: 116–37). On the other hand, 36 per cent of burglars had 15 or more previous convictions, although not necessarily for burglary. All in all, while specialisation may be rare, the evidence suggests that proliferation in offending is not. This prompts the question whether specialisation is necessarily worse than versatility if the number of previous convictions is similar.

Turning to the second issue, it is also possible to query what it is possible safely to deduce from the fact that an offender has been engaged in a recent spell of concentrated offending. The legislation seems to invite a crudely punitive response, but Appendix 3 of the Halliday report cited unpublished Home Office modelling which suggested that active offenders could be subdivided into three categories:

- persistent, 'high-rate', offenders (those who have high rates of offending, as measured by convictions, and a high likelihood of reconviction . . .);

- persistent, but 'low-rate' offenders (those whose convictions are at a low rate, ie spread out over time, but who have a high likelihood of reconviction . . .); and
- 'short-career' offenders (those with few convictions and low likelihood of reconviction . . .) (Home Office 2001: 92).

It is at least arguable that this typology supplies grounds for a more nuanced approach to sentencing than that which section 143(2) appears to permit. In particular, the case for subjecting those in the last group to additional punishment may be open to doubt. By contrast, the legislation can be read to imply that those in the first should be punished more severely than those in the second, whereas the prognosis for the latter might challenge the merits of that assumption. If the point is taken that previous convictions make a current offence more serious, why, as a matter of principle, should the fact that they are spread out lessen their impact on the current sentence by comparison with that which they would have if accumulated in a concentrated period of time?

Leaving aside these uncertainties over the policy behind current legislation, it is important not to overlook the existence of significant underlying stability. The punishment of persistence has proved an enduring feature of English sentencing law and, placed in that historical context, its renewed emphasis in the 2003 Act is unremarkable. If anything stands out as novel, it is the Criminal Justice Act 1991.[36] As discussed above, in so far as section 29(1) was intended to ensure respect for the principle of progressive loss of mitigation, it sought to arrest the practice of sentencing 'on the record'. That understanding, however, points to yet another unresolved issue that infuses the debate regarding the proper role of previous convictions in sentencing.

Consistently from 1991 onwards, English statutes have been couched in terms of previous convictions making a current *offence* more serious (or not, as the case may be). However, the proposition that the former can have any effect on the latter deserves scrutiny because it is not self-evident what it means. Nor, consequently, is it clear what precisely it is that the legislation is targeting for punishment.

On one view, the term 'offence' refers to the harmful act or omission that the offender has committed. If that is what successive provisions have referred to, then there is a difficulty because it is impossible to see how previous convictions can affect its seriousness in any way. Logically, the harm must be just the same if perpetrated by a first-time offender as it would be if perpetrated by one committing the offence for the hundredth time. This helps to explain why purer forms of desert theory incline towards a 'flat-line' or progressive-loss-of-mitigation approach (see eg Fletcher 1978: 460–66). Alternatively, the term 'offence' might be

---

[36] For discussion of the reasons, see Dunbar and Langdon (1998).

understood to have a broader meaning that incorporates aspects of the offender's mental state in relation to the harmful conduct or omission, as well as the conduct or omission itself.

The benefit of such a conception is that it creates room for the idea that the offender who commits a crime having already acquired one or more previous convictions is more blameworthy than the novice. Exactly why this should be so can be discussed in its turn,[37] but it is an inherently more plausible notion than that the existence of previous convictions alters the quality of the conduct that is the subject of the current offence. Nevertheless, it may be regarded as having a serious flaw. If the extra punishment is somehow to be justified in terms of the opportunity that the previous convictions have occasioned for the offender to develop a deeper degree of awareness, or comprehension, of the wrongfulness of what has been done, it begins to sound as though it is the offender's *attitude* that is being punished. And, if that is right, then the argument is verging towards the proposition that the offender is earning a sentence premium on account of who she or he is; not what she or he has done. It is not only the most devoted desert theorists who find that spectre distasteful.

A further set of policy issues arises from the growing bodies of empirical research into the phenomena of recidivism and desistance.[38] As the former is the subject of a separate contribution to this volume,[39] it will not be discussed here. However, it is appropriate to provide some brief, rudimentary indication of the consequence of the evolving literature on desistance for the issues that have been debated in this chapter. For example, one of the most important points that emerges from that work is that desistance from offending is better conceptualised as a process than as a clean-cut change. Therefore, even though an individual may remain actively engaged in crime, a pattern of de-escalation, whereby offences are becoming less harmful and/or less frequent, may be the marker of ongoing reform. Conversely, of course, if the offender's record reveals the opposite tendencies, that might suggest a strengthening commitment to a criminal lifestyle. Appraised in terms of the Criminal Justice Act 2003, the language of section 143(2) is not really apt to capture trends in either harmfulness or frequency as pertinent dimensions of decision-making.

To cite a second example, the literature also suggests that the outlook of an offender is an important factor in the desistance process. She or he may be trying genuinely to stop committing crimes, but failing for a variety of reasons. This suggests that, rather than the crudely negative method through which section 143(2) allows attitude to be taken into account, what the law should require instead is a more careful and reflective assessment that seeks to reinforce offenders' efforts to desist. There

---

[37] See eg the contributions by Lee, Bennett and Roberts in this volume.
[38] For a useful review, see Farrall and Maruna (2004: 357–436).
[39] See further Kazemian (in this volume).

is some evidence that a reform of this kind would operate to draw the legislation closer to practice.

Recent studies of sentencing decisions around the 'cusp' of custody have shown the importance of both previous convictions and qualitative assessments of an offender's character. Thus Hough, Jacobson and Millie found that criminal history was a major factor that inclined judges and magistrates towards a custodial sentence in borderline cases. At the same time, however, they found that where there was evidence of an offender's determination to change—'that a prolific offender was willing and able to change his or her offending behaviour'—a court might well be willing to make a community order rather than custody (Hough, Jacobson and Millie 2003: 36–41). Similarly, in their Scottish study, Tombs and Jagger found that previous convictions did incline the courts towards custody, but that the moral quality of the offender was all the more important. Typically, judges held offenders 'to fall into two types—the redeemable (those displaying signs of remorse and hope) and the irredeemable (those demonstrating neither)' (Tombs and Jagger 2006). Thus a large part of the cusp decision was the assessment of whether or not an offender was motivated to stop offending. Taking that survey in combination with the earlier English study by Hough et al, it emerges clearly that the offender's criminal history was a powerful reason for imposing custody in borderline cases, almost as powerful as the nature of the offence, but that courts were often prepared to alter their provisional sentence to a community order where they found some sign of hope (Millie, Tombs and Hough 2007: 243, 255). These findings show that, before the 2003 Act came into force in England, judges and magistrates took a more qualitative approach to previous convictions than that now required by the 2003 Act. It remains to be seen whether the 2003 Act has in fact altered sentencing practice.

E. CONCLUSION

This chapter has assessed the role that previous convictions play in the sentencing of repeat offenders in England and Wales, tracing the development of the current law and providing a critical analysis of the policy that underpins it from a variety of perspectives. Throughout the discussion it has sought to distinguish between those aspects of law and policy that appear to have had some stability over time and those that have been subject to evolution and change. By way of conclusion it is appropriate to provide a flavour of the way in which fluctuations in the prevailing political climate have shaped the manner and direction in which legal provision has evolved and to reflect on what may happen in the future.

Looking back, English sentencing law has shown a recurrent concern with focusing punishment on persistence. What, then, caused Parliament to depart from this established position and enact the anomalous provision in section 29 of the Criminal Justice Act 1991? Although implausible to attribute to a single trigger, the unusual political circumstances that existed at the time that the legislation was passed provide a powerful explanatory factor. The then Conservative government was *and felt* secure in office. Consequently, it was able to adopt a stance that was fiscally conservative but, relatively speaking, morally liberal. Faced with the escalating costs that were associated with a rising prison population, it was able to capitalise upon its reputation for being tough on law and order in order to adopt a policy tack that cut against the conventional line. As the rapid amendment of section 29 by the 1993 Act attests, that ripe political moment turned out to be fleeting; law and policy soon reverted to the more traditional position once a sense of electoral vulnerability returned.[40]

Given that the legislation then remained unchanged for a decade, equivalent curiosity might attach to the political factors that influenced the resurgence of emphasis on persistence as a primary target of punishment in the Criminal Justice Act 2003. Enacted during New Labour's second term of office, the statutory proposition that repeat offending should be singled out for serious attention resonated with core elements of the New Labour 'project'. These include its particular conception of community, the notion of responsible citizenship and the insistence that the criminal justice system should be 'rebalanced' in favour of the interests of victims. Furthermore, regarded in electoral terms, such a policy offered the prospect of an 'easy sell' to the electorate as public sympathy toward recidivists is liable to be in extremely short supply.[41] Therefore, again, the policy makes sound sense when understood in terms of the prevailing politics.

Switching focus to the future, the political climate will, of course, remain key. However, there are ever clearer signs that a further contextual factor will be too: the increasingly sophisticated state of technological development (using the term 'technological' in a broad sense). Earlier, in discussing the potential implications of recent research into desistance, it was pointed out that the terms of section 143(2) do not sit comfortably with the emerging findings in that empirical field. There is, therefore, an increasingly visible gap between what the law says and the contemporary state of scientific knowledge about those to whom it applies. As such, it is becoming apparent that the technological underpinning of section 143(2) is, in this respect, deficient. In an era of alleged commitment to 'evidence-led policy',[42] there is a ready argument that the law should be reformed to promote its cohesion with this body of empirically based knowledge.

---

[40] See further Baker (1996).
[41] For detailed discussion, see Tonry (2003).
[42] A deceptively nebulous concept: see Pawson (2006).

Nor is this only way in which technological advance is relevant to prospective developments.

Perhaps the most basic point of all about taking account of previous convictions in sentencing is that it cannot be done unless the means to connect today's offender with those convictions that she or he may have accumulated in the past are available. Over time the tools for performing that match have become increasingly sophisticated and the capacity for gathering and storing relevant data has grown exponentially. Consequently, what was once an ambition to be able to establish a person's identity, and to be able to pronounce with certainty that she or he was or was not the same individual who was held responsible for some past offence, has long since been taken for granted. Modern information technology, of course, enables the capture of a much more comprehensive set of data about an individual and renders it all but instantly available, and in a manner that is capable of annihilating geographical constraints. Thus there seems to be a developing impetus, and capability, for criminal records to become more akin to offender profiles.[43] Coupled with the contemporary preoccupation with security,[44] it points to the potential for a radical reordering of society and reconfigured institutions of rights responsibilities and citizenship, perhaps on a significant geographical scale.[45]

That vision, above anything else, underscores the significance of the issues that are discussed in this volume. It is remarkable how the taking account of previous convictions has become such a well-established and pervasive element of sentencing schemes when so many complex and fundamental questions about the practice remain unresolved. Yet it is possible that little challenged assumptions regarding its utility and validity are be about to become entrenched within our social structure in unprecedented ways.

REFERENCES

Ashworth, A (2010) *Sentencing and Criminal Justice*, 5th edn (Cambridge, Cambridge University Press).

Baker, E (1996) 'From "Making Bad People Worse" to "Prison Works": Sentencing Policy in England and Wales in the 1990s' 7 *Criminal Law Forum* 639.

Baker, E and Clarkson, CMV (2002) 'Making Punishments Work? An Evaluation of the Halliday Report on Sentencing in England and Wales' *Criminal Law Review* 81.

---

[43] For a detailed discussion of this process, see Thomas (2007). See also Magee (2008).

[44] There is a proliferation of recent literature on this subject. For a useful and succinct analysis of the key ideas, see Zedner (2009).

[45] See the rapid advance in measures to enable criminal record data to be shared across the EU, discussed, for example, in Stefanou and Xanthaki (2005).

Baker, E and Roberts, JV (2005), 'Globalisation and the New Punitiveness' in J Pratt et al (eds), *The New Punitiveness: Current Trends, Theories, Perspectives* (Cullompton, Willan).

Council of Europe (1993) *Consistency in Sentencing*, Recommendation R (92) 17 (Strasbourg, Council of Europe).

Dunbar, I and Langdon, A (1998) *Tough Justice: Sentencing and Penal Policies in the 1990s* (London, Blackstone).

Farrall, S and Maruna, S (eds) (2004) 'Desistance from Crime and Implications for Policy' 43 *Howard Journal of Criminal Justice* (special issue) 357.

Farrington, D (1997) 'Human Development and Criminal Careers' in M Maguire, R Morgan and R Reiner (eds), *Oxford Handbook of Criminology*, 2nd edn (Oxford, Oxford University Press).

Fletcher, GP (1978) *Rethinking Criminal Law* (Boston, Little Brown).

Franko Aas, K (2005) *Sentencing in the Age of Information: From Faust to Macintosh* (London, Glasshouse Press).

Home Office (1990) *Crime, Justice and Protecting the Public*, Cm 965 (London, HMSO).

—— (1996) *Protecting the Public: The Government's Strategy on Crime*, Cm 3190 (London, HMSO).

—— (2001) *Making Punishments Work: Report of a Review of the Sentencing Framework for England and Wales* (Chair: John Halliday) (London, Home Office).

—— (2008) *Government Response to the Magee Review of Criminality Information*, Cm 7511 (London, TSO).

Hough, M, Jacobson, J and Millie, A (2003) *The Decision to Imprison: Sentencing and the Prison Population* (London, Prison Reform Trust).

Jones, P (2002) 'The Halliday Report and Persistent Offenders' in S Rex and M Tonry (eds), *Reform and Punishment: the Future of Sentencing* (Cullompton, Willan).

Magee, I (2008), *The Review of Criminality Information* (London, Home Office).

Millie, A, Tombs, J and Hough, M (2007) 'Borderline Sentencing: A Comparison of Sentencers' Decision-Making in England and Wales, and Scotland' 7 *Criminology and Criminal Justice* 243.

Ministry of Justice (2009) *Sentencing Statistics 2007, England and Wales* (London, Ministry of Justice).

Pawson, R (2006) *Evidence-based Policy: A Realist Perspective* (London, Sage).

Roberts, JV (2008) *Punishing Persistent Offenders* (Oxford, Oxford University Press).

Roberts, JV, Hough, M, Jacobson, J and Moon, N (2009) 'Public Attitudes to Sentencing Purposes and Sentencing Factors: An Empirical Analysis' (November) *Criminal Law Review* 771–82.

Sentencing Advisory Panel (2008) *Sentencing for Theft from a Shop* (London, Sentencing Guidelines Council).

Sentencing Guidelines Council (2008) *Theft and Burglary in a Building other than a Dwelling* (London, Sentencing Guidelines Council).

South African Law Reform Commission (2000) *Sentencing: A New Sentencing Framework* (Pretoria, Law Reform Commission).

Stefanou, C and Xanthaki, H (eds) (2008) *Towards a European Criminal Record* (Cambridge, Cambridge University Press,).

Lord Taylor (1993) 'Judges and Sentencing' *Journal of the Law Society of Scotland* 129.

Thomas, DA (1970) *Principles of Sentencing* (London, Heinemann).

Thomas, T (2007) *Criminal Records: A Database for the Criminal Justice System and Beyond* (Basingstoke, Palgrave Macmillan).

Tonry, M (ed) (2003) *Confronting Crime: Crime Control Policy under New Labour* (Cullompton, Willan).

Tombs, J and Jagger, E (2006) 'Denying Responsibility: Sentencers' Accounts of their Decisions to Imprison' 46 *British Journal of Criminology* 803.

von Hirsch, A and Jareborg, N (2009) 'The Swedish Sentencing Law', in A von Hirsch, A Ashworth and J Roberts (eds), *Principled Sentencing: Readings on Theory and Policy*, 3rd edn (Oxford, Hart Publishing).

Wasik, M (1987) 'Guidance, Guidelines and Criminal Record', in M Wasik and K Pease (eds), *Sentencing Reform* (Manchester, Manchester University Press).

Wasik M and von Hirsch, A (1994) 'Section 29 Revisited: Previous Convictions in Sentencing' *Criminal Law Review* 409.

Zedner, L (2009) *Security* (Abingdon, Routledge).

Legislation and statutory material

Coroners and Justice Act 2009
Crime and Disorder Act 1998
Crime (Sentences) Act 1997
Criminal Justice Act 1948
Criminal Justice Act 1967
Criminal Justice Act 1991
Criminal Justice Act 2003
Powers of Criminal Courts (Sentencing) Act 2000
Prevention of Crime Act 1908

Cases

R v Bailey (1988) 10 Cr App R (S) 231
R v Bexley & others (1993) 14 Cr App R (S) 462
R v Bleasdale (1984) 6 Cr App R (S) 177
R v Davies [2006] 1 Cr App R (S) 213
R v Fox (1980) 2 Cr App R (S) 188
R v Kelly [1999] 2 Cr App R (S) 176
R v Offen (No.2) [2001] 2 Cr App R (S) 44
R v Queen (1981) 3 Cr App R (S) 245
R v Spencer and Carby (1995) 16 Cr App R (S) 482
R v Stephens [2000] 2 Cr App R (S) 320
R v Turner [2000] 2 Cr App R (S) 472
R v Woods [1998] 2 Cr App R (S) 237

Previous Convictions and Proportionate Punishment under Swedish Law

PETTER ASP

A. INTRODUCTION AND OVERVIEW

THIS CHAPTER FOCUSES on the role assigned to prior convictions under the Swedish sentencing system. The purpose, however, is not only to describe the development of Swedish law in this respect, but also to use the Swedish system as a point of departure for reflections on the proper role of previous convictions under a proportionate sentencing scheme. The chapter begins with some brief historical remarks (section B), followed by a presentation of the role of previous convictions under current Swedish law (section C) and of the new proposals of Straffnivåutredningen (the Committee on the level of punishments; section D). Thereafter (in section E) I comment upon these developments and try to justify the conclusion that prior convictions should not be used as a reason for increasing the quantum of punishment, but that it is unavoidable giving prior convictions a role when it comes to revoking initial (and, in itself, disproportionate) leniency.

B. HISTORICAL BACKGROUND

Under Swedish law previous convictions have in modern times always been considered to be of importance for sentencing purposes. Explicit rules on the role of previous convictions date back to the sixteenth century (eg Träskman 1999: 200; Durling 2005: 41). This means that rules on previous convictions have been relevant as least as long as there has been a criminal law system in the modern sense of the word.

Under the old penal code (Strafflagen), which was in force for exactly 100 years from 1865 to 1965, the rules on previous convictions were very specific and applicable only in relation to a limited number of cases. They had their primary, if not exclusive, focus on the crimes of theft and robbery (Aspelin and Lundqvist 1987: 119). The rules stated, for example, that a person who committed petty theft (with two prior convictions) should be sentenced as if he had committed an ordinary theft. As regards ordinary theft, the rules provided for a separate penalty scale for the first, second and third convictions, respectively, which meant that the applicable penalty scale depended on the number of previous convictions (chapter 20, sections 10 and 11). These rules were eventually given a broader scope of application.

In 1965, when the new Swedish criminal code was enacted, a general rule on previous convictions for offences punishable by imprisonment was introduced. According to this rule, which the courts were not obliged to make use of, the maximum penalty prescribed for a certain offence could be increased by up to two years in cases of recidivism. The section was interpreted to mean that recidivism was a factor that should be taken into account to justify a more severe sentence (independently of whether there were reasons to go beyond the statutory maximum penalty) (Berg et al 2009: 26:14).

Before continuing this chronology it should be noted that Swedish criminal law theory was, during the first 60 years of the twentieth century, heavily influenced by sociological thinking. This meant that the focus was on treatment and rehabilitation. This influence was reflected in the fact that it was sometimes questioned whether one should even use the term 'punishment'—for example, a major reform proposal of 1956, dealing with the sentencing system, was called Skyddslag ('The Protective Act') (SOU, 1956: 55). When criminal law is founded upon the concept of rehabilitation, it is quite natural to focus on the needs of different offenders. In this regard recidivism may (and will), of course, be considered an important factor when making predictions. This was reflected in the law, for example, by the introduction of rules which allowed for the incarceration (for an undetermined period of time) of offenders who were considered to be 'incurable' (first introduced in 1927) (Aspelin 1999: 121).

In the 1970s there was a strong reaction, partly stemming from influences abroad, against this line of thinking (eg Nytt Straffsystem 1977:7; Aspelin 1999: 122). One of the main concerns was that the focus on the needs of the offender meant that intrusive sanctions could be imposed on the basis of prognoses and that natural and basic requirements of justice and desert were disregarded (eg Nytt Straffsystem 1977:7: 193). One might say that the reaction was inspired by the principle of just deserts, but it was combined with an explicit ambition to minimise the use of punishment. This desire had its roots in the ideas of rehabilitation; in this sense the new ideology inherited some of the core values of the old one.[1]

The reaction was successful, and in 1989 a new sentencing system, explicitly founded upon what is often called neoclassical ideas of proportionality and equivalence, was introduced (SOU 1986: 13–15; Proposition 1987/88: 120). In theory this was a revolution (most important of all was the fact that sentencing was transformed from being a matter of more or less pure clinical practice to being an area ruled by law), but in reality the differences were not that striking. This can be explained partly by the fact that proportionality never lost its importance regarding the quantum of punishment (ie when deciding the size of fines or the length of a prison sentence (Jareborg 1992: 152)), and partly by the fact that the new system incorporated many exceptions based on old case-law. In what follows I will describe the role of previous convictions under this system. It is an account of the treatment of previous convictions within a pragmatic and non-fundamentalist proportionate sentencing scheme.

C. THE EXISTING SWEDISH SYSTEM

In this section I will describe the role of previous convictions under the existing Swedish sentencing system. As noted, this system uses proportionality and equivalence as its basic rationales. The system is, however, especially as regards offences of medium severity (ie offences deserving more than a fine, but not more than one or two years of imprisonment), full of far-reaching exceptions. Sentencing in Sweden is composed of two different components:

(a) on the one hand, there is the *measurement* of punishment, ie the meting out of a specific quantity of punishment (and only fines and imprisonment are defined as punishments under Swedish law);
(b) on the other hand, there is the *choice of sanction*, ie the choice between different types of sanctions (fines, conditional sentence, probation, imprisonment, etc).

---

[1] This ambition to minimise the use of punishment actually led to the abolition of the rule on previous convictions in 1976. The head of the Department of Justice stated that the scrapping of the section on harsher sentences for recidivists was a way of underlining that one should not only try to avoid making use of sentences of imprisonment, but also try to make sure that the time spent in prison—in cases where imprisonment is considered absolutely necessary—would be as short as possible (see NJA II 1975 s 730). The reform did not exclude the possibility of taking previous convictions into account in sentencing, but it meant that it had to be done within the normal penalty scale applicable to the offence in question. A couple of years later, when the sanction of indeterminate incarceration ('internering') was abolished, the rule on previous convictions was reintroduced. It was considered necessary to facilitate at least the possibility of keeping dangerous recidivists locked up for a relatively long period of time. See NJA II 1981 s 102.

In the legislation these components are divided into two chapters: chapter 29 of the Criminal Code focuses on the measurement of punishment, and chapter 30 upon the choice of sanction. When deciding on a sentence in a standard case (I exclude the sentencing of young people and those who suffer from mental illness) one moves between these two chapters in a fairly well-structured way.

Prior convictions are of importance to sentencing in three ways:

1. as a reason for choosing imprisonment;
2. as a reason for revoking parole; and
3. as a reason for an increased quantity of punishment (as a reason for a larger fine or for a longer prison term) (eg Ulväng 2005: 332).

1. Prior Convictions as a Reason for Choosing Imprisonment

The point of departure for standard cases of sentencing is the seriousness of the offence(s) in question. In the law, the term 'penal value' is used. This follows from chapter 29, section 1:

> 1 § The punishment shall be imposed within the statutory limits according to the penal value of the crime or crimes . . .
> The penal value is determined with special regard to the harm, offence or risk which the conduct involved, what the accused realised or should have realised about it, and his intentions and motives.

As is evident from this extract, this definition implies that penal value is, by and large, a combination of the harmfulness of the criminal conduct and the culpability of the offender. This definition of penal value corresponds very well to common understandings of the seriousness of crimes.[2]

The penal value of an offence is measured in terms of day fines and imprisonment. The scale used for measuring penal value starts with minimum fines, proceeds via maximum fines and the statutory minimum of imprisonment (which is 14 days) (the point at which fines turns to minimum imprisonment is illustrated by the bottom line in Figure 1) and then continues via imprisonment for 1 year (the second line), 5 years (the third line), 10 years (the fourth line) up to imprisonment for life (the fifth line). Thus, an offence has, for example, a penal value of 80 day fines, or a penal value of 2 years of imprisonment. For different offences, different segments of the total scale form the penalty scale for the specific offence. For regular assault the penalty scale is, for example, imprisonment for 14 days up to 2 years.

---

[2] There are some peculiarities in the system—eg drug offences are treated much more harshly than any other comparable offences; it is explicitly stated in the preparatory notes that the penal value of drug offences must be judged having regard to factors other than the seriousness of the offence.

Figure 1. The penalty scale (in totality)

Having assessed the seriousness of a particular offence, there are two simple main rules:

(a) If the penal value is on the level of fines (ie under the bottom line), then a day fine, with some minor exceptions, will be imposed. Thus, one can say that as regards the choice between fines and imprisonment the choice of sanction is in practice made by application of the rules on measurement of punishment (in chapter 29); another way of expressing the same idea is to say that measurement of punishment and choice of sanction is in practice the same thing as regards the choice between fines and imprisonment (Jareborg 1992: 152).

(b) If the offence deserves more than a fine (ie the penal value has reached the level of imprisonment), then the rules on choice of sanction in chapter 30 should be applied.

At this stage, the general rule is that the court should choose a sanction other than imprisonment, unless it finds additional reasons for imposing a prison sentence.

Thus, there is a general presumption against imprisonment. This means that the expectation when deciding the sentence is that one shall not— even if the offence has a penal value that corresponds to a certain amount of imprisonment—impose a sentence of imprisonment. Thus, the primary principle when making the choice of sanction is that the offender's interest should be privileged. This is because the emphasis of the law shifts from the penalty scale (which indicates imprisonment) to the the existing alternatives to imprisonment. This is shown in Figure 2 by the box surrounded by a dotted line. Within this area a number of different sanctions—represented by boxes—are available. The two standard alternatives are conditional sentence and probation.

This presumption against imprisonment can be rebutted for three reasons only. First, it may be rebutted (and the offender sentenced to imprisonment) if the penal value is high. As a rule of thumb this requires that the penal value corresponds to 12 months (or more) of imprisonment,

Petter Asp

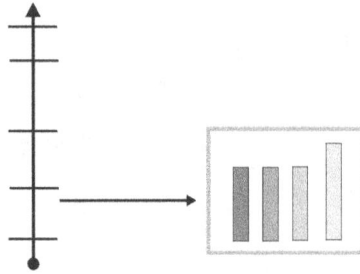

Figure 2: The presumption *against* imprisonment

so for particularly serious offences the presumption against imprisonment
is revised and more or less reversed (Proposition 1987/88:120: 100). This
is reflected in Figure 2; as can be seen, the alternative sanctions are, as
a main rule, available only at the lower end of the scale, ie between 14
days and 1 year of imprisonment.

Second, the presumption may be rebutted if the offence has such
'character' that imprisonment is considered to be appropriate for general
preventative reasons (despite the fact that the penal value is fairly low).
This exception has a very unclear theoretical basis, but is very important
in practice. One might say, quoting a Danish professor, that the main
function of the 'character' exception seems to be to provide justification
for prison sentences in cases where the judge cannot otherwise provide
reasons for such a sentence. Virtually all frequent types of criminality—eg
many crimes related to sex, drugs (including alcohol) and violence—are
considered to have such 'character' that it alone justifies incarceration.
The most important exception to this 'character' limb of the preponder-
ance against imprisonment is theft and other offences against property (eg
Berg et al 2009: 30-20; Borgeke 2008: 239; recently the Supreme Court
has actually decided that certain types of theft can also have this special
'character', thus further widening the importance of the 'character' rule).

Third, and this is where previous convictions become relevant, the presumption may be rebutted if the offender has previous convictions. When
determining whether the existence of a prior record should counteract the
presumption against imprisonment, four considerations are particularly
important:

(a) The time that has elapsed between the last offence and the new one.
Previous convictions normally become irrelevant after approximately
three or four years. However, if the offender has been imprisoned for
a long time, the courts take into account not only the time that has
elapsed between the two offences, but also the time that has elapsed

between the release of the person and the new offence (ie the time in prison is not taken into account).
(b) Whether the prior convictions are in the same genre as the new offence; if the offences are strikingly different, the prior record is normally considered to be immaterial.
(c) Whether the new offence is of similar gravity to the previous ones. If the fresh crime is manifestly less serious than the previous convictions, then the record will normally be disregarded.
(d) The number of times the offender has reoffended. If the offender has been sentenced on more than one occasion, this increases the importance of the prior record, and vice versa (eg Berg et al 2009: 30-26a; Borgeke 2008: 266).

The above-mentioned reasons for rebutting the presumption may of course interact in different ways. For example, if the penal value is high, but not so high that it in itself constitutes a reason for choosing imprisonment (eg 10 months), then one needs less of a prior record to rebut the presumption than if the offence is a minor one.

If the presumption against imprisonment is actually neutralised, then the system employs yet another provision to avoid imprisonment. This requires consideration of whether there are 'special reasons' for choosing a non-custodial sanction. The reasons are 'special' in the sense that they make it possible to choose a non-custodial sanction in cases where the court has found that there are reasons for sentencing the accused to imprisonment. One of the most important special reasons applied within the system is that the accused has agreed to combine a non-custodial sanction with community service. This second step does not, however, alter anything as regards the importance of the prior record. It will still be one of the three reasons—high penal value, special 'character' and prior record—for rebutting the presumption against imprisonment.

To summarise: the first role that prior convictions have is as a reason for choosing imprisonment rather than a non-custodial sanction.

2. Prior Conviction as a Reason for Revoking Parole

In addition to being a reason for choosing imprisonment as the punishment for the new offence, a prior record—or more correctly the fact that the person reoffends while being conditionally released—may be a reason for declaring the conditionally granted liberty forfeited, ie a reason for revoking parole (eg Berg et al 2009: 34-22; Borgeke 2008: 453).

A person serving a prison sentence in Sweden is normally granted conditional release after having served two-thirds of the jail term. This conditionally granted liberty shall, as a rule, be declared forfeit if the person reoffends within the probationary period (the probationary period equals with the length of the conditionally granted liberty, but is, as a minimum, one year).

The court may abstain from revoking the conditionally granted liberty or do so only partly if the new offence is less serious than the prior ones, or if a long time has elapsed between the prior offences, or if forfeiture otherwise would be unreasonable. However, the fact that a parolee reoffends during the probationary period creates a presumption for forfeiture. Thus, the second important and fairly direct way in which recidivism may be of importance at the sentencing stage is as a reason for revoking parole.

3. Prior Convictions as a Reason for Meting Out a Harsher Sentence

The two above-mentioned uses of previous convictions in sentencing are, by and large, considered to be consonant with the basic rationales of the system, ie with the principles of proportionality and parity. As such, they are not considered to be majorly problematic from a principled point of view. This is due to the fact that in both cases the offender is, by law, being privileged. He or she is treated with leniency (either by being sentenced to a non-custodial sanction instead of being given a prison sentence, or by being granted parole) and each provision renders previous convictions only of importance as long as one has not reached the 'normal level' which corresponds to the penal value of the offence(s). In this sense, one might say that these two avenues enabling account to be taken of previous convictions are fully reconcilable with the tolerance theory advocated by, among others, Andrew von Hirsch (1985: 77–91).

One should also add that on the practice of taking prior record into account the case-law is fairly uniform and stable (the district court included). The Criminal Code does, however, also make it possible to take previous convictions into consideration when evaluating the punishment, ie when determining the number of day fines or length of a prison sentence. This follows from chapter 29, section 4, which reads as follows:

> 4 § Apart from the penal value, the court shall in measuring the punishment, to a reasonable extent take the accused's previous criminality into account, but only if this has not been appropriately done [i] in the choice of sanction [ie when rebutting the presumption against imprisonment] or [ii] revocation of parole [ie when deciding whether conditionally granted liberty shall be forfeited].

Thus, one might say that scope exists to take prior convictions into account for the purpose of increasing the quantum of punishment, but that this possibility shall be used only exceptionally (when the prior record cannot be taken into account properly when choosing between imprisonment and a non-custodial sanction, or when deciding on whether or not conditionally granted liberty shall be forfeited).

The extent to which this section is applied differs considerably between different courts and different judges (eg SOU, 2008:85: 302). Some judges consider that the section is more or less obsolete and that prior convictions shall never (or very seldom) affect the length of a prison sentence. It is reasonable to assume that this dismissive attitude flows from the understanding that chapter 29, section 4 creates an irrational deviation from the basic principles (proportionality and parity) of the sentencing system.

Others find it 'natural' to take previous convictions into account and make use of this power fairly frequently. The recidivist premium applied, however, is usually not excessive (in the sense that it does not amplify the base of the sentence; the chief factor when deciding the length of a prison sentence remains the penal value).

However, the possibility for previous convictions to affect sentence severity has been subject to criticism, first and foremost from people who subscribe to the principle of proportionality and thus deem the rule in chapter 29, section 4 to be an irrational deviation from the central principles of the system (eg Ulväng 2005: 347; SOU, 2008:55: 517, 541). Another criticism is that the case-law is uneven and that the legislation provides too little guidance on how to treat previous convictions when determining a sentence (SOU 2008:55: 303).

In addition, the formulation of the system has been criticised for contradicting the rules on revoking parole. The three-step process described above—taking previous convictions into account, first, as a reason for choosing a prison sentence, second, as a reason for revoking parole, and third, as a reason for increasing the quantum of punishment—means that a person who has been conditionally released and has abstained from reoffending during the probationary period (and thus will not have his or her parole revoked), might nevertheless get a recidivist premium (SOU 2008:55: 304).

To summarise, there are three different ways of taking previous convictions into account:

(a) in choosing imprisonment instead of a non-custodial sanction, where previous convictions may solely or jointly justify rebutting the presumption against imprisonment;

(b) in declaring conditionally granted release forfeited, where previous convictions are a reason for revocation of parole; and—only if the prior record is not taken into account properly via (a) and (b)—

(c) in taking it into account as a reason for increasing the number of day fines or the length of a prison sentence.

4. Prospective Judgments

Thus far I have described the most important situations in which the historical fact that an offender has a prior criminal record might be directly relevant for deciding his or her sentence, or for revoking parole. In so doing, I have focused on situations in which the perspective is purely retrospective and in which the prior record is an explicit and legitimate factor for establishing a certain legal consequence.

A prior record might, however, be of importance in other more indirect ways. For example, when choosing between the two main forms of non-custodial sanctions (conditional sentence and probation), the choice is dependent upon whether there is reason to expect that the offender will commit new crimes in the future. The law clearly indicates that the choice rests upon a prospective judgment, but often the decision in practice is, at least partly, reliant upon whether or not the offender has a prior record (eg Borgeke 2008: 46).

The same holds true for situations where the question is whether or not a suspected offender should be held in custody. Here too the risk of future crimes being committed by the accused should be considered, but whether or not the suspect has a prior record will often affect the outcome. Hence, one should not underestimate the importance of a prior criminal record when it comes to the application of rules which are supposed to have a prospective character.[3]

D. THE COMMITTEE ON THE LEVEL OF PUNISHMENTS

In the previous section I have given an account of the role of previous convictions under the current Swedish legislation. There is, however, reason to believe (and fear) that there will shortly be reform in this area.

In 2007 the Swedish government appointed a legislative committee with the task of considering certain issues regarding sentencing. One of the objectives was to consider methods of adjusting the level of punishment for assault and other offences including violence against persons. The position of the government is that such offences are punished too leniently—ie disproportionately—in relation to, for example, tax offences and other types of property crime or crimes against the state.[4] Another

---

[3] One can, of course, also speculate whether a prior record does not at times affect the fact finding of the court (eg whether a prior record, in cases where the facts are unclear, may at times be seen as an indication of intent on the behalf of the accused or as an indication that he has participated in committing a certain offence) (eg Sitte Durling 2005: 128). This is not, however, the place for such speculations.

[4] In my view this position is tenable, but this does not necessarily mean that the only solution is to increase severity for these offences. Neither does it imply that this rather slight imbalance within the sentencing system is one of the bigger problems of the criminal

aim was to take measures to increase the differentiation within the system; Swedish courts have, with some exceptions, a tradition of using only the lower part of the available penalty scale, and even though this tradition can rationally be defended, it is considered to be a problem by leading politicians. In this respect, previous convictions were mentioned as one way of achieving the aim of increased differentiation.

The Committee undertook extensive discussions (in which I participated as an expert) on the role of previous convictions and, as indicated above, it was by no means clear that the Committee would find it necessary to make a proposal for reform vis-à-vis prior convictions. In the end, however, the Committee did so, and the proposed change focused solely on the rule in chapter 29, section 4 on previous convictions as a reason for increasing the quantum of punishment.

The Committee found that there are several problems connected with the present legislation. Among other things, it does not give enough guidance; it means that a person who has behaved well during his probationary period can have the reward (of not having his parole revoked) neutralised by a harsher sentence; and there is reason to take previous convictions into account not only indirectly as a reason for revoking initial leniency (ie for choosing imprisonment and for revoking parole) but also directly and regularly as a reason for a more severe sentence (SOU 2008:55: 301).

Thus, the proposals of the Committee are intended (i) to provide better guidance in relation to the factors that should be taken into account when deciding whether or not to take previous convictions into account for determining the quantum of punishment; (ii) to abolish the 'give and take back' arrangement arising from the three-step rule; and (iii) to make it clear that previous convictions shall be used not only for revoking initial leniency, but also for increasing the sentence.

Furthermore, the Committee listed five general reasons supporting the proposition that the opportunities to take prior convictions into account for the purpose of deciding the quantum of punishment should be increased. These reasons can be summarised as follows:

(a) There are such possibilities in most countries and it is believed to be 'fair' to take previous convictions into consideration.
(b) There is a need to show that society's tolerance decreases as a person reoffends.
(c) The degree of punishment must be differentiated in order to feasibly promote both the principle of parsimony and the need for 'credibility'. In other words, we should be able to demonstrate parsimony by imposing a shorter prison sentence the first time, and promote

---

justice system of Sweden. For example, the totally unreasonable repression of drug offences is far more pressing.

credibility the second or third time by increasing the length of the imprisonment.

(d) Imprisoning a person who reoffends for a longer period serves incapacitative purposes.

(e) There is systematic support for such in the Swedish sentencing system; if it were not possible to increase the quantum of punishment due to a prior record, the rule that provides for an extension of the penalty scale in cases of recidivism would not be necessary (SOU, 2008:55: 309).

In sum, the Committee proposed that the power to take previous convictions into account when determining the quantum of punishment should be broadened, above all (i) by making it clear that this type of factor should not be secondary in relation to the revocation of parole; and (ii) that the law should provide better guidance as to when previous convictions should be taken into account. The proposal can be summarised as follows:

(i)   previous convictions should be taken into account as a reason for an increased quantum of punishment when a person:
      (a) repeatedly commits crimes of the same type, and
      (b) when a person commits a second serious crime of the same type (serious would be indicated by a jail term of about one year)
(ii) previous convictions should be taken into account irrespective of whether conditionally granted release can be forfeited or not;
(iii) the principle of proportionality shall be observed by the introduction of a proportionality limit: the court shall, when applying the section, make sure that the total sentence length is not unreasonably harsh in relation to the penal value of the offence (SOU 2008:55: 33, 311, 395).

It should also be noted that the Committee—perhaps somewhat inconsistently (since it also argues that 'indirect' recidivist premiums, ie revocation of initial leniency, is one thing, and direct recidivist premiums quite another)—actually uses a limiting desert model (SOU 2008:55: 306) (which resembles Norval Morris's (1998) concept of limiting desert) for the purpose of justifying the recidivist premium. The reasoning can be described as the following:

(i)   proportionality provides only an approximate answer;
(ii) even though one adheres to proportionate sentencing, there is reason to make the first prison sentence as lenient as possible having regard to the seriousness of the offence;
(iii) this means that there is an additional quantum of punishment remaining within the boundaries dictated by proportionality;
(iv) this quantum of punishment can be added in the case of a recidivist.

I find this line of reasoning unconvincing—in my view it misrepresents the idea of ordinal proportionality, and will also contribute to the creation of a system which blurs the boundaries between different types of reasons. The consequence of this is the subject of a paper a defence lawyer and I wrote arguing against this proposal of the Committee (SOU, 2008:55: 399).

E. PLAIDOYER FOR GIVING PRIOR RECORD
AND INDIRECT IMPORTANCE ONLY

In the final part of this chapter I will attempt to outline my view on how previous convictions could coherently be integrated within a sentencing system governed by a proportionality rationale.

Before getting into the specifics of previous convictions I would, however, like to draw attention to the fact that one's position on the proper role of previous convictions will always depend upon stances taken on other, more fundamental issues concerning the criminal justice system. Hence, I would argue that any proposition concerning the role of previous convictions is derived from assumptions regarding the proper role, function and morality of the penal system; on different conceptions of desert, culpability and responsibility. This implies that one should perhaps start a debate on the role of previous convictions at sentencing, not by discussing previous convictions as such, but rather by discussing these fundamental and—in relation to previous convictions—almost axiomatic questions.

My thoughts build on at least two assumptions of this nature. First of all I would argue that there is, at the very bottom of the criminal law system, a basic principle of fair retribution,[5] the importance of which often seems to be underestimated when it comes to disputes on sentencing. I would contend that the distribution of punishment in known cases must always be justified by reference to what the person being punished actually has done—ie by reference to some notion of deservedness—and I will try to demonstrate the existence of such a principle by showing that all elements of the criminal law and justice system actually serve the purpose of securing deservedness.

If one starts at the procedural level it seems clear that many basic procedural principles (it is especially evident as regards the principle in *dubio pro reo*, which will be used as the prime example here) serve the basic function of ensuring we do not convict an innocent person. For example, the purpose of *in dubio pro reo* (and many other principles of criminal procedure) is to secure deservedness in the sense that the person accused should actually 'have done what he or she is accused of having done'.

---

[5] For a fuller account see Asp (2008).

Further, it seems quite plain that the importance that we attach to the principle is founded on the interest of justice rather than, for example, economic interests or convenience. The distress we feel when an innocent person has been punished is not due to the fact that it is a waste of money to punish the wrong person. It is due to the fact that it is a clear injustice to punish a person who did not deserve the punishment in question (he or she might of course deserve to be punished for something else). We may have problems with accepting retribution as the general justifying aim of the criminal law system, but great weight is obviously attached to retribution as a limiting principle of distributing penalties. Perhaps I am stating the obvious, but this is exactly what I want to do. My purpose is to highlight the fact that there seems to be almost unanimous agreement that it is unacceptable to convict a person who is innocent and therefore does not deserve punishment.

If we are—as I suggest—interested in deservedness, the simple fact that someone has 'done' the thing he is accused of is not, however, in isolation or on its own worth that much. For instance, it seems obvious that it is problematic to speak of deserved punishment in a case where we punish a person who has committed a criminal act whilst being asleep, or in a state of automatism. Ensuring that a person has actually done X is of little matter if one does not also ensure that the person is culpable for having done X. For the purpose of establishing that the accused is responsible we have, within the general part of the criminal law, many rules of imputation: rules that are supposed to guarantee deservedness not only in the sense of 'having done X' but also in the sense of 'being responsible for X'. Thus I would argue there is a clear link between the importance of deservedness and the rules on imputation in the general part of the criminal law.

Neither the procedural rules nor the rules on imputation can, however, do the job unless we ensure that we are not criminalising things which are not worthy of being proscribed in the first place. Applying *in dubio pro reo* and strong requirements of imputation does little for deservedness if we criminalise a walk in the park or the eating of an apple. If the tenet of deservedness should be of any value, we must also ensure that the law criminalises things worthy of penal censure.

Thus, the importance of deservedness not only explains the importance attached to basic rules on the procedural level and in relation to blameworthiness, but also demonstrates that we should attach great weight to the principles of criminalization. As Douglas Husak notes: 'None of the other normative concerns on which legal philosophers have tended to focus could hope to compensate for the injustice that inevitably occurs when a state punishes conduct that should not have been criminalized in the first place' (Husak 2002: 346; Husak 1995: 153).

Notwithstanding this, I would argue that it is necessary to take yet another step and assert that the notion of deservedness is of fundamental importance not only on the three levels discussed above, but also at the level of sentencing. This is due to the simple fact that the criminal justice system does not only use a digital on/off-perspective (guilty/not guilty, etc), but comprises a scale of crimes (everything from a petty theft to a murder) and penalties (everything from a minor fine to imprisonment for life). Due to this huge span of crimes and punishments, the question of deservedness must always be discussed as a question of degree. Questions of deservedness are, within criminal law, discussed in a normative context where one judgment will inevitably be related to another. One could, for example, question whether it is meaningful to speak of deservedness in a system where:

A, who has committed a murder (using a knife), gets 1 month imprisonment;
B, who has committed a murder (using an axe), gets 10 years of imprisonment;
C, who has shoplifted a chocolate bar, gets 25 years of imprisonment;
D, who has shoplifted a pack of chewing gum, gets 1 year of imprisonment; and
E, who has burned down the Royal Albert Hall, gets 1 month of imprisonment.

No matter whether the system in question fully lives up the principle of *in dubio pro reo* and challenging standards of imputation, it seems self-evident that it would be a difficult task to explain to C why his or her sentence is deserved.

To summarise, I am submitting that if we assign importance to deservedness—and the underlying principle of *in dubio pro reo* shows that we do—we cannot be satisfied merely with the finding that the accused has actually done what he or she is accused of having done, but we must also prove that he or she is culpable for having done that something, that the act is genuinely worthy of being criminalised at all, and that the quantum of punishment imposed upon them is deserved having regard to what the offender has actually done. If one accepts this line of reasoning, then it is clear that the principle of proportionate punishment is not just one rationale for sentencing amongst others, but rather a logical continuation of more ubiquitous values that actually define the criminal law itself.

Disproportionately harsh punishment is problematic due to the fact that it gives the sentenced person more punishment than he or she deserves. The fact that proportionality in this way can be derived from the brutishness of the criminal law system and from the importance of deservedness as a justification for the infliction of hardship and censure also explains why it is not necessarily equally problematic to be lenient—ie to deviate from proportionality by imposing a more lenient sentence than is deserved.

Even though proportionality is a determining rather than a limiting principle it thus seems clear that it is one thing to deviate from proportionality
by being lenient and quite another thing to deviate in the other direction.
Only the second type of deviation is in direct conflict with the basic value
of deservedness as a limit to justified punishment.

All this implies that previous convictions should be taken into account
only insofar as such a rule could be justified having regard to the factors
of deservedness that are actually applicable in the individual case. In my
view no such justification has—despite repeated attempts (most recently
in this volume)—been provided. One could try to argue for a broader
notion of deservedness, but then one will immediately face the problem
that once we take the broader context into account, we will certainly
find many arguments for treating people that reoffend more leniently (eg
people who reoffend are often socially underprivileged and live under
circumstances that make it more difficult for them to comply with the
law). Moreover, if you ask why it is wrong to commit an offence, the
most plausible answer is still 'because it violates the interests of others'.
If one tries to argue that it is partly due to some sort of disobedience in
relation to the state, one not only has to justify a form of personal relationship between the state and the offender (which nowadays seems, at
best, implausible), but also explain why the criminal process preceding the
first conviction should be considered to be of such importance. I am not
claiming that it is unreasonable to argue in another direction, but since
applying a recidivist premium results in more punishment, patently the
burden of proof (or the onus) is on the party who favours the use of a
recidivist premium to justify it. I do not think that this burden has been
overcome. The person who reoffends already receives at least twice the
sentence as the first-time offender (since he is actually sentenced twice);
why should he get even more?

My second assumption is that there are good reasons to show some
general initial leniency when operating the criminal justice system. Initial
leniency could be justified with reference both to notions of mercy and
human fallibleness, and also to utilitarian considerations pertaining to the
harmfulness of prisons and to the costs incurred by the use of imprisonment.[6] The criminal justice system is brutish and we all know how easy
it is to make mistakes. In addition, we know that imprisonment is costly
(we know how much it costs per day to keep someone in jail), and we

---

[6] It should be observed that such initial leniency does not—as a recidivist premium—necessarily need to be justified by reference to the individual circumstances of each and every
case, ie it does not necessarily have to involve judgments in an individual case about the
appropriateness of affording leniency. One could also use general knowledge about humanity,
general knowledge about the drawbacks of imprisonment, etc, as a basis for constructing
rules that (generally) allow for leniency for the first (second, third, etc) iteration. In other
words: a general rule providing for leniency can be justified without proving that the justifications behind the rule apply in each and every case within the realm of the rule.

also know that imprisonment does not always make it easier for people to return to a normal life.

As displayed by the Swedish system, one can show initial leniency in different ways, inter alia, (i) by choosing a less intrusive type of sanction than the one actually deserved under the proportionality scheme; or (ii) by not executing a sentence fully (ie by making the sentence conditional or by allowing conditional release).

The point of highlighting the concept of initial leniency is that rules regulating such leniency will almost inevitably have to be supplemented with rules providing a possibility to revoke the leniency. Thus, within a system which observes a policy of initial leniency, the fact that someone reoffends (in a way which is considered to be relevant) will have consequences: the person will indirectly be told that his behaviour is not acceptable and the fact that he has reoffended will mean that he is no longer eligible for the initial leniency discount. This means that previous convictions will automatically have an important role to play within a system based on (i) the principle of proportionality and (ii) a principle of initial leniency.

All this is more or less a variation on the theory of progressive loss of mitigation as developed by von Hirsch. This theory posits that previous convictions have a role to play, but not as reason for imposing a more punitive sentence than the one deserved having regard to the offence committed, but rather as a reason for not showing leniency in the way a first-time offender would be. This scheme for taking previous convictions into account is compatible with, but does not follow from, the principle of proportionality (at least if understood in the way developed above).

This means that the really crucial question is not whether reoffending should not count at all (it will as a reason for revoking initially shown leniency), but rather whether there are reasons to take a criminal record into account in yet another way: to enable a recidivist premium (which is independent of any initially shown leniency)? I would answer in the negative. As indicated above, the basic reason is that I cannot help but find the ideological basis for this still weak and undeveloped. After centuries of discussion it is still unclear why previous convictions should justify imposing a harsher sentence in relation to the first offence. However, since it is obvious that reasonable people disagree on this question, I would like to add a couple of prudential reasons for not accepting a recidivist premium that goes beyond the revocation of initially shown leniency.

Firstly, a system where great weight is attached to previous convictions will inevitably undermine the 'message' conveyed by sentences pronounced within a proportionate sentencing regime as crimes are ranked ordinally in relation to their severity. The amalgamation of deservedness relating to the act and deservedness relating to the actor will blur the moral message of the criminal justice system and make it difficult to comprehend; acts of equal severity will be met by different sanctions depending on whether or not the offender has a prior criminal record. Since the desire to make previous convictions relevant to sentencing can be accomplished by other means than a recidivist premium, there are good reasons for avoiding any such sentencing premium system.

Secondly, proportionality requires an offence ranking, and the ranking of offences is a difficult task whether you are discussing the relation between classes of offences (ie between the offence of assault and the offence of perjury) or the relation between two concrete acts. Further difficulties arise due to the fact that the system will have to deal not only with single offences, but also with multiple offending. Proportionality is, even though it gives better guidance than most other rationales for sentencing, a difficult concept to translate into practice. If, in addition, we amalgamate factors of different types (offence seriousness and the relevance of previous convictions), things becomes extremely complicated. Thus I would argue that preserving proportionality in itself can be considered as a cogent reason not to operate a recidivist premium.

Thirdly, there are within a proportionate sentencing scheme strong reasons for having a system of bulk discounts for multiple offences. Such a system will, if it is combined with a system providing for recidivist premiums, simply make the chronology of the course of crimes and respective court hearings too important. In practice, too much importance will be attached to the time when the last sentence was passed. This can be illustrated by the following argument in three steps:

(a) Due to the fact that life is short we cannot, at least not in practice, simply cumulate punishment for all offences. On the contrary, if one wants to preserve the idea of ordinal proportionality (preserve the internal ranking of offences so that, for instance, 400 petty thefts are not treated as being more serious than a murder, and avoid hitting the sanction ceiling) some forms of bulk discounts are simply necessary (Jareborg 2002: 56; Ulväng, 2005: 257).

(b) The only difference between a case of multiple offending and a case of recidivism is that the latter presupposes that there is a conviction before the present offences have come to court. When there is no conviction(s) the offender will get a discount; when there is a conviction the offender will instead get a recidivist premium.

(c) This means that if we combine a system of bulk discounts with a system of recidivist premiums, we might get very divergent results depending on the way offences and convictions are structured in time. As a (fully realistic) example, 4+4 will be 6 if there is no sentence before the second offence, but 4+4 will be 10 if there is. The differences can be even bigger if you consider a case where you have a larger number of offences. Thus 4+4+4+4 might be 8 if there is no conviction in between the crimes, while the same series of offences might add up to 25 (4+6+7+8) if you add an increasing recidivist premium.

Thus, one can say that the combination of bulk discounts and a recidivist premium will lead to a situation where the chronological structure will be very important. I do not think that it is possible to eliminate the impact of the chronological structure—the outcome of the criminal process will be affected by factors such as if and when an offence is detected, etc—but there is no reason to exacerbate this effect by combining a bulk discount policy with a system of recidivist premiums. To do that is to attach too much importance to (what I have called) the chronological structure.

Fourthly, putting strong emphasis on previous convictions (in a way that goes beyond revoking initial leniency) is perhaps the best way of making the criminal justice system discriminatory in terms of social status. The recidivist premium will generally speaking hit the underprivileged hardest. One could argue that this is a characteristic of the criminal jsutice system in general, but if one recognises this, it only makes it more crucial not to enhance this feature of the system. To use recidivist premiums could be seen as a way of underlining an 'us and them' attitude within the criminal justice system.

F. SUMMARY

To summarise, I have tried to argue that there are both principled and pragmatic reasons for not applying a recidivist premium. As such, my message has been that even if you are inclined to think that a recidivist premium is justified, there are strong pragmatic reasons against actually providing for such a rule. In short, I have sought to argue that enacting a recidivist premium will undermine the concept and the implementation of the principle of proportionality, and that the principle of proportionality, having regard to its fundamental importance in securing justice and deservedness, should be given priority.

REFERENCES

Asp, P (2008) 'Principen om rättvis bestraffning—alltings grundbult' *Tidskrift utgiven av Juridiska föreningen i Finland* 530.
Aspelin, E (1999) 'Straffets grunder—historisk bakgrund' *Svensk juristtidning* 108.
Aspelin, E and Lundqvist, A (1987) 'Synpunkter på återfallets betydelse i straffsystemet' (Det 31 nordiska juristmötet, Helsingfors) 111.
Berg, U, et al (2009) *Brottsbalken. En kommentar Kap 25–38* (Stockholm, Stockholm Norstedts Juridik).

Borgeke, M (2008) *Att bestämma påföljd för brott* (Stockholm, Norstedts Juridik).

Husak, D (1995) 'The Nature and Justifiability of Nonconsummate Offenses' 37 *Arizona Law Review* 151.

— — (2002) 'Reflective Equilibrium between Punishment and Crime' in P Asp et al (eds), *Flores juris et legume. Festskrift till Nils Jareborg* (Uppsala, Iustus).

Jareborg, N (1992) *Straffrättsideologiska fragment.* (Uppsala, Iustus).

— — (2002) *Scraps of Penal Theory* (Uppsala, Iustus).

Morris, N (1998) 'Desert as a Limiting Principle' in A von Hirsch and A Ashworth (eds), *Principled Sentencing: Readings on Theory & Policy*, 2nd edn (Oxford, Hart Publishing).

Sitte Durling, C (2005) *Tidigare brottslighet. Om rättsverkningar av återfall i brott.* (Stockholm, Juridiska institutionen, Stockholms universitet).

Träskman, PO (1999) 'Om återfall i brott' 2 *Svensk juristtidning* 200.

Ulväng, M (2005) *Påföljdskonkurrens problem och principer* (Uppsala, Iustus).

von Hirsch, A (1985) *Past or Future Crimes* (New Brunswick, Rugters University Press).

Official Rreports

Nytt Juridiskt Arkiv (NJA) II 1975.

Nytt Juridiskt Arkiv (NJA) II 1981.

Nytt straffsystem, Idéer och förslag, Rapport 1977:7.

Proposition 1987/88:120. om ändring i brottsbalken m.m. (straffmätning och påföljdsval m.m.).

Statens offentliga utredningar (SOU) 1956:55 Skyddslag.

Statens offentliga utredningar (SOU) 1986:13–15. Påföljd för brott.

Statens offentliga utredningar (SOU) 2008:85. Straff i proportion till brottets allvar.

12

Assessing the Impact of a Recidivist Sentencing Premium on Crime and Recidivism Rates

LILA KAZEMIAN

T HE ROLE OF the criminal record in sentencing practices remains the subject of ongoing debate among scholars and policy-makers. Information about offending history is integrated in most sentencing guidelines, either to make an assessment of the offender's degree of culpability or to make predictions about future offending. It is well established that repeat offenders tend to be punished more harshly when compared to first-time offenders facing charges for the same offence (Kowalski and Caputo 1999), and that sentence enhancements (or sentencing premiums) for repeat offenders are widespread in different jurisdictions and countries (Roberts 1997). The recidivist sentencing premium is a particularly important topic in the study of sentencing practices and policies, as the majority individuals at the conviction stage are repeat offenders (Roberts 2008). The 'three-strikes' laws implemented across the United States (as well as in England, in a modified version) are an example of policies that seek to give enhanced sentences to repeat offenders.

In recent years, some important changes have occurred in England and Wales with regard to the role of criminal history in determining the severity of the sentence (Roberts 2008). While the 1991 Criminal Justice Act (and its amended version in 1993) stated that prior convictions should not be used as a criterion for sentence enhancement, this particular provision was subsequently subject to some significant modifications. The Home Office Sentencing Review of 2001, which led to the 2003 Criminal Justice Act, stipulates that the severity of the sentence should be determined on the basis of two factors: the seriousness of the current offence, and the *recent and relevant criminal history* of the defendant. With regard to the latter factor, '[T]he severity of sentence should increase to reflect a persistent course of criminal conduct, as shown by previous convictions and sentences' (Home Office 2001: iii). The emerging role of criminal history in sentencing decisions warrants a thorough discussion of the impact of a recidivist sentencing premium on crime and recidivism rates. More specifically, it is important to examine whether such a policy can be justified within a utilitarian framework.

This chapter attempts to shed some light on this question, and to explore some of the key issues relevant to the implementation of a recidivist sentencing premium (RSP). The fundamental concern raised by the RSP, as well as other similar practices, relates to the crime reduction effects of cumulative sentencing policies. While there have not been any evaluations of policies advocating incremental increases in sentence,[1] this chapter aims to assess whether extended sentences for repeat offenders can potentially have desirable effects on crime and recidivism rates. Because sentencing premiums are generally relevant to custodial sanctions, it is particularly important to investigate the impact of incarceration on crime and recidivism. The first section of the chapter lays out the rationale for using a RSP, from both theoretical and practical viewpoints. The second section highlights some of the major caveats of the recidivist sentencing premium. The empirical evidence relating to the relationship between incarceration and crime and recidivism is also presented. The chapter concludes with a discussion of the implications of a recidivist sentencing premium for repeat offenders, and for criminal justice policies more generally.

A. THE APPEAL OF A RECIDIVIST
SENTENCING PREMIUM

The RSP entails the recourse to enhanced sentences for repeat offenders, based on the premise that recidivists present a higher risk of reoffending (Roberts 2008).[2] There is a large body of research that has emphasised the inextricable link between past and future offending (eg Piquero, Farrington and Blumstein 2003). These studies have argued that past offending is one of the strongest predictors of future offending, and that there is a great deal of continuity in offending behaviour. As such, an extensive criminal history is often associated with increased risks of recidivism. In the area of policy, the link between culpability and criminal history is found to be a guiding principle in sentencing practices worldwide (Roberts 2008).

The RSP offers the same appealing claim that has been laid out in

---

[1] There is a large body of research that has assessed the effectiveness of three-strike policies, which target repeat offenders. However, these policies do not imply an incremental increase in sentence severity to reflect each additional conviction.

[2] Beyond the imposition of longer sentences, another strategy used to enhance the incarceration time of repeat offenders is to increase the period of eligibility for parole and early release (Roberts 1997).

the selective incapacitation literature: the idea of incapacitating high-rate offenders who persistently engage in illicit behaviour. Conflicting arguments arise with regard to the use of cumulative sentencing policies. The incapacitation model justifies recourse to the RSP on the basis that repeat offenders are more likely to recidivate than first-time offenders, and should thus be incapacitated in order to prevent further offending. Proponents of the deterrence perspective argue that recidivists require more dissuasion than first-time offenders. Desert theorists emphasise that the severity of the sentence should be proportional to the gravity of the current offence, and reflect the offender's level of culpability. As such, this model gives limited importance to the offender's criminal history. The debate surrounding the use of a RSP has included advocates of these different theoretical models, and a further examination of the arguments developed in each paradigm follows.

1. The Relevance of a Recidivist Sentencing Premium from a Utilitarian Standpoint

The utilitarian rationale relies on a cost–benefit analysis of the implications of extended sentences; its primary concern relates to whether the social benefits of enhanced sentences surpass the social costs (Fletcher 1982). Fletcher (1982: 55) adds that '[F]rom a utilitarian point of view, the recidivist premium finds its warrant in the greater social danger posed by repeating offenders'. Chu, Hu and Huang (2000: 129) formulate a similar idea, and argue that 'It is expected that observed repeat offenses may be a signal related to potential criminals' unobservable characteristics, and more severe penalties on repeat offenders are needed to deter people having these unobservable characteristics.' This idea of *unobservable characteristics* has been addressed by various criminal career, life-course and developmental researchers (eg Nagin and Farrington 1992). Some have argued that these *latent traits* (or 'criminal propensity') remain stable across the various periods of the life course (Wilson and Herrnstein 1985; Gottfredson and Hirschi 1990), thus explaining the strong relationship between past criminal behaviour and future offending.

From an incapacitation viewpoint, enhanced sentences for recidivists are valuable because the offenders are removed from the community for a given period of time, thus preventing them from committing further crimes. The RSP may be viewed as a selective incapacitation policy, as it seeks to increase the incarceration time of offenders who are highly active in crime (see Greenwood and Abrahamse 1982, for one of the major studies on selective incapacitation). The incapacitative justification for a RSP presumes a greater risk of recidivism for repeat offenders, and a need to remove these individuals from the community to prevent further offending.

Another viewpoint within the utilitarian perspective draws on deterrence principles, which stipulate that repeat offenders require additional dissuasion (ie harsher punishment and longer sentences) to desist from crime. Advocates of the specific deterrence position argue that long prison sentences dissuade individuals from engaging in offending behaviour. The general deterrence camp maintains that enhanced sentences are not only useful in deterring the repeat offender, but also discourage other potential offenders from engaging in this type of behaviour.

Other arguments have been developed in favour of the RSP. The Home Office review of the sentencing framework, known as the Halliday Report, claimed that longer sentences for recidivists would result in increased time for treatment. von Hirsch (2002) explains that this claim is justified only if it can be demonstrated that: (a) intervention programmes are effective tools in reducing recidivism; and that (b) repeat offenders are as responsive to intervention programmes as other offenders. Some have justified the use of enhanced sentences for repeat offenders on the basis of the principle of fairness, arguing that '[T]he probability of erroneously convicting repeat offenders is lower than that of convicting first-time offenders' (Chu et al 2000: 136). Regardless of the framework, arguments of a utilitarian nature conflict with some of the basic principles put forth in the retributive model, and the use of a RSP is inconsistent with the core beliefs of desert theory.

2. The Retributive Approach to the Recidivist Sentencing Premium

Among retributive theorists, there are three perspectives (Roberts 2008). The first (the *'exclusionary' school*) argues that criminal history should not play any role in the determination of the severity of the sentence, and that only two factors (seriousness of the offence and offender's culpability) should be considered in sentencing decisions. The second perspective grants some influence, though limited, to prior convictions. This alternative position is based on the premise that recidivists are more culpable than first-time offenders (Lee, 2009). The third perspective holds that first offenders and those offenders with modest criminal records are entitled to some mitigation according to the principle of the progressive loss of mitigation.

Stigler (1970: 528–29) draws attention to the fact that 'The first-time offender may have committed the offense almost accidentally and (given any punishment) with negligible probability of repetition, so heavy penalties (which have substantial costs to the state) are unnecessary.' Some even regard a first offence as an 'aberration or out-of-character misjudgment' (Roberts 1997: 313). As such, first-time offenders should be entitled to a reduced sentence, but '[O]nce the mitigation accorded first offenders is exhausted, criminal record should play no further role at sentencing' (Roberts 2008: 470). This idea of *progressive loss of mitigation* supports the recourse to a discount for first-time offenders, but also implies that the discount is attenuated with each additional offence. With cumulative offences, the discount is eventually eliminated.

The use of a RSP conflicts with the exclusionary perspective and the progressive-loss-of-mitigation principle. Accordingly, the motives underlying the recourse to such policies can only be of a utilitarian nature; to justify the use of enhanced sentences for repeat offenders, these sentencing strategies must reduce recidivism, deter from offending, and/or lower crime rates through incapacitation. The empirical evidence on these issues will be presented in a subsequent section.

B. THE RECIDIVIST SENTENCING PREMIUM: SOME CAVEATS

Some of the limitations of this sentencing policy will be highlighted in this section. These include the issue of prediction, replacement effects, the expansion of the criminal justice net, deterrence effects, and the measurement of criminal history.

1. Does Information about Criminal History Enable Accurate Predictions about Future Offending and Risks of Recidivism?

The case for a RSP can only be maintained if it can be established that criminal history is key in the prediction of future offending behaviour. The debate over the use of prediction models in the criminal justice system has been ongoing for many years. Advocates of the prediction models argue for the relevance of incapacitation policies, stating that such policies can potentially reduce crimes rates without further taxing already scarce criminal justice resources. Desert theorists maintain that such policies violate the fundamental principles of proportionality and fairness. In prediction models, emphasis shifts from the offence to the offender. One obvious example illustrating the inconsistency between the two paradigms relates to sentencing in cases of murder and homicide. In many instances, these offences occur under exceptional circumstances. Although an individual guilty of murder would most likely present a low probability of recidivism, the gravity of the acts begs a harsh sentence, over and above the assessment of the individual's risk of harm to the community. In this example, there is a clear inconsistency between the prediction and desert models.

While it has been established that there is some continuity in offending behaviour and that past offending is a strong predictor of future
crime, an increasing number of researchers seem to agree that there is
both stability and change in offending during the course of an offender's
life (Moffitt 1993; Sampson and Laub 1993; Farrington and West 1995;
Horney, Osgood and Marshall 1995; Ezell and Cohen 2005). While criminal history information may offer some estimate of future risk, it does
not always draw an accurate portrait of risk because of the failure to
account for change in behaviour. A sentencing system that relies heavily
on criminal history emphasises the importance of stability in behaviour,
but fails to recognise the potential for change. Such a system overlooks
the fact that individuals are capable of desisting from crime and successfully reintegrating into the community.

Various difficulties arise when attempting to establish the link between
criminal history and future offending. The predictive power of criminal
history on future offending is attenuated with time, and is more influential during the earlier stages of a criminal career (Cline 1980; Sampson
and Laub 2003; Kazemian and Farrington 2006). In their follow-up of a
sample of Boston males to age 70, Sampson and Laub (2003: 584) argued
that '[L]ife-course-persistent offenders are difficult, if not impossible, to
identify prospectively using a wide variety of childhood and adolescent
risk factors'. Ezell (2007) found that life events in adulthood were better
predictors of future arrest than criminal history information. Kazemian
and Farrington (2006) also found similar results, illustrating the difficulty
in making accurate long-term predictions of criminal career outcomes.
Bushway and Smith (2007: 378) discussed the so-called 'asymmetry in the
risk prediction literature', referring to the idea that it is generally easier to
make accurate predictions about low-rate offenders than high-rate offenders (Gottfredson and Gottfredson 1986; Visher 1986).

Auerhahn (2006) has highlighted the difficulties in predicting violent
behaviour and dangerousness, arguing that 'Virtually all research that
presents a scheme to predict dangerous behavior . . . is not technically
predictive . . . these are better thought of as "post-diction" studies' (772).
Post-diction studies refer to retrospective classifications of individuals into
groups based on past behaviour. According to Auerhahn (2006), these
studies are not truly predictive by nature, and qualifying them as such
results in an overestimation of the effectiveness of the prediction instruments. Auerhahn (2006) further argues that our ability to make accurate
predictions about violent or 'dangerous' behaviour is very limited, and
concludes that 'To claim that we can predict dangerousness in individuals is false; and to subject offenders to deprivations of liberty based on
such predictions is at the very least, ethically questionable and potentially
detrimental when considered from a systemic perspective' (777).

Some recent research has suggested some improved accuracy of prediction when assessing between-individual versus within-individual differences (Kazemian, Farrington and Le Blanc 2009). If prison space is limited, background variables may provide a better (though far from perfect) insight on how to strategically allocate institutional resources between individuals. However, criminal history information is less likely to provide information about progress in the desistance process and towards termination of criminal behaviour.

The effectiveness of a RSP is conditional upon the ability to identify and incapacitate individuals while criminally active (von Hirsch 1988; Spelman 1994; Auerhahn 1999). If offenders were to naturally end their criminal careers during the period of incarceration, the preventive effects of the premium may be overestimated (Cohen 1983; Chaiken and Chaiken 1984; Blumstein, Cohen, Roth and Visher 1986). As such, given the distribution of the age–crime curve, it appears that the RSP may exert a differential impact on recidivism based on the age of offenders.

Our failure to make accurate predictions about offending behaviour has stimulated some highly controversial ideas about sentencing practices. For instance, Harcourt (2006) suggested resorting to randomisation in the allocation of punishment, guided by a fixed sentencing range. For example, individuals convicted of first-degree murder can serve anywhere between 15 and 25 years, and Harcourt (2006: 19) proposed that the judge 'simply draw a number between 15 and 25 from an urn'. Such drastic solutions underline the desperate state of prediction models.

2. Replacement Effects

The utilitarian paradigm supports the use of a RSP on the basis that the incapacitation of repeat offenders leads to the prevention of crimes that would have otherwise been committed. However, one of the major limitations in evaluations of sentencing policies relates to the assumption that replacement does not occur (see Miles and Ludwig 2007, for a thorough discussion on the topic). von Hirsch and Gottfredson (1983) highlighted the importance of replacement effects. If an offender is incarcerated, it is possible that co-offenders would either recruit a new partner or simply continue committing offences (Chaiken and Chaiken 1984). In this scenario, the crime reduction effects of the RSP would be overestimated. As such, the premium is likely to be an ineffective incapacitative strategy in the case of network offending, or other forms of group crime.

3. Penal 'Net-Widening'

A RSP creates an additional burden on the criminal justice system, and entails increased costs (von Hirsch 2002). This type of policy involves longer sentences for repeat offenders, as well as longer supervision periods after release. The recourse to enhanced sentences for repeat offenders results in a widening of the criminal justice net. Because the majority of convicted individuals are repeat offenders (Roberts 2008), the RSP is likely to have a substantial impact on sentencing decisions and incarceration, and is liable to create a greater burden on the criminal justice system. Moreover, because of the expansive nature of such policies, a RSP does not necessarily target the serious and dangerous offenders, who tend to be the main concern of policy-makers and scholars alike.

3. The Negative Effects of Incarceration

While incarceration seeks to reduce crime through incapacitation and deterrence, prison time may also have some undesirable effects, such as increased labelling and stigmatisation, limited opportunities to rebuild social ties, increased exposure to other offenders, and insufficient exposure to programmes that seek to prevent to recidivism. The narratives from Maruna's (2001: 154) study revealed that the criminal justice system did not deter offenders from crime, nor did it prompt them to desist, but rather trapped them in an endless 'cycle of crime and prison'. Sampson and Laub (1993: 165) refer to an *'indirect* role of incarceration in generating future crime'. It may, through a process of stigmatisation, have a negative impact on later job stability and employment opportunities.

4. Issues Relating to the Measurement of Criminal History

Roberts (1997: 307) discusses some of the issues that arise in the measurement of a criminal record. Some of these questions include whether juvenile adjudications should be considered when sentencing adults, whether criminal history should be assessed on the basis of arrests, convictions or sentences, whether the nature of prior offences should be considered, whether recency should be taken into account and when prior conviction should cease being considered. More importantly, Roberts asks whether there is an alternative method of conceptualising the criminal record that does not involve *repeated punishment for the same offence* (307).

Sentencing guidelines do not use a dichotomous measure of criminal record or a simple count of past convictions (Roberts 1997), but rather employ weighting schemes that give more influence to violent offences, and to felonies (as opposed to misdemeanours). Roberts (1997) notes that without this weighting scheme, an offender who commits many misdemeanours would acquire a high criminal history score. Some jurisdictions (eg Minnesota) have imposed a cap on the weight granted to misdemeanours in order to avoid a high criminal history score driven by frequent, minor offences.

Based on utilitarian principles, the RSP should be adjusted on the basis of an assessment of recidivism risk with each additional prior offence, in order to maximise deterrence and incapacitation effects (Roberts 1997). However, in most sentencing guidelines the premium increases incrementally and linearly with each additional prior, which overlooks risks of recidivism. In this model, 'The difference between first offenders and those in the next criminal history category is no greater than the difference between, say, criminal history categories 3 and 4' (Roberts 1997: 348). This may lead to 'a cumulative sentencing model in which the offender's record may be as important as the seriousness of the current offence in determining sentence severity' (Roberts 2008: 469). It is clear that this linear increase in sentence with prior convictions violates conflicts with the desert position, which suggests limiting the discount to first offenders.

The current structure of most sentencing guidelines is therefore inconsistent with the utilitarian goals sought by the RSP, and seems to emphasise punitiveness rather than assessment of risk (Roberts 1997). The hazard rate method, which is used to assess the risk of future offending, may be useful in developing sentencing guidelines that are more consistent with the utilitarian model (eg see Bushway, Brame and Paternoster 2004; Kurlycheck, Brame and Bushway 2006; Ezell 2007).

It is important to consider other features of criminal history at the sentencing stage, namely the nature and recency of the criminal record. For example section 143(2) of the 2003 Criminal Justice Act in England and Wales states that:

> In considering the seriousness of an offence ('the current offence') committed by an offender who has one or more previous convictions, the court must treat each previous conviction as an aggravating factor if (in the case of that conviction) the court considers that it can reasonably be so treated having regard, in particular to the nature of the offence to which the conviction relates and it relevance to the current offence, and the time that has elapsed since the conviction

How long should an individual be held accountable for past convictions? Investigating the impact of a criminal record on employment opportunities, Kurlycheck, Brame and Bushway (2006) use hazard rates to identify the point at which the risk of recidivism of individuals with a criminal history converges with that of individuals without a criminal record. They found that, '[I]f a person with a criminal record remains crime free for a period of about 7 years, his or her risk of a new offense is similar to that of a person without any criminal record' (80). This study highlights the idea that a recent criminal record offers greater predictive power of risk of reoffending when compared to an older criminal record. Similarly, Ezell (2007) found that even when controlling for prior differences in offending, the time elapsed since the last offence is strongly and negatively correlated with risks of future arrest; similar findings were found elsewhere (Kazemian and Farrington 2006). Roberts (1997: 335) concluded that 'Sentencing theorists of all stripes, then, agree that the relevance of a previous conviction declines over time.'

The consideration of age in sentencing decisions has been discussed by Bushway and Piehl (2007). The authors argued that age is an important factor in the assessment of a criminal record. This argument is based on the premise that the extent of the criminal record is dependent on the length of active criminal careers, and thus age must inevitably be considered in this assessment. The authors ask whether 'age deserves a place at the table as a legitimate factor for decisions about retribution and incapacitation, or if it deserves to be placed into the same category as race—an illegitimate, extralegal variable' (160). Age has also been found to be a significant predictor of residual criminal careers (Kazemian and Farrington 2006). Inevitably, the consideration of age in sentencing policies would violate the fundamental principle of proportionality put forth by desert theorists.

While sentencers may consider whether the nature of the current offence is similar to that of previous offences, empirical research demonstrates that offenders tend to be versatile and that criminal careers are generally characterised by limited specialisation (see Piquero et al 2003, for a review). The desistance literature provides some useful insight on this issue. It has been argued that desistance from crime is unlikely to occur abruptly; the patterns of intermittency observed in criminal careers underline the importance of perceiving desistance as a process, as opposed to a discrete state. Studies that rely on a dichotomous measure of desistance do not account for changes in rates of offending. In recent years, an increasing number of researchers have acknowledged the relevance of regarding desistance as a gradual process (Bushway, Piquero, Broidy, Cauffman and Mazerolle 2001; Laub and Sampson 2001; Maruna 2001). Focusing solely on termination from crime may mask the progress exhibited by individuals across various stages of the desistance process. Therefore, downward trends in offending patterns (such as deceleration or de-escalation) are highly relevant to the study of desistance. This idea raises an important question for the recidivist sentencing premium: should offenders be granted a discount if they demonstrate progress towards termination, ie a progression from serious to more minor forms of offending?

The caveats highlighted in this section have underlined the numerous points of contention between the RSP and the desert model. As a result, it is not surprising that the RSP is mainly guided by utilitarian principles. In order for the RSP to fulfil its mandate, it must be demonstrated that extended sentences for repeat offenders accomplish more than just the incapacitation of these individuals for a given period of time. Because the use of a RSP is justified on utilitarian grounds, then it must be demonstrated that incarceration does indeed exert a deterrent effect on crime and recidivism. While little is known about the crime reduction effects of cumulative sentencing policies (which entail an incremental increase in sentence for repeat offenders), various studies have investigated the impact of incapacitation on crime and recidivism rates. This question is central to the assessment of the effectiveness of a recidivist sentencing premium.

C. EMPIRICAL EVIDENCE ON THE IMPACT OF INCARCERATION ON CRIME AND RECIDIVISM

An increase in the carceral population may occur as a result of two practices: the growing number of individuals who are sentenced to a prison term (general incapacitation), or the imposition of longer sentences for offenders who are viewed as high-risk (selective incapacitation). There is a large body of research that has investigated the impact of incarceration on crime and recidivism, which is an important distinction. The impact on crime refers to the immediate or short-term effects of incarceration on aggregate crime rates, mainly through incapacitation and deterrence. The impact on recidivism is measured through recidivism rates when offenders are released and return to the community. This section highlights the different conclusions drawn about the impact of incarceration on different outcome measures, namely crime and recidivism, and the implications of the findings for a RSP.

1. Impact of Incarceration on Crime Rates

Various studies have demonstrated that increased incarceration rates result in short-term decreases in aggregate crime rates (Marvell and Moody 1994; Levitt 2004; Spelman 2006; Rosenfeld and Fornango 2007). It has been hypothesised that this negative association between incarceration and crime occurs as a result of incapacitation and deterrence effects (Levitt 2004). While he does acknowledge that his analysis overlooks other factors that would help to capture a more accurate picture of the social costs of incarceration, Levitt (1996: 348) found that the incapacitation of each additional offender prevents about 15 crimes per year, and concluded that

'[T]he marginal costs of incarceration are at or below the accompanying social benefits of crime reduction'. Spelman (2006) has suggested that a quarter of the decline in crime rates in the 1990s occurred as a result of higher incarceration rates. Fabelo (1995) found that a 30 per cent increase in incarceration is associated with a 5 per cent decrease in crime, highlighting the drastic increases in imprisonment rates required to produce any change in crime rates.

Blokland and Nieuwbeerta (2007) used data from a longitudinal Dutch study ('Criminal Career and Life Course Study') to create 'two hypothetical societies'. Their analyses include an *experimental society*, which is subject to a selective incapacitation policy. The *control society* is the group in which no new policy is implemented. Blokland and Nieuwbeerta (2007) contrasted the benefits (which refer to reductions in crime) and costs (increase in prison populations) of selective policies. They found that targeting high-rate offenders for incapacitation resulted in considerable reductions in crime, although this effect was somewhat attenuated over time (as a result of individuals being released again). Their analyses also showed a '25% decrease in crime under the strictest regime' (348), but this decline is accompanied by a substantial increase in the prison population (up to 45 times higher when compared to the prison population in the absence of a selective incapacitation policy). Blokland and Nieuwbeerta (2007: 351) concluded that 'Selective incapacitation conflicts with a number of fundamental principles of the Dutch criminal law system', and suggested resorting to alternative policies, such as policies seeking to further invest in probation and re-entry services. This recommendation is similar to that of Miles and Ludwig (2007), who argued that it is important to assess the *cost-effectiveness* of sentencing policies.

From the viewpoint of a policy-maker who is concerned with rapid reductions in crime rates, the idea that increased incarceration produces immediate reductions in crime is certainly appealing. However, there are limits to the incarceration–crime link, and these are highly relevant to policies seeking enhanced sentences for repeat offenders. Not all studies have found that incarceration reduces crime. Bernard and Ritti (1991) investigated the effectiveness of nine different selective incapacitation policies, using a sample of chronic offenders from the Philadelphia Birth Cohort Study (see Wolfgang, Figlio and Sellin 1972). Bernard and Ritti's (1991: 50–51) findings did not provide support for the effectiveness (or cost-effectiveness) of selecting incapacitation policies:

> [T]here is no evidence in the Wolfgang et al (1972) study to support the argument that selective incapacitation is a practical strategy for crime reduction. . . . Our least harsh hypothetical policy would have reduced serious adjudications by about 6% but only by incarcerating between two and six times as many juveniles as at present. Our most harsh policy would have reduced

serious adjudications by 35% but only by incarcerating between 9 and 22 times as many juveniles as at present.

Bernard and Ritti (1991) also argue that because high-rate offenders are already being sent to prison in disproportionate numbers (see also Canela-Cacho, Blumstein and Cohen 1997; Miles and Ludwig 2007), the actual impact of selective incapacitation policies on crime is not as pronounced as predicted. In light of these results, policies such as the RSP would not be expected to produce substantial crime reduction effects.

King, Mauer and Young (2005) have discussed the complex relationship between incarceration and crime, and raised issues that speak directly to the RSP. First, they argue that high-rate offenders that would be targeted by a RSP are already subject to increased incarceration (see argument above), and hence such a policy would ultimately punish lower-rate offenders. Second, the incarceration of drug or other network offenders makes little sense from a utilitarian viewpoint, because market offences are driven by demand and the offenders can be easily replaced by the network in the pursuit of its interests. The use of a sentencing premium among network offenders is thus unlikely to impact crime rates. In a similar vein, King et al (2005) have suggested that the effect of incarceration on crime rates is even more modest at the federal level in the United States, where 55 per cent of offenders are convicted of drug offences, and only 13 per cent are convicted of violent offences. The impact of a RSP would therefore be even less pronounced at the federal level.

The third point raised by King et al (2005) summarises the complex relationship between incarceration and crime. While incarceration rates have been rising rather steadily since the 1970s in the United States (especially between the mid-1980s to the early 1990s), this increase has not always been accompanied by a decline in crime rates. In fact, incarceration rates were on the rise in the 1980s, but so were violent crimes rates for offences such as robbery and murder; this phenomenon is often attributed to the expansion of drug markets during that period. These trends underline the fact that incarceration alone cannot explain the total variation in crime rates.

King et al (2005) also suggest that the excessive use of incarceration will, after a certain threshold, produce diminished returns and even unintended consequences. This is the case when replacement occurs, when the deterrent effect of incarceration is attenuated because an increasing number of people become exposed to prison experience, directly or indirectly (see also Nagin 1998), and when incarceration contributes to the development of other risk factors for crime (social disorder, dissolution of families, etc). While it is informative to better understand the effect of incarceration on crime rates, Gendreau, Goggin and Cullen (1999) raised an important question on this issue: to what extent do such aggregate figures inform us about individual behaviour?

2. Impact of Incarceration on Recidivism Rates

Whereas the incarceration–crime link is concerned with short-term effects on aggregate crime, the incarceration–recidivism link investigates the effect of imprisonment on reoffending behaviour after release from prison. This issue is of particular relevance to policies that call for enhanced sentences for repeat offenders. While there is an abundance of studies on the association between sentencing policies and crime, there is surprisingly little research evaluating the effect of sentencing policies on recidivism rates, and few studies have attempted to evaluate this research (Nagin, Cullen and Jonson 2009). One obvious reason for this gap in the literature is that recidivism studies require a post-release follow-up of the incarcerated individuals, who may not be released for long periods of time, particularly in the case of enhanced sentences. Nagin et al (2009) have highlighted some of the difficulties associated with the investigation of the effects of incarceration on reoffending, namely the direction of this association (does incarceration increase of decrease offending?), interactions with other factors (such as age of stage of criminal career), and the distinct profiles of individuals who are incarcerated versus those who are granted community sanctions.

While the literature on the incarceration–crime link has shown mixed results, empirical findings on the impact of incarceration on recidivism are rather bleak; the majority of studies have found that incarceration has either no effect or undesirable effects of subsequent offending (Nagin et al 2009). Villettaz, Killias and Zoder (2006: 1) conducted a systematic review of experimental and quasi-experimental studies having examined the 'effects of custodial and non-custodial sanctions on re-offending'. The authors found that in most quasi-experimental studies (14 out of 27) there are no significant differences in reoffending rates between those who receive custodial sanctions and those who receive non-custodial sanctions. In 11 of the 13 significant comparisons, non-custodial sanctions result in lower reoffending rates when compared to custodial sanctions. However, when the assessment is limited to experimental designs, no significant differences emerge in the reoffending rates between individuals sentenced to custodial and non-custodial sanctions.

Gendreau, Goggin and Cullen (1999) reported a meta-analysis of studies that have investigated the link between prison and recidivism. Their analysis was based on 50 studies (336,052 offenders) that examined the effect of both incarceration (compared to community sanctions) and length of time in prison on recidivism. The key finding was that both these conditions lead to increases in recidivism. The authors drew important conclusions that are highly relevant to the issue of enhanced sentences for recidivists (Gendreau et al 1999: 2).

'Prisons should not be used with the expectation of reducing criminal

behaviour.' Gendreau et al (1996: 7) argued that prison may promote offending behaviour by damaging the 'psychological and emotional well-being of inmates'. Some authors have highlighted the importance of identity transformation in the process of desistance (Meisenhelder 1977; Shover 1983; Gartner and Piliavin 1988; Shover 1996; Laub and Sampson 2001, 2003; Maruna 2001; Giordano, Cernkovich and Rudolph 2002; Bottoms, Shapland, Costello, Holmes and Muir 2004; Burnett 2004). The strains of prison life suggest that this environment may not be conducive to the development of a reformed, prosocial identity. It is not sufficient to condemn an inappropriate behaviour; the individual must be exposed to an alternative behaviour as a replacement.

In an earlier study of 100 convicted burglars in New Mexico, Bartell and Winfree (1977) found that recidivism rates were higher for individuals who were incarcerated versus those who were placed on probation. Walker, Farrington and Tucker (1981) analyzed data on 2,000 convicted males in England. Their results showed that incarceration was more effective than probation in reducing recidivism among first-time offenders, but that the opposite was true for repeat offenders (having between one and four previous convictions). This finding suggests that incarceration may not be the best response to reducing recidivism among repeat offenders. In a similar vein and of particular relevance to a RSP policy, it has been found that sentence length has either no effect or produces undesirable effects on recidivism outcomes (Beck and Hoffman 1976; Gottfredson, Gottfredson and Garofalo 1977). Maruna and Toch (2005: 171) noted that incarceration does not successfully fulfil its utilitarian mandate, and that '[T]he best research to date seems to indicate that most prison practices make little difference on offending outcomes, regardless of whether the intent is to scare straight or rehabilitate'.

Finally, various authors have highlighted the negative impact of incarceration on social bonds (family, work, school, community, etc), and its role in promoting the development of other risk factors associated with offending behaviour (Orsagh and Chen 1988; Sampson and Laub 1997; Laub and Sampson 2001; Travis and Petersilia 2001; Burnett 2004; Richards and Jones 2004; King et al 2005; Travis 2005).

'*Excessive use of incarceration has enormous cost implications.*' Over a decade ago, Cohen (1998: 17) estimated the financial costs associated with the criminal career of a life-course-persistent offender, including 'victim costs, lost quality of life, criminal justice costs, and offender productivity losses'. The author estimated that the typical criminal career costs anywhere between $1.3 and $1.5 million. Based on such results, it is not difficult to appreciate the substantial costs that may be incurred even with slight increases in recidivism rates (Gendreau et al 1996).

'*The primary justification of prison should be to incapacitate offenders (particularly, those of a chronic, higher risk nature) for reasonable peri-*

ods and to exact retribution.' This recommendation from Gendreau et al's (1996) study highlights the failure of incapacitation policies to exert anything more than a short-term effect on crime. In short, extended sentences for repeat offenders may, under certain circumstances, lead to crime reductions in the short term, but such policies are less likely to impact recidivism rates in the long term. Therefore, while cumulative sentencing policies (such as the RSP) violate principles of desert theory, they also fail to fulfil the mandate of the utilitarian model.

Despite the results presented in this section, Nagin et al (2009) have, however, cautioned that the current state of research is insufficiently developed and that limitations of studies of this nature are too substantial to draw firm conclusions about the effects of incarceration on subsequent offending. The assessment of post-release recidivism rates are a useful objective measure of the effectiveness of incarceration on later offending. However, without a parallel comparison with the magnitude of subsequent offending in the absence of imprisonment, it is difficult to assess the impact of incarceration on individual offending rates. Villetaz et al (2006) have also highlighted the need for experimental designs in order to adequately address these questions. The authors underlined other limitations of studies investigating the effect of custodial sanctions on reoffending, namely the limited follow-up periods, the lack of information about self-reported offending, the sole focus on the prevalence of offending and the oversight of other dimensions (frequency, de-escalation, etc), possible placebo effects, and a failure to account for the role of the perceived fairness of the punishment.

In summary, studies that have assessed the effects of incarceration on crime and recidivism seem to suggest that incapacitation may have only limited crime reduction benefits. It follows that policies seeking to incapacitate repeat offenders for longer periods of time (i.e., the recidivist sentencing premium) are likely to exert a negligible impact on crime and recidivism rates.

D. 'THREE-STRIKES' SENTENCING POLICIES

Three-strikes laws do not constitute a RSP in the traditional sense, as they do not prescribe an incremental increase in punishment with additional offences but rather entail a sharp, drastic increase in sentencing. However, some valuable insight can be drawn from the assessment of these policies aimed at high-rate offenders. Various studies have demonstrated the negligible (or even detrimental) effects of three-strikes laws on crime rates (Austin, Clark, Hardyman and Henry 1999; Dickey and Hollenhorst 1999; Marvell and Moody 2001; Kovandzic, Sloan and Vieraitis 2004; Chen 2008), despite substantial increase in costs (associated with the greater number of cases being processed at all stages of the criminal justice process, rising number of individuals incarcerated, and lengthier sentences) (Dickey and Hollenhorst 1999).[3]

The lack of effect of three-strikes laws on crime rates has been attributed to various factors. It has been argued that in the 1990s, crime declined as a result of pre-existing trends, and not the three-strikes law (Stolzenberg and D'Alessio 1997; Dickey and Hollenhorst 1999). Sentencing practices already punished repeat offenders more harshly, and thus the three-strikes law did not alter the distribution of punishment in a significant way (Stolzenberg and D'Alessio 1997; Austin et al 1999; Dickey and Hollenhorst 1999; Kovandzic et al 2004). This form of 'self-selective incapacitation' is referred to as *stochastic selectivity* (Canela-Cacho et al 1997), and results in an overestimation of incapacitation effects and limited crime reduction effects. The effectiveness of the three-strike policy is also affected by the duration of criminal careers and the distribution of the age–crime curve. When offenders reach a third strike, many are already in the process of aging out of crime (Stolzenberg and D'Alessio 1997; Dickey and Hollenhorst 1999; Kovandzic et al 2004). Another reason for the lack of impact of the three-strikes law relates to the fact that it does not target juvenile offenders, despite the fact that this group accounts for a large proportion of crime (Stolzenberg and D'Alessio 1997). It has also been suggested that the three-strikes legislation had virtually no effect on reductions in network and group crime, as a result of replacement effects (Kovandzic et al 2004).

Beyond the limited impact on crime, Dickey and Hollenhorst (1999) discuss the unintended consequences of the three-strikes law, namely the increased recourse to incarceration for less serious offences, the lack of uniformity in the application of the law in different jurisdictions (as a result of prosecutorial discretion in determining whether the three-strikes law should be applied), and the greater over-representation of minorities (particularly Blacks) among groups affected by this policy (Crawford, Chiricos and Kleck 1998; Austin et al 1999). Marvell and Moody's (2001) analysis of the effect of three-strikes legislation suggests that these laws lead to non-negligible increases in homicide rates, in both the short (10–12 per cent) and long term (23–29 per cent). The authors attributed this finding to the fact that 'criminals who fear the laws because they have two strikes would be expected to take extra steps to avoid punishment' (106), which may include resorting to violence to eliminate the threat of potential witnesses.

Austin et al (1999) estimated the correctional costs of a three-strikes policy, based on the incarceration cost per year, and the average minimum

---

[3] Similar practices have been implemented in England (Prolific and other Priority Offenders initiative) and in Canada (Habitual Offender Act).

sentence length. Correctional costs for three-strikers ranged anywhere from *at least* $471,477 to $1,036,519 for the most serious offences. In the case of "non-strikers", these figures ranged from at least $21,509 to $53,773. Dickey and Hollenhorst (1999: 2) argued that 'Research shows that the money spent on the additional prisons required to house them would prevent far more crimes if it were invested in prevention programs.'

In conclusion, according to Austin et al (1999: 138), the philosophy of 'the "three-strikes and you're out" movement was largely symbolic. It was not designed to have a significant impact on the criminal justice system.' This idea again supposes that while enhanced sentences for repeat offenders are meant to be guided by utilitarian principles, such policies appear to be predominantly guided by punitive principles. In the case of the three-strikes law, it is indeed true that 'the "toughest" sentencing policy is not necessarily the most effective option' (Chen 2008: 363). The key findings emerging from the three-strikes literature are directly relevant to cumulative sentencing policies and the RSP.

E. CONCLUSION

Lessons from empirical research seem to suggest that incarceration may exert an immediate impact on aggregate crime rates through the incapacitation of high-rate offenders, although this has not been a consistent finding across different periods and offence types. However, despite some methodological limitations, most studies seem to suggest that incarceration (and more importantly, incarceration length) does not significantly reduce recidivism. As such, the incremental increases in sentence set by the RSP are unlikely to lead to substantial, long-term reductions in crime and recidivism rates. This lack of impact of the cumulative sentencing model may be attributed to the imperfect continuity between past and future behaviour, the effects of offender replacement (particularly in the case of network offences), the increased tendency to incapacitate individuals who do not pose a serious threat to the community, and the various negative repercussions of incarceration on individual development and reintegration into the community. In short, the RSP is hard to justify on desert grounds, as it violates some of the basic precepts of the retributive model. While this policy is intended to serve a utilitarian function, the empirical evidence on the incarceration–reoffending link has suggested that cumulative sentencing policies such as the RSP do not fulfil this mandate. As such, it remains unclear within which framework such a policy would be justified.

It may be that the RSP is not implemented within a utilitarian framework, but that it is rather guided by principles of punitiveness (or 'revenge retribution'). This *vengeance as public policy* (Shichor and Sechrest 1996) approach has not been proven to exert a deterrent effect on crime. Sapir

(2008) maintains that harsh sentencing policies (such as the three-strikes law), mandatory minimums and similar legislation can be viewed as reactive policies. A predilection towards such policies diverts attention away from the need to invest in preventive policies, which aim to tackle the issues that deeply impact the onset and maintenance of offending behaviour: employment, education, immigration, substance use, re-entry, etc.

A recurrent theme in the legal literature and the discourse of economists is the presumption that offending occurs as a result of a rational, conscious choice. For instance, Emons (2007: 171) refers to offenders as 'agents who choose whether or not to become criminals'. From a utilitarian viewpoint, it is argued that 'recidivists should receive harsher sentences because they have not learned their lessons' (Roberts 1997: 317). The underlying principle for a RSP supposes a conscious decision to defy the law on the part of the offender. This philosophy may partly explain the predominance of the concept of punitiveness in sentencing practices. It is important to highlight that while all behaviours are the result of 'free choice', the choice itself may be bounded by a restrictive set of circumstances or opportunities.

In conclusion, the disagreements about the fate of the recidivist sentencing premium result from the lack of consensus regarding the guiding principles for punishment. The RSP conflicts with principles of desert theory, and produces results that are inconsistent with the utilitarian model. It is plausible to suggest that the recidivist sentencing premium (and other similar sentencing policies) delivers a moral message rather than serves a practical purpose. To claim otherwise overlooks the empirical evidence on the impact of extended sentences for repeat offenders on later offending.

REFERENCES

Auerhahn, K (1999) 'Selective Incapacitation and the Problem of Prediction' 37 *Criminology* 703.

—— (2006) 'Conceptual and Methodological Issues in the Prediction of Dangerous Behavior' 5 *Criminology and Public Policy* 771.

Austin, J, Clark, J, Hardyman, P and Henry, DA (1999) 'The Impact of 'Three Strikes and You're out'' 1 *Punishment and Society* 131.

Bartell, T and Winfree LT, Jr (1977) 'Recidivist Impacts of Differential Sentencing Practices for Burglary Offenders' 15 *Criminology* 387.

Beck, JL and Hoffman, PB, (1976) 'Time Served and Release Performance: A Research Note' 13 *Journal of Research in Crime and Delinquency* 127.

Bernard, TJ and Ritti, RR (1991) 'The Philadelphia Birth Cohort and Selective Incapacitation' 28 *Journal of Research in Crime and Delinquency* 33.

Blokland, AAJ and Nieuwbeerta, P (2007) 'Selectively Incapacitating Frequent Offenders: Costs and Benefits of Various Penal Scenarios' 23 *Journal of Quantitative Criminology* 327.

Blumstein, A, Cohen, J, Roth, JA and Visher, CA (1986) 'Dimensions of Active Criminal Careers' in (ed.), *Criminal Careers and 'Career Criminals'* (Washington DC, National Academy Press).

Bottoms, A, Shapland, J, Costello, A, Holmes, D and Muir, G (2004) 'Towards Desistance: Theoretical Underpinnings for an Empirical Study' 43 *The Howard Journal of Criminal Justice* 368.

Burnett, R (2004) 'To Reoffend or Not to Reoffend? The Ambivalence of Convicted Property Offenders' in S Maruna and R Immarigeon (ed), *After Crime and Punishment: Pathways to Offender Reintegration* (Cullompton, Willan).

Bushway, SD and Piehl, AM, (2007) 'The Inextricable Link between Age and Criminal History in Sentencing' 53 *Crime and Delinquency* 156.

Bushway, S and Smith, J (2007) 'Sentencing Using Statistical Treatment Rules: What We Don't Know Can't Hurt Us' 23 *Journal of Quantitative Criminology* 377.

Bushway, SD, Brame, R and Paternoster, R (2004) 'Connecting Desistance and Recidivism: Measuring Changes in Criminality over the Life Span' in S Maruna and R Immarigeon (eds), *After Crime and Punishment: Pathways to Offender Reintegration* (Cullompton, Willan).

Bushway, SD, Piquero, AR, Broidy, LM, Cauffman, E and Mazerolle, P (2001) 'An Empirical Framework for Studying Desistance as a Process' 39 *Criminology* 491.

Canela-Cacho, JA, Blumstein, A and Cohen, J,(1997) 'Frequency (L) of Imprisoned and Free Offenders' 35 *Criminology* 133.

Chaiken, MR and Chaiken, JM (1984) 'Offender Types and Public Policy' 30 *Crime and Delinquency* 195.

Chen, EY (2008) 'Impacts of "Three Strikes and You're Out" on Crime Trends in California and Throughout the United States' 24 *Journal of Contemporary Criminal Justice* 345.

Chu, CYC, Hu, S-c and Huang, T-y, (2000) 'Punishing Repeat Offenders More Severely' 20 *International Review of Law and Economics* 127.

Cline, HF (1980) 'Criminal Behavior over the Life Span' in OG Brim Jr and J Kagan (eds), *Constancy and Change in Human Development* (Cambridge, MA, Harvard University Press).

Cohen, J (1983) 'Incapacitation as a Strategy for Crime Control: Possibilities and Pitfalls' in M Tonry and N Morris (eds), *Crime and Justice: An Annual Review of Research* (Chicago, University of Chicago Press,).

Cohen, MA (1998) 'The Monetary Value of Saving a High-Risk Youth' 14 *Journal of Quantitative Criminology* 5.

Crawford, C, Chiricos, T and Kleck, G (1998) 'Race, Racial Threat, and Sentencing of Habitual Offenders' 36 *Criminology* 481.

Dickey, WJ and Hollenhorst, P (1999) 'Three-Strikes Laws: Five Years Later' 3 *Corrections Management Quarterly* 1.

Emons, W (2007) 'Escalating Penalties for Repeat Offenders' 27 *International Review of Law and Economics* 170.

Ezell, ME (2007) 'The Effect of Criminal History Variables on the Process of Desistance in Adulthood among Serious Youthful Offenders' 23 *Journal of Contemporary Criminal Justice* 28.

Ezell, ME and Cohen, LE (2005) *Desisting from Crime: Continuity and Change in Long-term Crime Patterns of Serious Chronic Offenders* (Oxford, Oxford University Press).

Fabelo, T (1995) *Testing the Case for More Incarceration in Texas: The Record so Far* (State of Texas, Criminal Justice Policy Council,).

Farrington, DP and West, DJ (1995) 'Effects of Marriage, Separation, and Children on Offending by Adults Males' in ZS Blau and J Hagan (eds), *Current Perspectives on Aging and the Life Cycle* (Greenwich, CT, JAI Press).

Fletcher, GP (1982) 'The Recidivist Premium' 1 *Criminal Justice Ethics* 54.

Gartner, R and Piliavin, I (1988) 'The Aging Offender and the Aged Offender' in PB Baltes, DL Featherman and RM Lerner (ed), *Life-Span Development and Behavior* (Hillside, NJ, Erlbaum,).

Gendreau, P, Goggin, C and Cullen, FT (1999) *The Effects of Prison Sentences on Recidivism* (Ottawa, Corrections Research Branch, Solicitor General of Canada).

Gendreau, P, Little, T and Goggin, C (1996) 'A Meta-analysis of the Predictors of Adult Offender Recidivism: What Works!' 34 *Criminology* 575.

Giordano, PL, Cernkovich, SA and Rudolph, JL (2002) 'Gender, Crime, and Desistance: Toward a Theory of Cognitive Transformation' 107 *American Journal of Sociology* 990.

Gottfredson, DM, Gottfredson, MR and Garofalo, J (1977) 'Time Served in Prison and Parole Outcomes among Parolee Risk Categories' 5 *Journal of Criminal Justice* 1.

Gottfredson, MR and Hirschi, T (1990) *A General Theory of Crime* (Stanford, CA, Stanford University Press).

Gottfredson, SD and Gottfredson, DM (1986) 'Accuracy of Prediction Models' in A Blumstein, J Cohen, JA Roth and CA Visher (eds), *Criminal Careers and 'Career Criminals'* (Washington DC, National Academy Press).

Greenwood, PW and Abrahamse, A (1982) *Selective Incapacitation* (Santa Monica, CA, Rand Corporation).

Harcourt, BE (2006) *Embracing Change: Post-modern Meditations on Punishment* (New York, New School Conference on Punishment).

Home Office (2001) *Making Punishment Work* (London, Home Office).

Horney, J, Osgood, DW and Marshall, IH (2005) 'Criminal Careers in the Short-term: Intra-individual Variability in Crime and its Relation to Local Life Circumstances' 60 *American Sociological Review* 655–73.

Kazemian, L and Farrington, DP (2006) 'Exploring Residual Career Length and Residual Number of Offenses for Two Generations of Repeat Offenders' 43 *Journal of Research in Crime and Delinquency* 89–113.

Kazemian, L, Farrington, DP and Le Blanc, M (2009) 'Can We Make Accurate Long-term Predictions about Patterns of De-escalation in Offending Behavior?' 38 *Journal of Youth and Adolescence* 384–400.

King, RS, Mauer, M and Young, MC (2005) *Incarceration and Crime: A Complex Relationship* (Washington DC, The Sentencing Project).

Kovandzic, TV, Sloan, JJ and Vieraitis, LM (2004) '"Striking Out" as Crime Reduction Policy: The Impact of "Three Strikes" Laws on Crime Rates in US Cities' 21 *Justice Quarterly* 207–39.

Kowalski, M and Caputo, T (1999) 'Recidivism in Youth Court: An Examination of the Impact of Age, Gender, and Prior Record' 1 *Canadian Journal of Criminology* 57–84.

Kurlycheck, MC, Brame, R and Bushway, SD (2006) 'Scarlet Letters and Recidivism: Does an Old Criminal Record Predict Future Offending?' 5 *Criminology and Public Policy* 483–503.

Laub, JH and Sampson, RJ (2001) 'Understanding Desistance from Crime' in M Tonry (ed), *Crime and Justice: A Review of Research* (Chicago, University of Chicago Press).

—— (2003) *Shared Beginnings, Divergent Lives: Delinquent Boys to Age 70* (Cambridge, MA, Harvard University Press).

Levitt, SD (1996) 'The Effect of Prison Population Size on Crime Rates: Evidence from Prison Overcrowding Litigation' 111 *Quarterly Journal of Economics* 319–51.

—— (2004) 'Understanding Why Crime Fell in the 1990s: Four Factors that Explain the Decline and Six that Do Not' 18 *Journal of Economic Perspectives* 163–90.

Maruna, S (2001) *Making Good: How Ex-Convicts Reform and Rebuild Their Lives* (Washington DC, American Psychological Association).

Maruna, S and Toch, H (2005) 'The Impact of Imprisonment on the Desistance Process' in J Travis and C Visher (eds), *Prisoner Reentry and Crime in America* (New York, Cambridge University Press).

Marvell, TB and Moody, CE (1994) 'Prison Population Growth and Crime Reduction' 10 *Journal of Quantitative Criminology* 109–40.

—— (2001) XXX 'The Lethal Effects of Three-Strikes Laws' *Journal of Legal Studies* 89–106.

Meisenhelder, T (1977) 'An Explanatory Study of Exiting from Criminal Careers' 15 *Criminology* 319–34.

Miles, TJ and Ludwig, J (2007) 'The Silence of the Lambdas: Deterring Incapacitation Research' 23 *Journal of Quantitative Criminology* 287–301.

Moffitt, TE (1993) '"Life-Course Persistent" and "Adolescence-Limited" Antisocial Behavior: A Developmental Taxonomy' 100 *Psychological Review* 674–701.

Nagin, DS (1998) 'Criminal Deterrence Research at the Outset of the Twenty-first Century' in M Tonry (ed), *Crime and Justice: A Review of Research*, vol 23 (Chicago, University of Chicago Press).

Nagin, DS and Farrington, DP (1992) 'The Onset and Persistence of Offending' 32 *Criminology* 501–523.

Nagin, DS, Cullen, F and Jonson, CL (2009) 'Imprisonment and Reoffending' in M Tonry (ed), *Crime and Justice: A Review of Research*, vol 38 (Chicago, Universty of Chicago Press) 115–200.

Orsagh, T and Chen, J-R (1988) 'The Effect of Time Served on Recidivism: An Interdisciplinary Theory ' 4 *Journal of Quantitative Criminology* 155–71.

Piquero, A, Farrington, DP and Blumstein, A (2003) 'The Criminal Career Paradigm' in M Tonry (ed), *Crime and Justice: A Review of Research* (Chicago, University of Chicago Press).

Richards, SC and Jones, RS (2004) 'Beating the Perpetual Incarceration Machine: Overcoming Structural Impediments to Re-entry' in S Maruna and R Immarigeon (eds), *After Crime and Punishment: Pathways to Offender Reintegration* (Collumpton, Willan).

Roberts, JV (1997) 'The Role of Criminal Record in the Sentencing Process' in M Tonry (ed), *Crime and Justice: A Review of Research*, vol 22 (Chicago, University of Chicago Press) 303–62.

—— (2008) 'Punishing Persistence: Explaining the Enduring Appeal of the Recidivist Sentencing Premium' 48 *British Journal of Criminology* 468–81.

Rosenfeld, R and Fornango, R (2007) 'The Impact of Economic Conditions on Robbery and Property Crime: The Role of Consumer Sentiment' 45 *Criminology* 735–70.

Sampson, RJ and Laub, JH (1993) *Crime in the Making: Pathways and Turning Points through Life* (Cambridge, MA, Harvard University Press).

—— (1997) 'A Life-Course Theory of Cumulative Disadvantage and the Stability of Delinquency' in TP Thornberry (ed), *Developmental Theories of Crime and Delinquency* (New Brunswick, NJ, Transaction).

—— (2003) 'Life-Course Desisters: Trajectories of Crime among Delinquent Boys Followed to Age 70' 41 *Criminology* 555–92.

Sapir, Y (2008) 'Against Prevention? A Response to Harcourt's against Prediction on Actuarial and Clinical Predictions and the Faults of Incapacitation' 33 *Law and Social Inquiry* 253–64.

Shichor, D and Sechrest, DK (1996) *Three Strikes and You're Out: Vengeance as Public Policy* (Thousand Oaks, CA, Sage).

Shover, N (1983) 'The Later Stages of Ordinary Property Offender Careers' 31 *Social Problems* 208–18.

—— (1996) *Great Pretenders: Pursuits and Careers of Persistent Thieves* (Boulder, CO, Westview).

Spelman, W (1994) *Criminal Incapacitation* (New York, Plenum).

—— (2006) 'The Limited Importance of Prison Expansion' in A Blumstein and J Wallman (eds), *The Crime Drop in America*, rev edn (New York, Cambridge University Press).

Stigler, GJ (1970) 78 'The Optimum Enforcement of Laws' *Journal of Political Economy* 526–36.

Stolzenberg, L and D'Alessio, SJ (1997), '"Three Strikes and You're Out": The Impact of California's New Mandatory Sentencing Law on Serious Crime Rates' 43 *Crime and Delinquency* 457–69.

Travis, J (2005) *But They All Come Back: Facing the Challenges of Prisoner Reentry* (Washington DC, Urban Institute Press).

Travis, J and Petersilia, J (2001) 'Reentry Reconsidered: A New Look at an Old Question' 47 *Crime and Delinquency* 291–313.

Villettaz, P, Killias, M and Zoder, I (2006) The Effects of Custodial vs Non-custodial Sentences on Re-offending: A Systematic Review of the State of Knowledge (Philadelphia, PA, Campbell Collaboration Crime and Justice Group).

Visher, CA (1986) 'The Rand Inmate Survey: A Reanalysis' in A Blumstein, J Cohen, JA Roth and CA Visher (eds), *Criminal Careers and 'Career Criminals'* (Washington DC, National Academy Press).

von Hirsch, A (1988) 'Selective Incapacitation Reexamined: The National Academy of Sciences' Report on Criminal Careers and "Career Criminals"' 7 *Criminal Justice Ethics* 19–35.

—— (2002) 'Record-enhanced Sentencing in England and Wales: Reflections on the Halliday Report's Proposed Treatment of Prior Convictions' 4 *Punishment and Society* 443–57.

von Hirsch, A and Gottfredson, DM (1983) 'Selective Incapacitation: Some Queries About Research Design and Equity' XII *New York University Review of Law and Social Change* 11–51.

Walker, N, Farrington, DP and Tucker, G (1981) 'Reconviction Rates of Adult Males after Different Sentences' 21 *British Journal of Criminology* 357–60.

Wilson, JQ and Herrnstein, RJ (1985) *Crime and Human Nature* (New York, Simon & Schuster).

Wolfgang, ME, Figlio, RM and Sellin, T (1972) *Delinquency in a Birth Cohort* (Chicago, University of Chicago Press).

Index

www.ingramcontent.com/pod-product-compliance
Lightning Source LLC
Chambersburg PA
CBHW071849270326
41929CB00013B/2152